The Flexible City

The Flexible City

Solutions for a Circular and Climate Adaptive Europe

Tom Bergevoet & Maarten van Tuijl

nai010 publishers

Content

Foreword

From flooding after rainfall in Amsterdam to heat stress in Athens. From excessive carbon dioxide emissions in Luxembourg to a lack of biodiversity in Prague. All over Europe, cities are struggling with the consequences of climate extremes. Our economic and growth-driven course brought us a lot, but our production and consumption have reached the limit of what our living environment can handle. The effects of climate change are especially felt in our cities, where the vast majority of people live.

Liveable Cities
The call for inclusive, liveable streets, neighbourhoods and cities therefore grows stronger every day. If we want to keep our cities liveable, we need to make them circular and climate-adaptive. Together, we need to use our space differently. Instead of more and bigger, we should aim for different and better. As the Board of Government Advisors, we have therefore drawn up the Agenda: *the 22nd-century starts now*. We believe in nature-inclusive and climate-adaptive cities. With our programme 'A new building culture', we strive to make biobased and nature-inclusive building become the new normal. A new building culture – from the cultivation of building materials to their application – needs to arise in which construction is in balance with nature, so that future generations can continue to live well. Fortunately, we have already reached a number of important agreements together, such as on limiting global warming (Paris 2015) or protecting biodiversity (Montreal 2022). But the pace of change is still too slow.

The Flexible City
The will is there in cities, but often the know-how is still missing or ambitions fail because of restricting regulations or a lack of financing options. That is why I am delighted that with *The Flexible City; Solutions for a Circular and Climate Adaptive Europe*, Tom Bergevoet and Maarten van Tuijl, in collaboration with their sponsors and a team of reporters, offer European cities the necessary tools and instruments to successfully implement circularity and climate adaptation. Their flexible city is a circular, climate-adaptive and future-proof city that can be easily reused and allows its inhabitants to shape their own living environment. It is a city that is emphatically part of a process of continuous transition. New developments do not lead to a fixed end position, but emerge from future-oriented, dynamic starting positions.

Together with an international team of reporters, the authors have put together a set of 36 tools to help shape that flexible city. From a stronger involvement of local communities in urban design to the initiation of circular food chains. Changes are not isolated; they are interconnected. Only by working together with different sectors, we will find circular and climate-adaptive solutions.

Reuse and Social Inclusion Take Centre Stage
It is encouraging to read how many circular and climate-adaptive initiatives are actually already in place in European cities. The authors offer a very comprehensive overview of these initiatives in their last chapter.

Those initiatives are illustrative of a new way of working and a new mindset, in which reuse, social inclusion and the time factor are central. Like an open-air car park on the banks of the Rhône in Lyon that has been transformed into a climate-adaptive park, providing room for the river. Or the circular housing project in Copenhagen converting 463 tonnes of waste from nearby demolished buildings into new living space, proving that circular construction can compete with regular prices, conventional qualities, strict guarantees and – on top of that – offer a whole new aesthetic.

May you enjoy reading this inspiring handbook for everyone who contributes to a future-proof European city: from officials and policymakers to developers, builders and users, and, of course, us as architects.

Francesco Veenstra, Chief Government Architect, The Netherlands

Prologue

In this prologue, a wide range of European cities is explored. All of them are facing urgent environmental challenges.

Though these challenges are all described and visualized in relation to a specific city, they are not unique to that particular city. Numerous other cities across Europe are facing similar challenges.

1800: Prague as a stony exception within a massive forest area, biodiversity is at a high level.

higher biodiversity: forests and parks
lower biodiversity: agricultural fields
urban area
landscape restoration

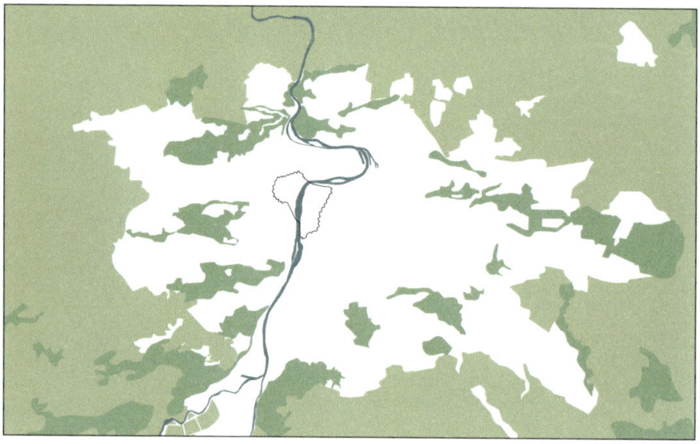

1970s: Prague's green infrastructure was broken in its most extreme form, biodiversity is at the lowest level.

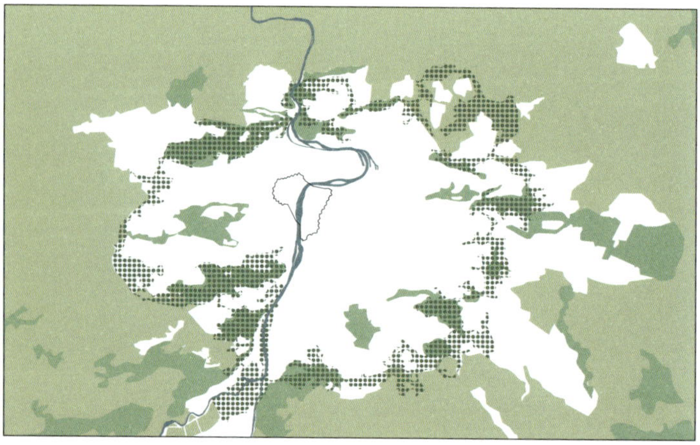

2020: Prague plans to restore the green structure around (and within) the city, boosting biodiversity again.

Biodiversity Decline

Prague, Czech Republic

Background

Up until the beginning of the nineteenth century, Prague was a stony exception nestled between fields and wooded areas with thriving biodiversity, unhindered by the effects of industrialization or urban sprawl. During the nineteenth and twentieth century, Prague's borders kept expanding with light industry and housing. Prague's green infrastructure was broken in its most extreme form during the Communist regime (1948-1989).

The regime built a ring of new satellite settlements called 'sídliště' in the greater metropolitan area of Prague – Jižní, Severní and Jihozápadní město. Open nature was replaced by large panel housing blocks separated by poorly maintained green spaces. While the interruption of the green belt around Prague was not completely devastating, it did have a lasting impact on the area's biodiversity.

Outside of the city, collectivization and large-scale farming caused a decline in biodiversity due to the ploughing of field borders, the use of fertilizers, pesticides and further expansion of agricultural land. This contributed to the loss of habitat of wild fauna and flora.

Current Situation

Being aware of the poor condition of its biodiversity, the Czech Republic intensified its efforts by legally adopting the Convention on Biodiversity in 1999. On top of that, Prague is currently developing the New Metropolitan Plan that proposes a greater protection of open green spaces by stabilizing the border of the built city, preventing further urban sprawl by earmarking dilapidated plots within the city for development and increasing the ecological stability. By mapping the territorial system of ecological stability (územní systém ekologické stability' – ÚSES), the plan connects biocentres and a biocorridor to enhance the blue-green infrastructure around the city.

Challenges

Next to the loss of natural habitat, climate change is also a threat to the biodiversity in Prague. Due to its structure and geographical location, the heat island effect is stronger in Prague than it is on average in European cities. On top of already existing strategy reports such as the Climate Change Adaptation Strategy (2017), the city recently published a Drought Plan (2023). Improving the green-blue infrastructure is crucial to reduce the heat island effect. However, Prague also has to create a legislative strategy for the mitigation of climate change to make measures enforceable.

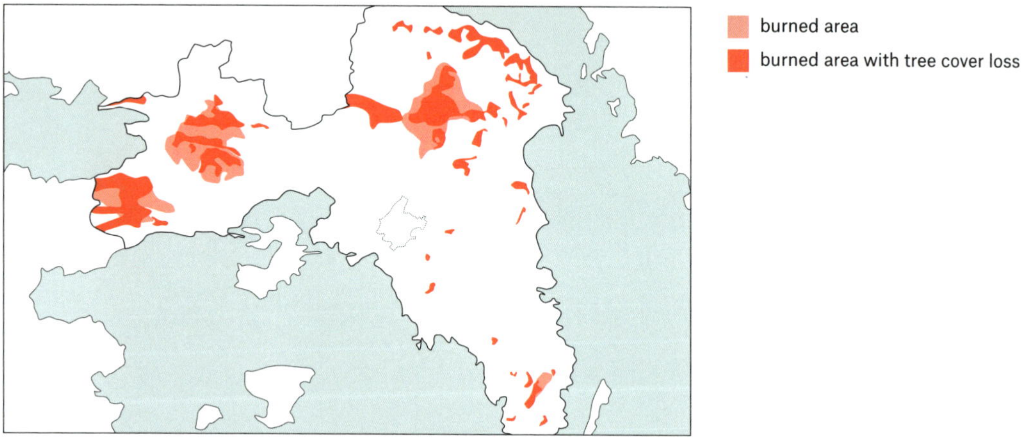

Attica region: burned areas and tree cover loss due to fires in 2021.

Athens metropolitan area: heat stress levels in 2021.

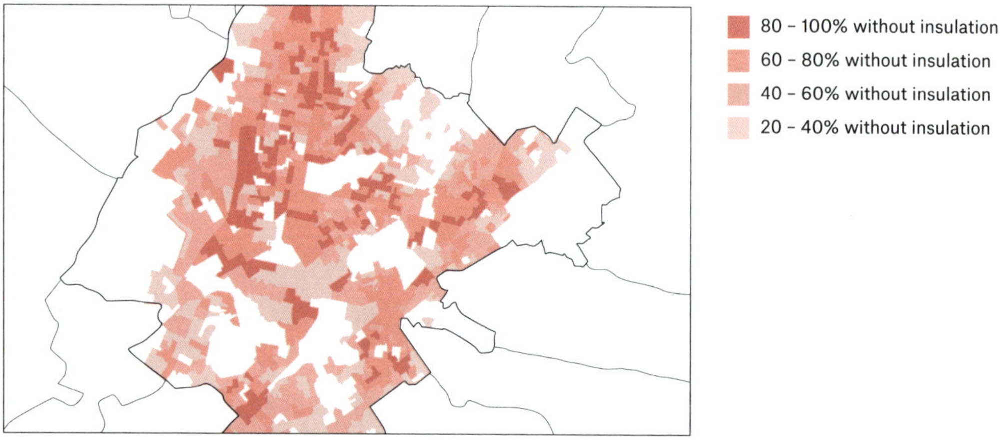

Athens: percentage of buildings without insulation.

Heat Stress
Athens, Greece

Background
Situated in the south of Europe, Greece has always been on the sunny side of the continent and a safe destination for holidaymakers looking for some sun. Recently however, this region has increasingly been facing the negative effects of global warming, such as forest fires, urban heat stress and energy-consuming measures to counteract it.

Current Situation
The country is experiencing a faster warming rate than the European average, resulting in more frequent heatwaves and prolonged droughts, which elevates the risk of fires. These result in tree cover loss, which intensifies urban heat stress and increases the risk of flooding in the affected areas. In addition to that, the current building stock is not ready to cope with the rising temperatures. Approximately half of all the residential buildings in the Attica region lack insulation, making them vulnerable to extreme heat during the summer. As a result, residents of these buildings are forced to rely heavily on air-conditioning devices, resulting in increased energy consumption during the hot months. Furthermore, only a small portion of this energy comes from renewable sources, exacerbating the problem.

Challenges
On its way to future-proof, this region is looking for more sustainable ways to deal with climate change and global warming, such as planting more vegetation in urban areas and looking for sources of renewable energy.

In an effort to combat urban heat stress and create more favourable microclimate conditions within cities, there are regional plans to protect existing urban green spaces, as well as to expand and increase their coverage. However, the constant growth of Athens and the lack of a holistic urban planning approach pose substantial challenges for successfully expanding green spaces within urban areas.

Anticipating the increased demand for cooling energy, the country is exploring the use of passive, less energy-intensive systems and is seeking ways to support the energy upgrading of the existing building stock. Through programmes like the 'Energy Refurbishment of Residences', funded by the European Regional Development Fund (ERDF) and national Greek funds, the government targets building owners directly and provides financial incentives for energy retrofitting measures for their homes. Despite these efforts, the transition to a low-carbon, energy-efficient building stock remains a major challenge and requires continued investment and engagement from all stakeholders.

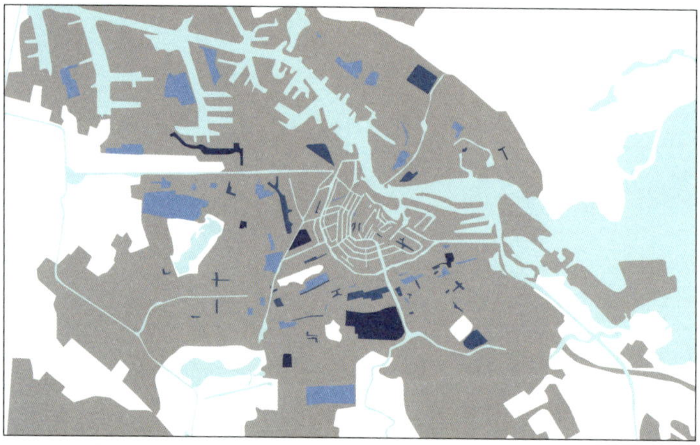

Amsterdam region: risk map regarding flooding due to heavy rainfall; in the highest risk areas, serious damage (property, roads, infrastructure) may be expected.

- very high risk of flooding
- high risk of flooding
- risk of flooding
- high groundwater level
- 100 - 840 mm flooding in the case of 120 mm rainfall in 2 hours

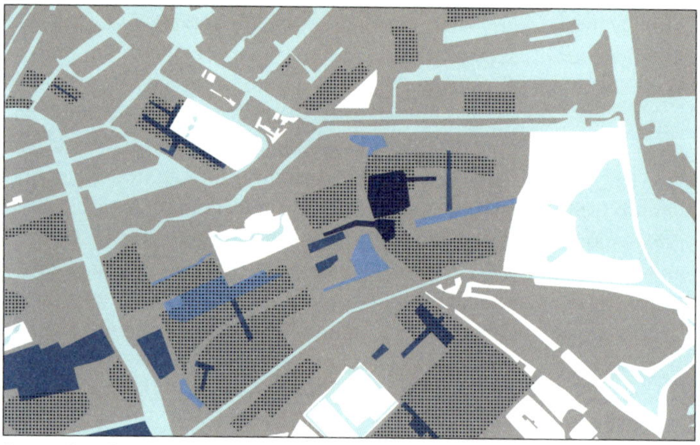

Amsterdam Central East part: risk areas related to groundwater levels.

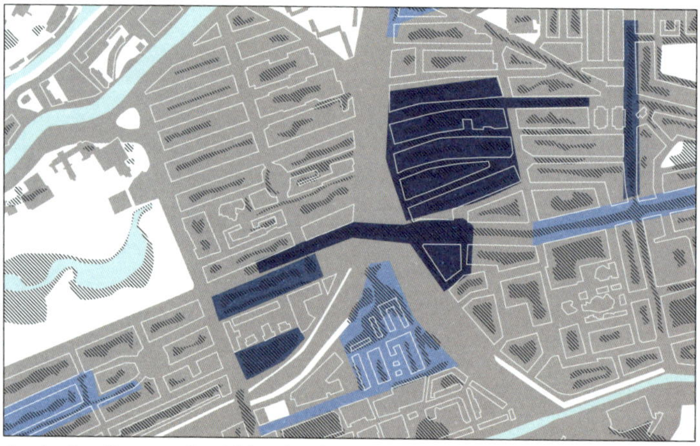

Amsterdam Oosterpark neighbourhood: expected flooding in the case of 120 mm rainfall in two hours.

Rainwater Floods

Amsterdam, the Netherlands

Background

The urban structure of Amsterdam derives from its ongoing struggle with water. A finely meshed canal structure and elevated dry grounds led to an urban tissue that could deal with its original swampy ground condition. Because most parts within this tissue were both accessible by land and by water, the city was very suitable for trade.

Since the Middle Ages, engineering knowledge and water management grew significantly. From the seventeenth century onwards, Amsterdam could therefore expand into its surrounding wetlands. These wetlands were transformed into polders, reclaimed land surrounded with dykes in which the groundwater level was permanently kept low through drainage and pumping stations. In these polders, wooden pile foundations were used for buildings These piles should always be completely below groundwater level to protect them from rotting.

Current Situation

Climate change leads to more extreme weather conditions, like droughts and heavy rainfalls. Huge city expansions in the twentieth century turned the former wetlands into stony surfaces with a discharge-orientated water infrastructure. The urban infrastructure is under stress due to the changing conditions of the extreme weather events. The city is facing serious challenges, where daily urban life is stressed by the abundance or absence of (rain) water. Increasing heat stress has an effect on the health of the urban population. Public squares and streets are made 'rainproof', reducing the effects of climate change by introducing local water storage and implementing more green. Private parties are encouraged to do the same with their real estate and gardens. Next to that, the municipality stimulates a transformation towards a blue-green roof-landscape as a crucial element of the 'Sponge City'. This also helps in times of drought when the wooden foundations are threatened and brackish seepage has an impact on the local biodiversity. Sea level rise is a complex threat in the long run that demands a solid strategy, a re-evaluation of the elevation strategy and the development of fitting coping mechanisms.

Challenges

The city understands it should once more rethink its relationship with water. Next to the current measures regarding climate adaptation, it should be able to deal with even more extreme differences in the near future. Embracing uncertainties is a strategy to deal with the inherent unpredictability of climate change. This might introduce a fundamentally different way of building and land use where the concept of The Flexible City is crucial. The municipality and Waternet (responsible for the complete water-cycle management in Amsterdam) are encouraging research, redeveloping a vision on the underground of the city and a fitting elevation strategy. This is where the principles of adaptive spatial and policy pathways can guide future investments in the urban development and transformation.

Copenhagen municipality: landfill areas.

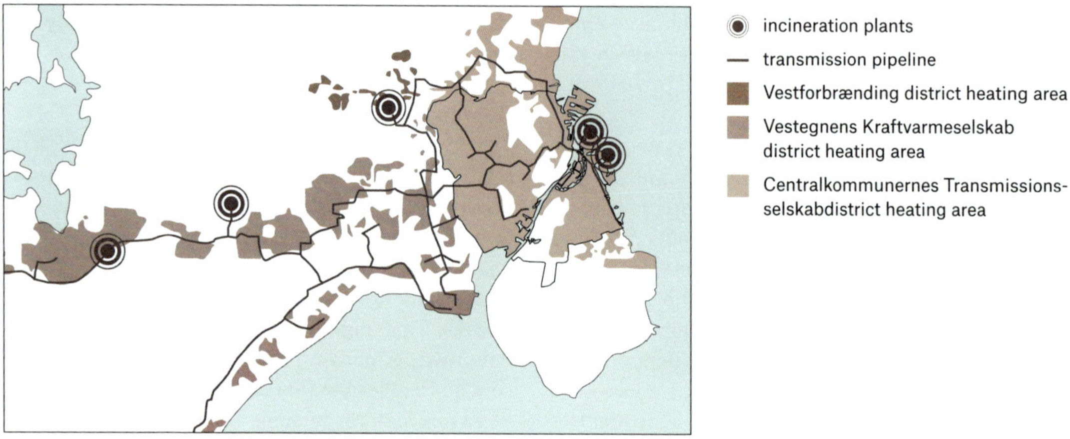

Copenhagen municipality and surroundings: waste incineration plants with their distribution networks for electricity and district heat.

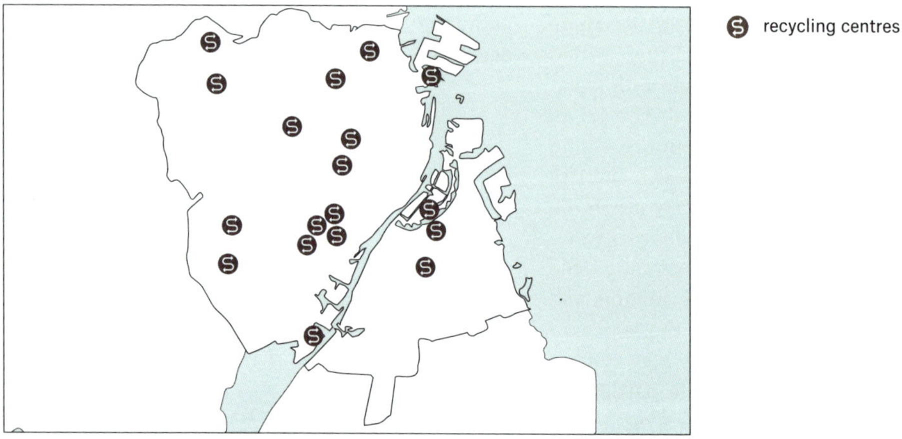

Copenhagen municipality: recycling centres, recycling hubs or swap centres, where Copenhageners can bring their unwanted belongings to be repaired or used as a resource for new products.

Waste Excess

Copenhagen, Denmark

Background

For centuries, Copenhagen's focus was only on the collection and disposal of waste, mostly by burning in incinerators or burying it in landfills, like in many other industrial cities in Europe. This form of waste disposal turned out to have significant environmental impacts, such as air pollution and soil contamination.

Current Situation

When concerns about the environmental impacts of waste disposal were raised in the 1960s and 1970s, more focus was placed on recycling and composting. Collection systems were introduced for recyclable materials such as paper, glass, and plastic. Waste sorting facilities and composting plants were founded, where the collected materials could be processed. Nevertheless, in 1970 the Amager Bakke waste incineration plant was built, a facility that still provides much of the city's heat and electricity needs by burning waste.

Since the 1990s, efforts were focused on reducing the amount of generated waste. This led to the development of several educational campaigns and programmes to raise awareness of the issues among residents.

Challenges

Copenhagen announced in 2012 that it wants to be the world's first carbon-neutral capital city by 2025. This means a significant shift away from traditional waste disposal methods towards more recycling, composting and waste reduction. One way of achieving this is through the 'Circular Copenhagen – Resource and Waste Plan 2024', which envisages an annual reduction in carbon emissions of 59,000 tons by tripling the amount of recycling between 2019 and 2024. Another important goal is to reuse more construction materials, now making up around 30 per cent of Denmark's waste production.

The amount of incinerated waste should be reduced too. This requires the (partial) decoupling of heat and power generation from waste management. If the system does not succeed in transforming and using alternative materials such as wooden pallets from sustainable forestry, the goals of a higher recycling rate and further decreasing waste volumes will not only conflict with the economic viability of the waste incineration plant, but also with the reliable supply of the Copenhagen district heating system – the largest of its kind in the world.

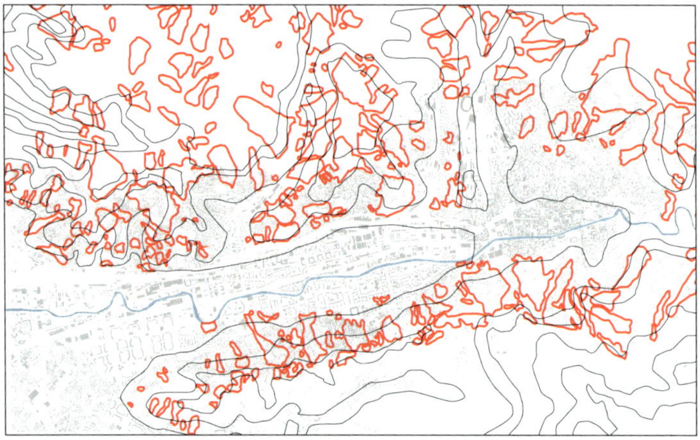

Sarajevo is located in a valley surrounded by hills and mountains, parts of which are instable and vulnerable to landslides after heavy rains.

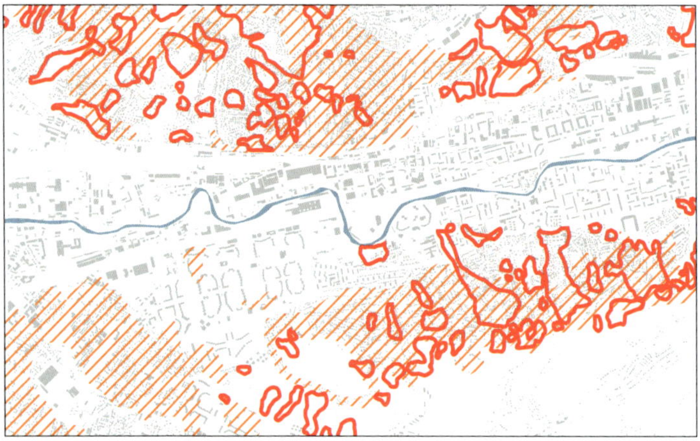

Illegally built neighbourhoods in these hills are often built within the risk area's for landslides.

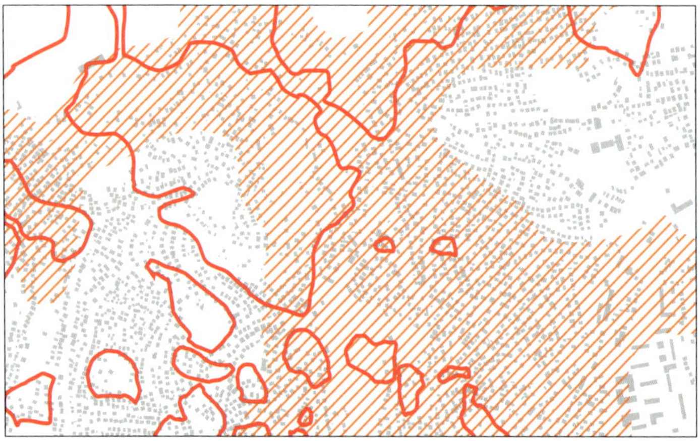

Illegally built neighbourhoods around Buća Potok were built without a zoning plan and a with a lack of supervision.

Social Segregation

Sarajevo, Bosnia and Herzegovina

Background

Sarajevo, the capital of Bosnia and Herzegovina, is located in a valley surrounded by hills and mountains. Over the centuries, the city developed to the west, over the flat banks of the river Miljacka. The mountains have always been of great importance to the identity of the city in many ways – as protection against invaders, as a setting for the 1984 Winter Olympics, but also as points of attack in the war of 1992-1996 – but there were hardly any houses on the north and south sides as they were too steep and unstable.

Current Situation

In the hills on the north side of the city, in the municipality of Buća Potok, workers' houses were placed in 1970-1980s, temporarily, because the location was considered unsuitable for permanent residence. When many refugees and other newcomers came to Sarajevo after the 1992-1996 war, expecting to find a better perspective in the capital, they ended up in Buća Potok, in the hills around the temporary workers' homes. With cheap building materials and simple construction methods, they built their own houses, not being aware of the dangers of the unstable subsoil. As there was no zoning plan and a lack of supervision, many houses were built illegally shortly after the war, with the risk of landslides during heavy rainfall. Because of their disorganized nature, these illegal neighbourhoods were called Bosnian favelas.

Challenges

The government authorities have always found the social segregation between the legal, safe areas in the valley on the one hand and the illegal and unsafe areas in the hills on the other undesirable. In recent years, the municipality has carefully mapped illegal buildings, assessed them for safety and legalized them where possible.

Buildings on and around all 850 risk areas for landslides have been assessed and additional safety measures were implemented where necessary. The combination of measures is different for each location. In Buća Potok, for example, the houses have been connected to the city sewer system and the network of rainwater drainage pipes has been improved and expanded. Existing retaining walls on the site have been examined by the municipality and the construction institute of Canton Sarajevo and repaired wherever necessary. New retaining walls have also been installed on the site.

Once the situation is safe for all homes, the municipality wants to upgrade the infrastructure and public space in the legalized districts. Roadworks are in order to make the roads here clearer and safer. Public space of sufficient quality is to be created between the buildings. All homes should be easily accessible from the public area.

In this way, the illegally built districts will eventually become a fully-fledged part of the urban fabric.

- smaller-sized food distribution point
- bigger-sized food distribution point
- food distribution point with lower ecological impact
- food distribution point with higher ecological impact

Antwerp, medieval city: pre-industrial food distribution locations in the city had a small ecological footprint.

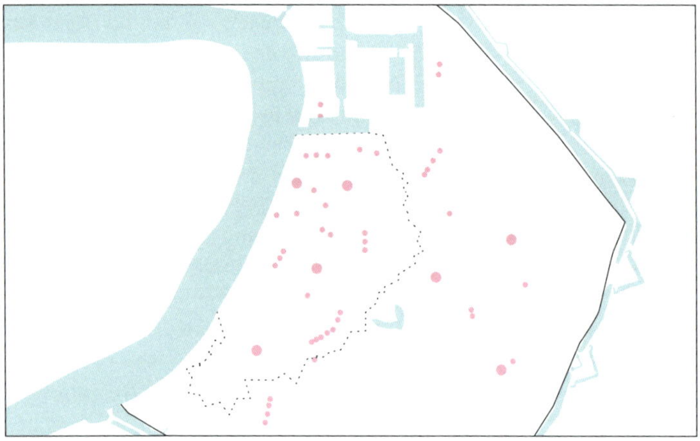

Antwerp, 1900: industrial locations of food distribution with a growing ecological footprint.

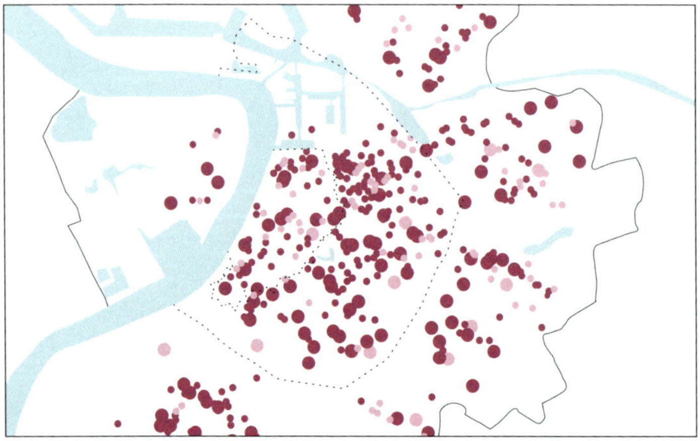

Antwerp, today: post-industrial locations of food distribution have a problematic ecological footprint due to high consumption rate.

Food Consumption

Antwerp, Belgium

Background

In medieval times the citizens of Antwerp had many vegetable gardens and stables with cattle for their own food production within the city walls. This urban agriculture declined in the sixteenth century when Antwerp saw a rapid population growth. Food was distributed from many specialized outdoor markets in the city for meat, vegetables, fish and eggs, where nearby farmers and fishermen would come selling their products and taking urban (human and household) waste back to their farms in return to use as manure. Until the 1900s, Antwerp kept recycling most of its urban waste as manure for its nearby countryside.

In industrial times, faster ways of transportation, such as trains, cars and steamboats, made products from further away more accessible for ordinary consumers in Antwerp. From 1900, new ideas about hygiene changed the outdoor marketplaces of Antwerp into covered indoor spaces, changing over time into indoor retail shops. The introduction of plastic packaging made household waste worthless as manure. Farmers turned to fertilizer instead, interrupting the local circular chain of food and waste. Excrements and waste were now simply dumped on sites in the periphery, creating pollution problems for future urban settlements.

Current Situation

From the 1950s, supermarkets became the places to supply for fresh products. Modern inventions like the car and the refrigerator allowed Antwerpers to do their shopping for a week. The last places for food production left the city centre, making the food industry invisible in Antwerp.

Nowadays, growing, harvesting, packing, transporting, selling, preparing, eating and disposing food in Antwerp involves a huge international network with a problematic ecological footprint. Some 21 to 37 per cent of the Belgian greenhouse gas emissions derive from the national consumption of food.

Challenges

By developing the Antwerp food strategy, the city of Antwerp introduces a cross-domain food policy and strategic framework enabling the various links in the food system to become more sustainable. For example, a public plant-based protein transition should substantially reduce animal protein consumption by 2036. The city wants to reintroduce urban agriculture, stimulating vegetable gardens as community assets inside buildings and on rooftops, making the production of food more visible again. Furthermore, it wants to prioritize regional products, reduce food losses and food packaging.

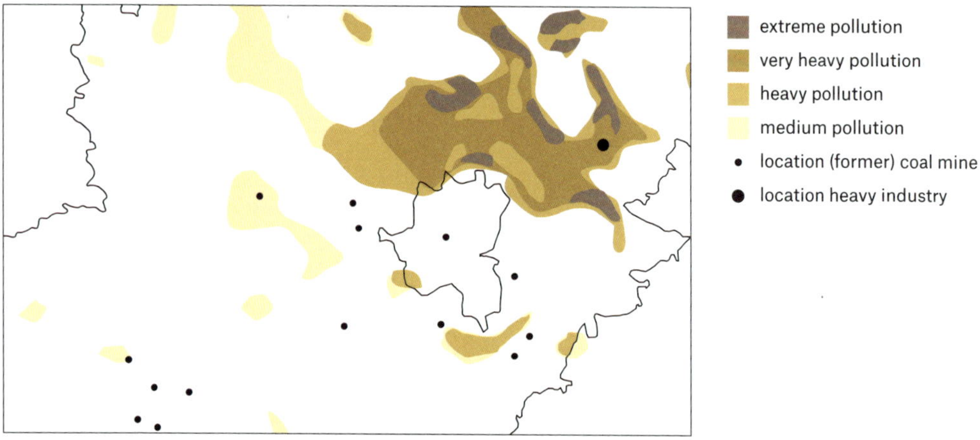

Silesian Voivodeship: soil pollution related to historical mines and heavy industries.

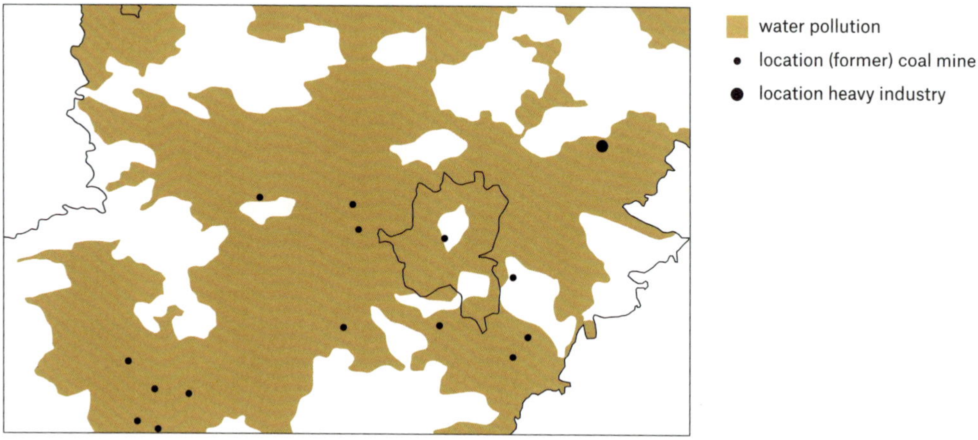

Silesian Voivodeship: water pollution related to historical mines and heavy industries.

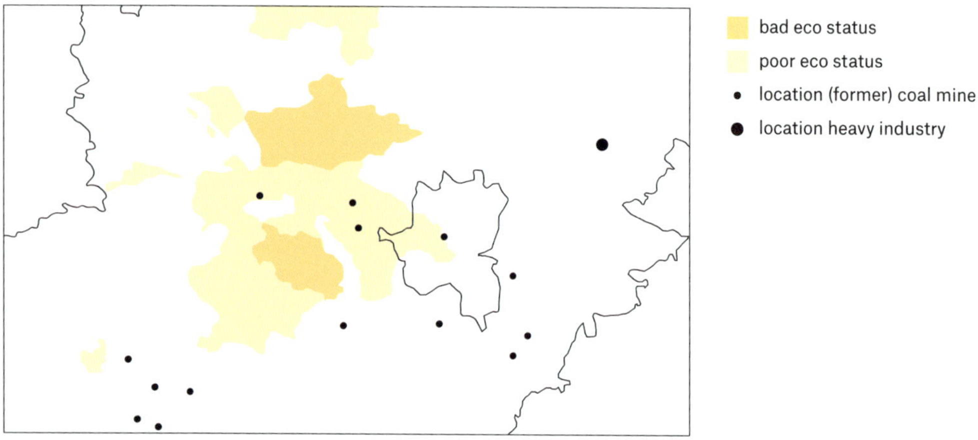

Silesian Voivodeship: current ecological status related to historical mines and heavy industries.

Soil Pollution

Katowice, Poland

Background

The region of Katowice is rich in natural resources. There were over fifty coal mines, most of them built in nineteenth century and exploited until 1989. After the fall of the Iron Curtain in 1989, coal mining turned out to be unprofitable and also environmentally degrading, which led to the closing of mines. Since 2021, only one coal mine is still in use. Nowadays, the revitalization of post-mining areas is the main target and mission in the region.

Current Situation

Katowice, traditionally associated with heavy industry, gradually strives to become a leader in innovation. Employment in the heavy industry is visibly going down, whereas more jobs in the IT sector are created. The city created plans to supercharge the city transformation in the coming years. For example, as part of the revitalization plan of a former coal mining area, the Culture Zone was established – an area unique for the entire country. The city has extensive experience in counteracting the effects of long-term environmental degradation. The air quality and living standard of its residents has clearly improved in recent years. However, the official environmental reports for Silesia show that the chemical condition of surface waters and the soil in post-industrial sites is still unsatisfactory.

Challenges

Recently, both the urban infrastructure and the architectural condition of the city have improved significantly. Now, the environmental condition is a matter of the highest importance. Polluted sites are to be turned into attractive city parts in order to attract new investors. The city has already achieved several goals, including the greening of 50 per cent of the city's area. But the cleaning of the soil and water in Silesia is still a great challenge. Water supply and management need to be thoroughly modernized, especially because metal pollution is a growing problem. As heavy metals are hard to remove, chemical solutions or liming are still often used to clean the soil. In some cases, however, natural methods, for instance using specific plants to purify the soil, can be a great alternative.

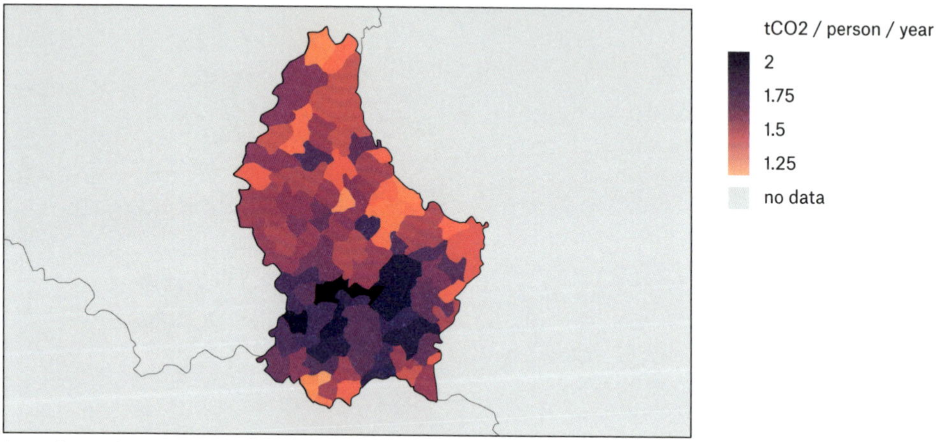

Luxembourg: local CO2 emission – food consumption (2020).

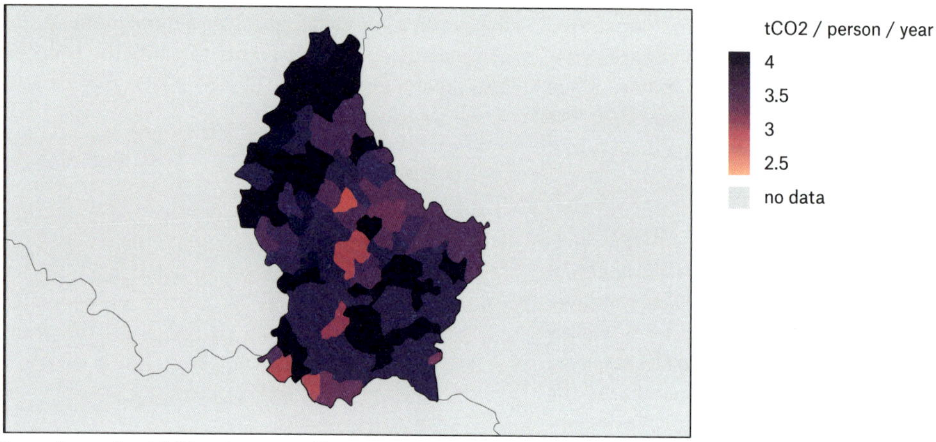

Luxembourg: local CO2 emission – traffic and transportation (2020).

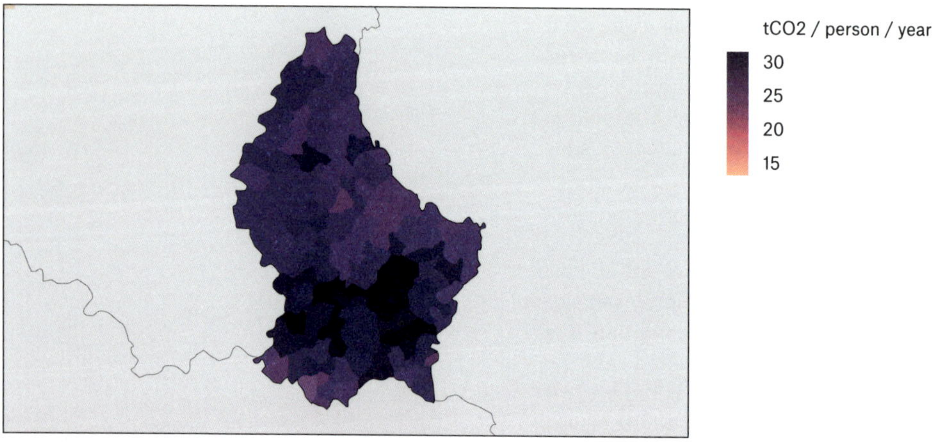

Luxembourg: average local CO2 emission (2020).

Carbon Emissions

Luxembourg, Luxembourg

Background

Luxembourg is the most prosperous country of Europe, which is attributed to the quick transition from a steel and coal-producing industry to a service-based one. Too small to create a self-sustaining internal market, Luxembourg has elaborated its political, financial and trade interconnections within Europe. Despite its small size, the country plays an important role in European politics and economy, hosting many EU institutions and a substantial financial sector. The service industry accounts for around 85 per cent of the gross domestic product (GDP).

Current Situation

Luxembourg has both the highest GDP per capita and the highest carbon dioxide emissions per capita in Europe. Air pollution can be primarily attributed to fuel tourism (54 per cent of energy demand comes from the transport sector, including drivers from neighbouring countries visiting Luxembourg to fill up their tanks) and energy-intensive technological networks (data centres). Luxembourg has determinedly positioned itself as an infrastructure hub in central Europe, driven by keen tax incentives.

Luxembourg has developed into a major freight route with cheaper fuel prices (attracting a high level of cross-border sales) and an extensive motorway network, alongside one of the largest cargo airlines in Europe (CargoLux). Concurrently, the country is a communications powerhouse hosting the world's largest satellite services company, SES. Talks are underway for Google to build an energy-intensive data centre in Luxembourg, which would consume 12 per cent of the country's current energy use. Emissions can also be traced to the country's rapid transition to a services-based economy relying heavily on cross-border workers; almost 50 per cent of Luxembourg's workforce commute daily from neighbouring countries, more than three out of four of them driving by car despite nationwide free public transport. Finally, Luxembourg's energy system is characterized by high import dependence (95 per cent in 2018) and a reliance on fossil fuels (78 per cent in 2018).

Challenges

In the last decade, Luxembourg has moved towards decoupling its economic and demographic growth from its energy consumption. Luxembourg has generous support schemes for renewable energy sources and energy efficiency, two critical pillars of a clean energy transition. The government's plan to gradually introduce carbon pricing could stimulate the behavioural changes and investments required for transitioning to a lower-carbon energy system. Nonetheless, the country's attractive low taxes on energy represent a hurdle to a sustainable transition to lower carbon consumption.

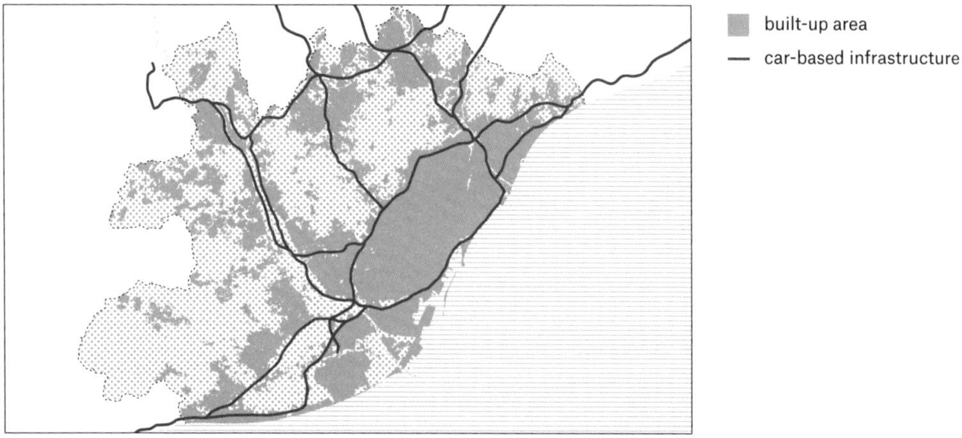

Metropolitan Area of Barcelona: car-dominated infrastructure, connecting satellite towns to the city centre.

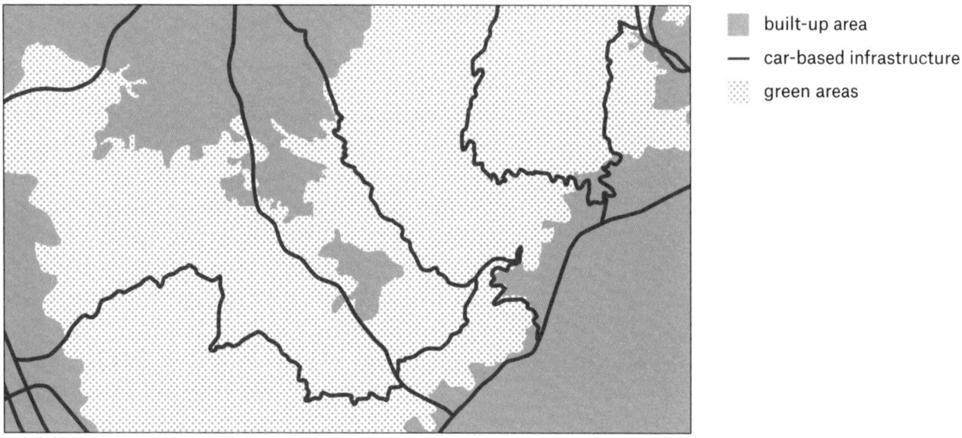

Metropolitan Area of Barcelona: car-dominated infrastructure, cutting through green areas, disrupting ecological structures.

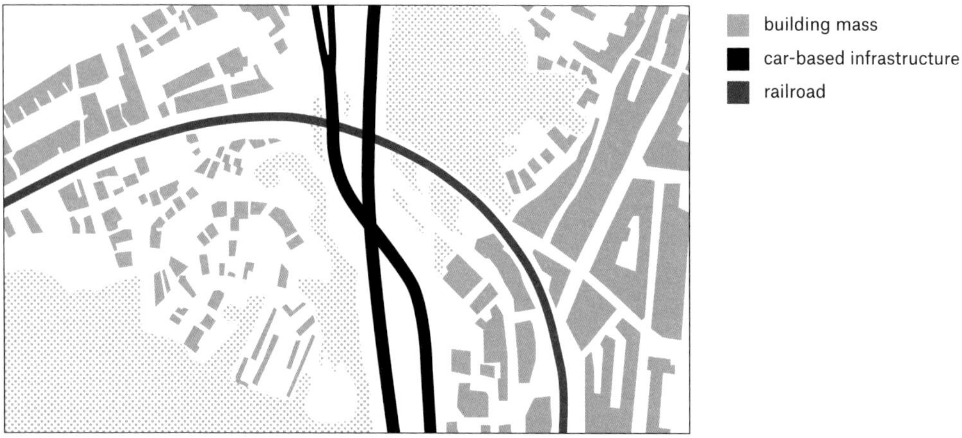

Metropolitan area / Montcada i Reixac town: car-dominated infrastructure, cutting through urban tissue, reinforcing poor interconnectivity and causing social segregation.

Car-based Infrastructure

Barcelona, Spain

Background

The metropolitan area of Barcelona arose from an arrangement of several historical small towns and villages around the central city of Barcelona. After the Second World War, the small roads that used to connect the historic settlements were turned into much bigger motorways, resulting in a poly-nuclear urban arrangement dominated by car infrastructure. Over the years the small towns have almost grown together to form one urban continuum to the centre of Barcelona, connected by lines of infrastructure.

Current Situation

Nowadays many infrastructural lines, such as motorways and railroad tracks, cut through the urban tissue and the surrounding green areas, creating huge barriers. This reinforces poor social and ecological interconnectivity and spatial segregation. Socially, the monocultures emanating from this segregation are a threat to the inclusive society Spain wants to be. Ecologically, the obstructing infrastructure isolates species, adding to the loss of biodiversity. Additionally, the heavy dependency on the car causes air and noise pollution around the infrastructure, affecting health and quality of life. Along the roads, many leftover spaces are neglected and became areas with a low urban quality.

Challenges

Being aware of the problems infrastructural lines cause, the Area Metropolitana de Barcelona (AMB) approved a Metropolitan Urban Masterplan (PDMU) in March 2023 that redefines the urban mobility model. One of the main objectives of this Masterplan is the introduction or stimulation of alternatives for car traffic. The final goal is to downgrade the existing car-dominated infrastructure.

The masterplan prioritizes active mobility like walking and cycling and public transport. As the suburban towns have clear centres with a high population density, there is a good base for intensifying the existing infrastructure of public transport. By improving the network for bicycles, cycling can become a good alternative for short car rides.

After car traffic is contained or reduced, the Masterplan aims to bring back the human scale to several significant roads and public spaces within the urban tissue. Re-interpretation of the historic roads, which gradually turned into large-scale motorways during the twentieth century, key spaces within the local infrastructure can be made suitable for pedestrians and other forms of slow traffic again.

1. The Inflexible City

Since the beginning of the twentieth century, the way we develop our towns and cities is modern and mainly economically driven. This has eventually led to a complex of environmental crises. The way our towns and cities are made is now threatening those very towns and cities.

To turn the tide, our cities have to be changed into circular environments, removing the causes of these environmental crises. At the same time, we have to make our cities climate-adaptive, counteracting the harmful consequences of those crises. Despite ambitions, progress in our cities is too slow. Changing our urban environment, planning habits and future expectations is tough. Conflicting interests, legal obstructions, uncovered costs and technical challenges complicate the much-needed changes.

In this chapter, we explain why more flexibility is necessary to help make our cities circular and climate-adaptive.

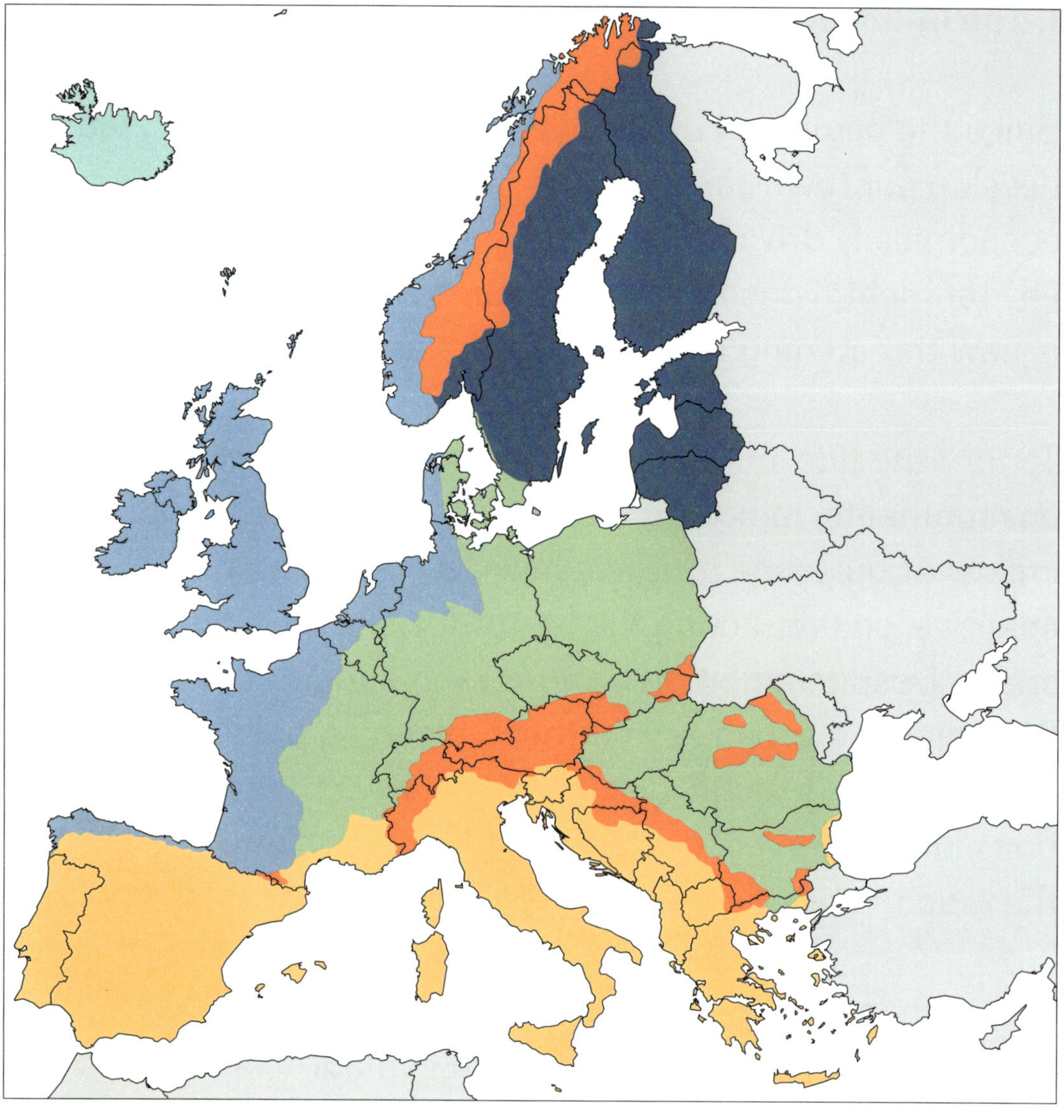

The impact of climate change on Europe (source: European Environment Agency)

Arctic: temperature rises much more than the global average; higher risk of biodiversity loss; risks to the livelihoods of local people

Boreal region: more heavy rain, less snow and ice; more rain and river flows; more risks of forest pests; winter storms do more damage

Atlantic region: more heavy rain; higher river flow; higher risk of flooding; higher risks of damage due to storms in winter; more bad weather

Continental region: more weather extremes; less rain in summer; higher risk of river floods; higher risk of forest fires; more energy needed for cooling

Mediterranean region: more heat extremes; less rain and river flows; higher risk of droughts; higher risk of biodiversity loss; higher risk of forest fires; more competition for water; lower crop yields; more energy needed for cooling; most economic sectors negatively affected; more people die because of heat waves

Mountain area: temperature rises more than the European average; fewer and smaller glaciers; high risk of species extinction; more risks of forest pests; more risks of rock falls and landslides; declining ski tourism

no data

1.1 Europe Facing Challenges

Since the beginning of the twentieth century, we have become increasingly prosperous. While the worldwide population has grown from less than 2 billion people in 1900 to 8 billion people in 2023[1], the income per capita has been increased by a factor six in the same time[2]. Triggered by this increase of purchasing power, companies strained themselves to meet the growing demand for goods. Their industrialized production lines got scaled up and globalized in order to provide us with products, both affordable and with the highest quality. Since 1900, the worldwide industrial production grew with a factor twenty[3].

But this growth has a downside. With our production modes and consumption patterns, we have reached the limits of what our planet can handle. Currently, several environmental crises tumble over each other. Greenhouse gas emissions cause global warming. Waste is spoiling our resources. Expanding urbanization and intensive agriculture decrease biodiversity. Pollution is impoverishing our soils. Excessive consumption unsettles the availability of finite resources. The negative impacts of our way of living have become a threat for that same way of living.

Those threats are numerous. Climate change for example, caused by global warming, leads to all kinds of environmental dangers. Coastal areas are threatened by floods, while continental regions are vulnerable to temporary heat stress or periods of drought. In mountain areas, rising temperatures accelerate the extinction of species. Mediterranean regions are endangered by forest fires and failed harvests. All over Europe, waste and pollution are threatening our health. Basic human needs such as dry feet, environmental safety and a continuous food supply are increasingly under pressure. Most likely, not all of us will be able to afford protective measures, so the gap between the rich and the poor is expected to widen. Climate refugees will cause demographic shifts. In the near future, social inclusion will be harder to effectuate.

There is a growing urge to counteract these crises around the world. At conferences like those aimed at limiting global warming (Paris 2015) or protecting biodiversity (Montreal 2022), countries try to come to future-proof agreements. Though not all governments are willing to take restrictive measures, Europe appears to be one of the most ambitious continents at these conferences. Frequently, the European Union pleads for rigorous changes by setting ambitious targets.

Being important facilitators of our way of life, cities are key in accomplishing the desired changes. The European Union realizes that achieving the agreed targets starts with reconsidering the way we develop our cities. However, converting ambition into action is not easy and measurable results are lagging behind. Changing the way our cities behave means changing large-scaled systems, proven mechanisms and conventional habits. Counteracting the negative impact of our way of living and tackling the complex of environmental crises means that European cities, towns and villages will face challenges in the coming decades that differ fundamentally from the challenges that we have faced in the past. If Europe wants to make its ambitions come true, far-reaching reforms are needed in the spatial development of our cities, towns and villages.

1. source: UN World Population Prospects
2. source: Our World in Data
3. source: Macrotrends

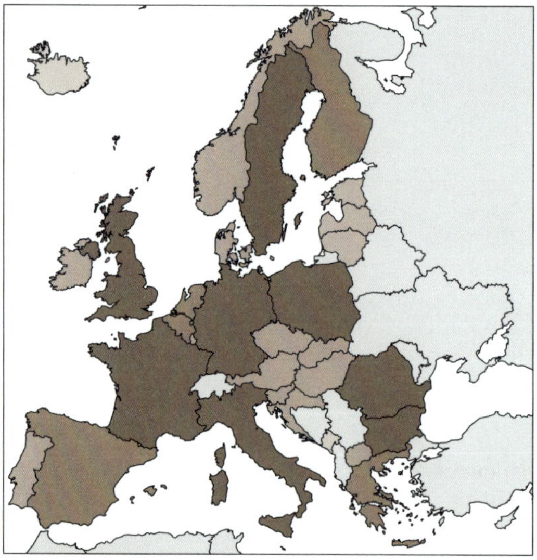

Total waste production in tons
(source: ResearchGate)

- 385,507 - 2,000,000
- 2,000,000 - 60,000,000
- 60,000,000 - 150,000,000
- 150,000,000 - 400,000
- no data

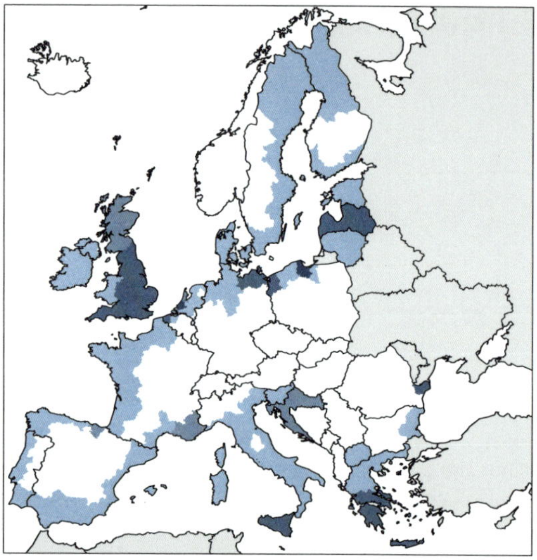

Flooding of coastal areas across Europe, scenario 2080s
(source: European Environment Agency)
People flooded (thousands / year)

- <6
- 6 - 10
- 10 - 50
- 50 - 150
- no data

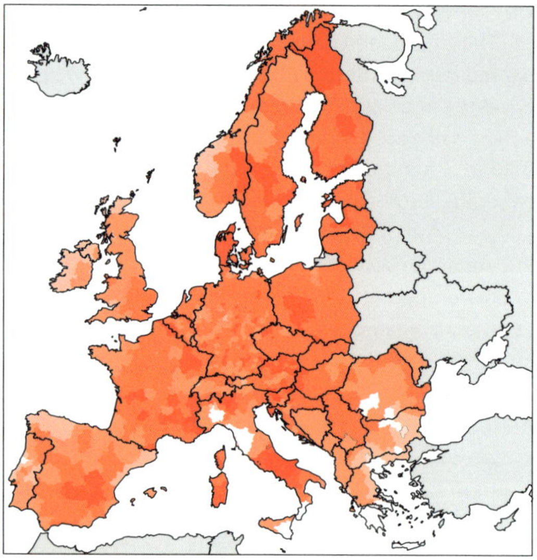

Observed trends in annual temperature from 1960 to 2021
(source: European Environment Agency)
°C / decade

- 0.0 - 0.1
- 0.1 - 0.2
- 0.2 - 0.3
- 0.3 - 0.4
- 0.4 - 0.5
- > 0,5
- no data

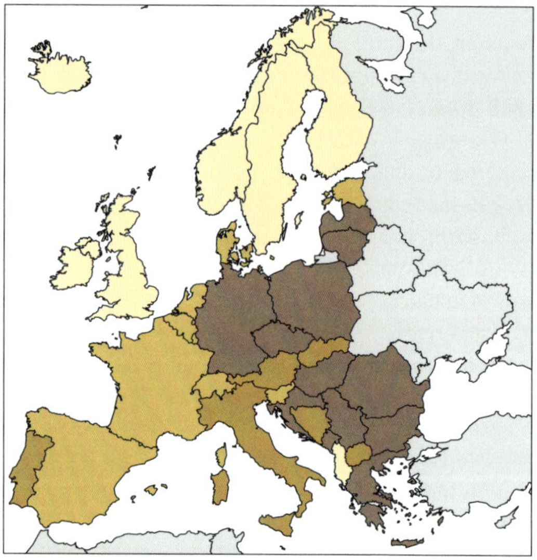

Premature deaths caused by air pollution in Europa
(source: European Society of Cardiology / European Heart Journal)
number of deaths / 100,000 people

- < 100
- 100 - 130
- 130 - 150
- > 150
- no data

1.2 The Need for Circular and Climate Adaptive Solutions

If we want to save our planet with all its resources for future generations, we have to counter its decline, caused by an accumulation of environmental crises like global warming, the spoiling of natural recourses, pollution and the extinction of species. It is not easy, however, to distinguish each one of these crises clearly from the other. They are often closely related and reinforce each other. A good example of this is the burning of fossil fuels to generate energy, which simultaneously results in the exhaustion of finite resources and the acceleration of global warming due to greenhouse gas emissions. Another example of the entanglement of environmental crises is the expansion of paved surfaces within our cities. As a result, it is increasingly difficult for rainwater to seep into the soil, making floods more likely. At the same time there is less space for vegetation to mitigate heat stress and enhance biodiversity. So, instead of taking action to address one single crisis, it is better to address to the whole complex of related crises in a coherent, holistic way. Instead of focusing on one single crisis at the time, we should focus on what actions we can take to remove the causes of environmental crises and to adapt to the consequences of these environmental crises.

An example of the removal of a cause of environmental crises is the reduction of greenhouse gas emissions, which will help slow global warming. By generating energy from infinite sources like sun or wind instead of by burning fossil fuels, these emissions can be reduced. Another example is using more recycled or biobased materials and fewer finite resources, to minimize waste and pollution. Actions that reduce the causes of environmental crises are circular actions, as they turn linear processes into circular ones. Based on infinite resources like sun, wind, recycled materials or biobased products, circular processes can be repeated time after time without aggravating the complex of environmental crises.

Actions to adapt to the consequences of environmental crises do not remove their causes, but mitigate their negative effects. An example is the raising of dykes, to prevent areas from flooding. Another example is the implementation of green in cities, attenuating heat stress. Also the retainment of water, protecting areas against periodic drought is an example of an action that limits negative environmental effects. Though these actions don't stop the climate from changing, they keep our environment liveable despite climate change. Therefore, these actions are called climate-adaptive actions.

From this perspective, the solutions our cities need to counteract environmental crises are classified into circular and climate-adaptive solutions. Implementing circularity and climate adaptation in our cities asks for a reconsideration of the way we develop, use and exploit them. It asks for adjustments in our way of planning. More than before, planning needs to become contextually sensitive, as circularity is most credible when relying on local resources and climate adaptation starts with a careful analysis of local threats and opportunities. More than before, planning should enable its users to implement circularity and climate adaptation in their own surroundings, buildings and networks. And more than before, planning must allow for unpredictability. The availability of circular resources is less predictable and so are weather conditions or the rising of the sea level.

Though Europe is willing to implement circularity and climate adaptation in its cities, this is easier said than done. In practice, making Europe's towns, villages and urban areas circular and climate-adaptive asks for a recalibration of our planning conventions.

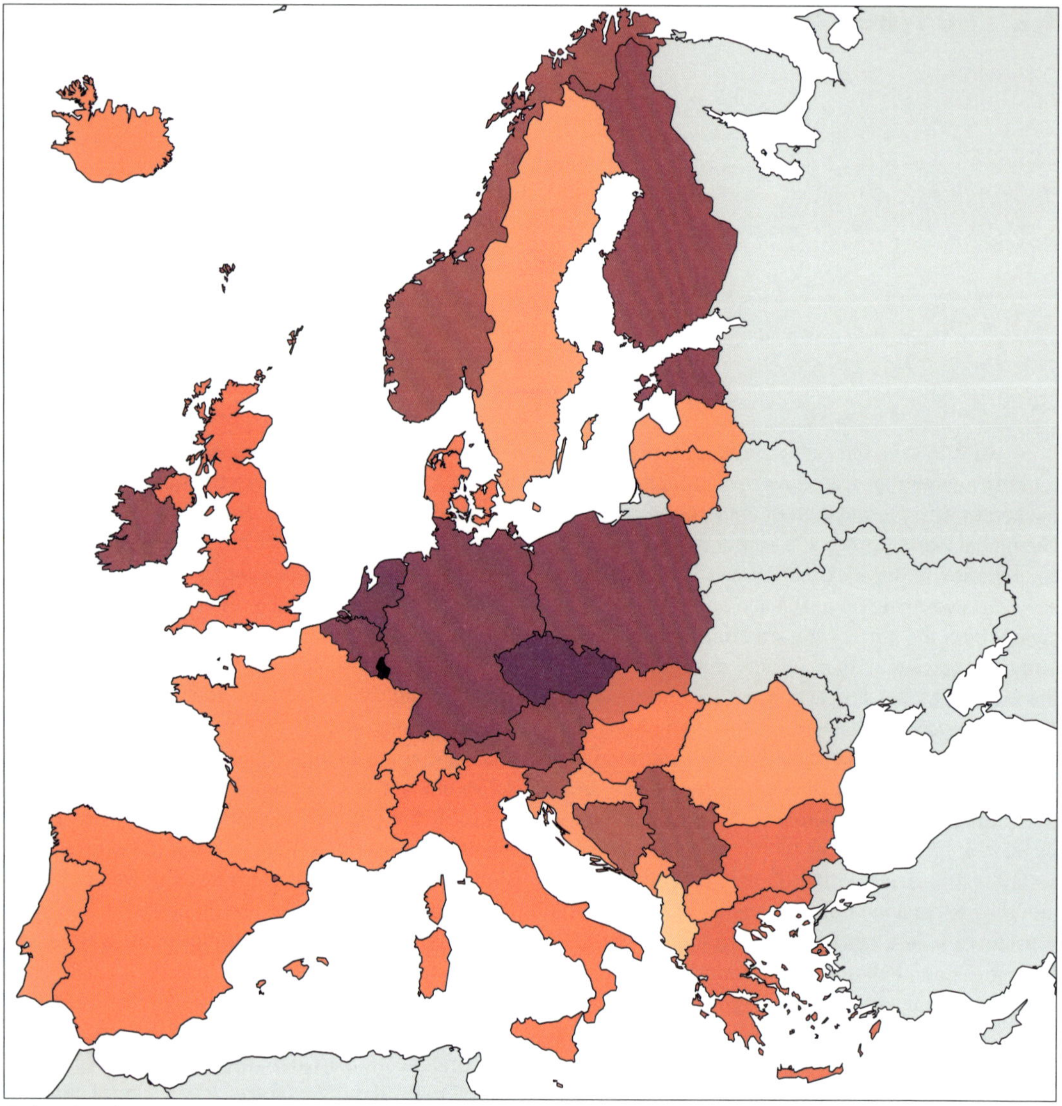

Carbon dioxide emissions per capita, 2019 (source: The World Bank)
(Carbon dioxide emissions are those stemming from the burning of fossil fuels and the production of cement. They include carbon dioxide produced during consumption of solid, liquid and gas fuels and gas flaring.)

tCO2 / person / year

16

0

no data

1.3 System Crisis

If we want to understand how our planning system has to be changed to make our cities, towns and villages circular and climate-adaptive, we first need to understand that system.

Our current planning system is, to a great extent, based on the principles of modern urbanism. Inspired by the possibilities of industrial production and encouraged by social engagement, modernist urbanism arose in the beginning of the twentieth century. After attempts in various European countries to somehow define its principles, like the German definition of a minimum subsistence level (*Existenzminimum*) and the Dutch 1901 Housing Act, an international group of leading architects and town planners drew up the Declaration of La Sarraz in 1928, which can be seen as a complete resume of modernist urbanism principles. The declaration pleas for the industrial standardization of building output, allowing high-quality housing to be built cheaply. This housing should be built in new districts outside the historic city limits, according to urban patterns following the generic functional paradigms of light, air and space rather than site specific, environmental features. Residential areas were separated from working areas and an extensive, car-based infrastructure made sure that people could travel to work efficiently.

In the first half of the twentieth century, the principles of modernist urbanism were adopted by European governments, construction companies, property developers, designers and the users of space. This resulted in a hyper-efficient construction economy that was fully equipped to produce standardized suburban housing on a grand scale, from its organizational structures to its professional mindset, and from the legislation to the business models and production methods. As a result, nearly every European city, town and village got considerably extended in the twentieth century following the economic principles of modernist urbanism.

From the 1970s on, however, there has been a growing awareness that the way we build our cities has severe negative environmental effects. Industrial production based on fossil fuels results in significant greenhouse gas emissions. Building with steel, concrete and brick relies heavily on finite resources. The one-sided focus on efficiency in construction processes ends up in vast amounts of waste and pollution. Expanding towns and cities comes at the expense of their green peripheries, while nature is already under pressure. Focussing on short-term profits rather than on long-term goals, such as a careful contextual fit, eventually leads to urban tissues suffering more and more from environmental threats such as heat stress or floods. The way we are used to planning our cities clearly does not match with the principles of circularity and climate adaptation.

Despite this awareness, the way we plan, construct and use our cities has not fundamentally changed. Apparently, it is hard to change planning conventions. The set of instruments within our planning system is just not flexible enough to implement circular and climate-adaptive solutions. There is a crisis in the system. The way we plan European towns and cities is too inflexible to counteract environmental crises.

If we want to make our towns and cities circular and climate-adaptive, we will have to look for a more flexible set of instruments that makes it possible to implement the necessary transformations, that empowers users to develop new habits and that ensures a sustainable, future-proof urban environment.

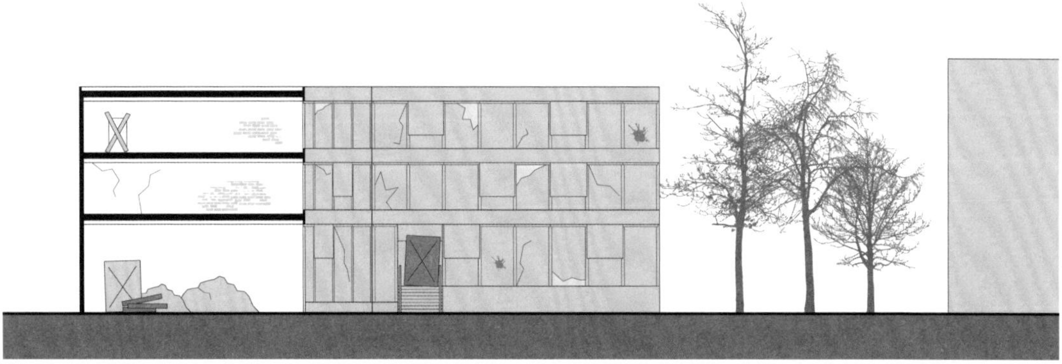

1. An old office building is abandoned.

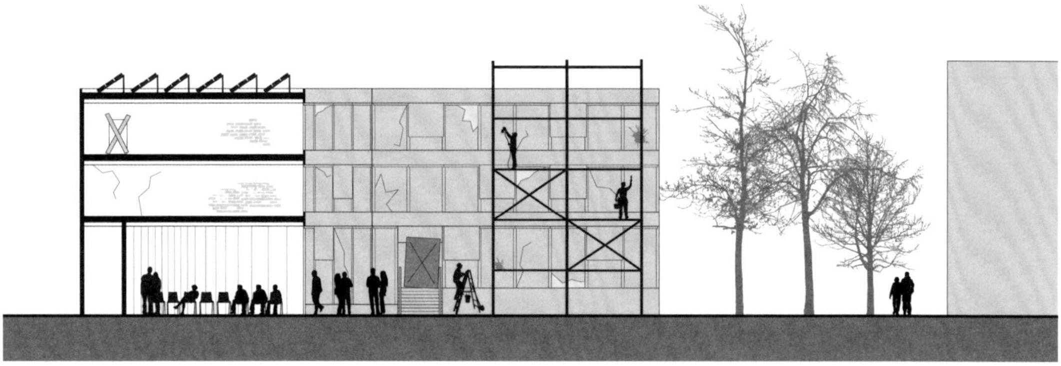

2. The building is insulated, renovated with circular materials and provided with a source for circular energy.

3. Being energy-sufficient and nicely renovated, the building is in full use again.

1.4 From Building to Recycling

Contextual Indifference

The large stock of European property that was built since the beginning of the twentieth century was not designed to be circular or climate-adaptive. If we don't want these buildings to become a source of future problems, we will have to make them circular and climate-adaptive. And, even more important, if we don't want this problematic building stock to grow even further, we have to change our planning habits too.

As a circular use of resources was not part of modern construction, finite materials such as steel, brick or concrete formed the base of the modern building stock, despite their environmental impact. While being mined, produced and transported, these materials make a major contribution to global warming and additionally, their resources get exhausted. As a result, large parts of our cities consist of materials that are not circular and have a big environmental impact. Future transformation or demolition of these buildings will lead to more greenhouse gas emissions and waste.

Turning these city districts into circular environments means making processes circular that were originally linear. Local resources should be identified so that circular processes can be initiated or continued. Building materials, ready to be reused or upcycled, could be such resources. Rainwater that is locally retained or energy from sun and wind can be seen as local resources too. Keeping circular chains relatively small contributes to a smaller environmental footprint. Local production of food and biobased materials reduces greenhouse gas emissions because distances are smaller. A conscious use of finite resources also means a halt to further sprawling of our cities, protecting the surrounding nature. Densifying our cities in a smart way is how we can create more space for living and working.

The focus on efficiency and short-term profits frustrates the ability to respond to contextual features like the water-permeability of soil, local water loops, ecologic qualities or seasonal sensitive circumstances, such as weather conditions. Modern urbanism meant the rolling out of roads and buildings on top of the underlying landscape, regardless of contextual features. As a result, large parts of our cities are not climate-resilient. Vulnerable to floods, droughts or heat stress, these existing districts are the problems of the future.

Incorporating climate adaptation means a close reading of existing features that might cause future threats, such as elevation differences in the underground, the potential for water storage or the ratio between stony surfaces and green. Precious local qualities, such as public infrastructure, private properties or local biodiversity, that are vulnerable to environmental threats should be carefully analysed and protected through appropriate measures. Bringing in climate adaptation means considering the underlying landscape as a base that matters and should be taken as the starting point for any further development.

Local Flexibility

Making our cities circular and climate-adaptive asks for planning instruments that enable us to adapt existing local structures, systems and habits to relate them better to their context. In contrast to the contextually and environmentally indifferent way we used to plan cities, local circumstances become a key factor in making our cities circular and climate-adaptive. As these local circumstances may initially seem to be inflexible and hard to change, we need instruments that enforce more local flexibility to help us incorporate circularity and climate adaptation into our cities.

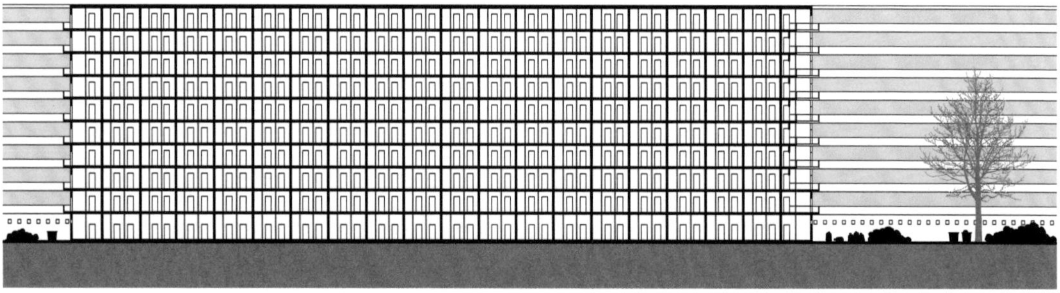

1. A worn-out apartment building suffers from increasing energy costs: residents move out.

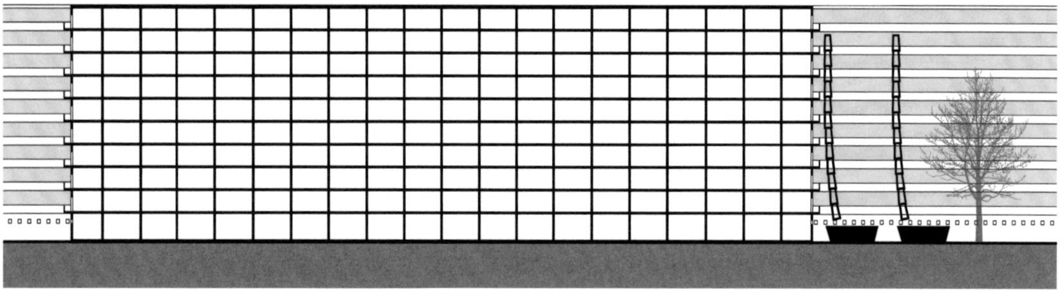

2. Instead of demolishing it, the owner renovates the building and provides it with circular energy supply, reintroducing it to the market with options for residents to co-invest.

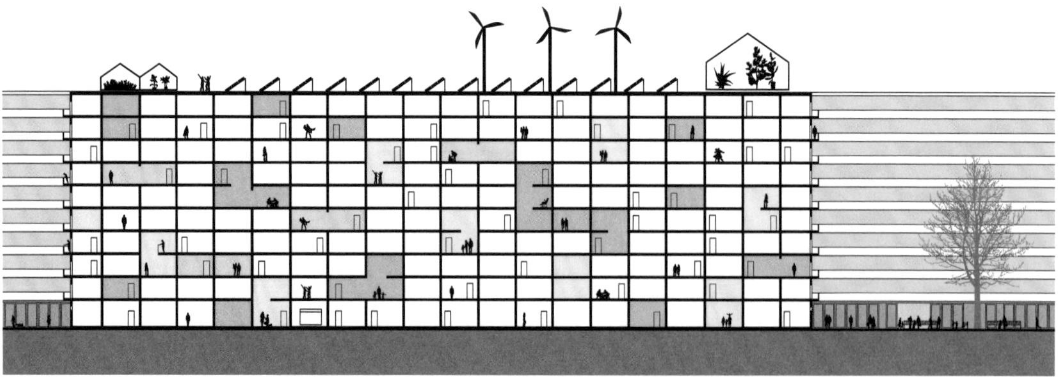

3. Attracted by its sustainability and options to co-invest, new residents move into the building.

1.5 From Supply to Demand

Consumerism

Aiming for the lowest cost and the highest quality, the economy of modern urbanism has been a mostly supply-driven affair. Optimized, linear production chains led to a consumption of finite resources and a production of waste on a scale never seen before. Subsequently, citizens were pushed into a role of mere consumers, accepting the range of products emanating from optimized production processes and degenerating them to disposables within a limited period of time. During the last decades of the twentieth century, unparalleled amounts of waste were produced by consumers all over Europe. On top of that, citizens struggled to develop a sense of ownership for their immediate surroundings, because building developments took place with only little consideration for their contexts.

Of course, parties on the supply side, such as planning authorities and manufacturers of building materials, can play a major role in reducing the environmental footprint of urbanism. But users, representing the demand side of the supply-chain, can have at least as much impact. By liberating themselves from their role as mere consumers and becoming critical about the space and products they use, they can eventually force planners and suppliers to limit the environmental footprint of cities. Making the demand side of production chains more determinative, considerable steps can be made turning our towns and cities into circular and climate-adaptive environments.

Moreover, users can have a stronger impact by being more than just critical consumers of space. As the negative effect of various environmental crises directly threatens their daily living environment, their safety and their health, the urge for change is most directly experienced by the people working and living in these environments. By regaining responsibility for their own living environment and implementing the needed circular and climate-adaptive changes themselves, local communities of users assure that actions are taken suitable for their specific environment and needs. Possessing the property, participating in local networks and being part of the local economy, users and their communities are in a good position to effectuate measures such as the adjustment of building structures to natural water systems, the reinforcement of local ecology and the reduction of car-based infrastructure. Local communities can initiate circular processes themselves, for instance by harvesting of building materials in order to reuse them, or locally producing food. Smaller scaled, circular supply chains will easily lead to a smaller environmental footprints. From this perspective, smaller supply chains can easily turn users into producers of their own goods, eventually strengthening their economies and increasing local profits.

Use-driven Flexibility

In order to implement circularity and climate adaptation in our cities, our urban development and production chains should become more use-driven. We should reconsider the supply-driven set of instruments our cities are currently developed with. A set of instruments is needed that enables users to liberate themselves from their roles of mere consumers, becoming critical about the supply and regain a sense of ownership of their own environment. As users get more responsibility for the layout of their own living environment and the supply of space, circularity and climate adaptation can be better implemented.

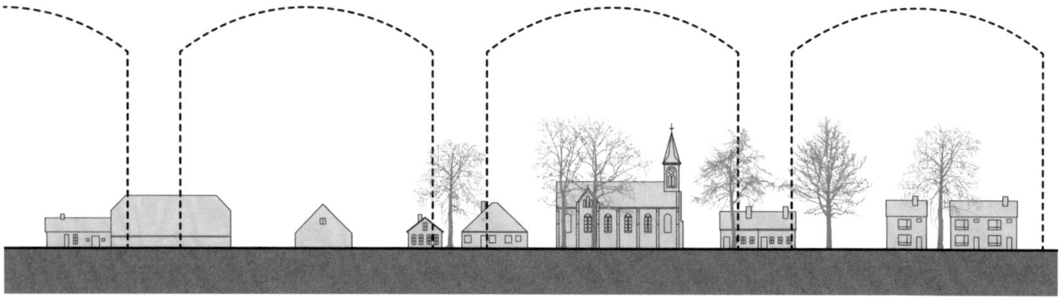

1. An entire village was cleared to make way for the large-scale expansion of a seaport.

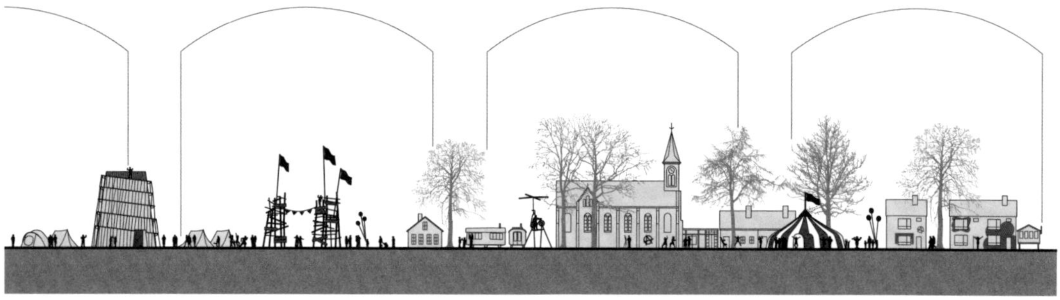

2. As the economy turned circular faster than expected, the port development stagnated; new residents settled in the village.

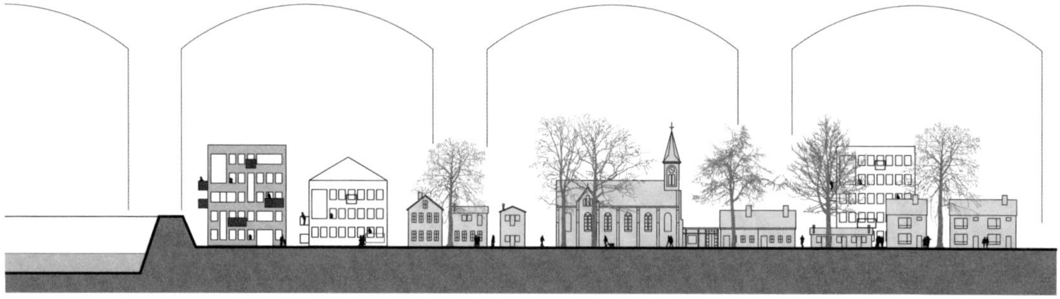

3. The village developed into a unique, flourishing community surrounded by an extensive seaport.

1.6 From Blueprint to Unpredictability

Stagnation

Based on blueprints, modernist urban planning derives from the perception that society is predictable, plannable and controllable. Subsequently, the availability of resources is perceived as being endless and natural phenomena such as the fluctuation of water levels, seasonal droughts and the climate are considered predictable. We all know, however, that both the availability of resources and our climate are increasingly characterized by unpredictability. The realization that the future can no longer be controlled or predicted to the same extent as before is making our current way of urban development problematic, as it is still mainly based on the principles of predictability. Awareness of the uncertain availability of resources and possible future environmental threats is sapping the confidence of investors, developers, users and other relevant players. While the urge for changes is growing, projects implementing circularity and climate adaptation are seen as increasingly high-risk from a fear that investments will not be recouped in time. As a result, the necessary shift towards circular and climate-adaptive towns and cities is stalled.

A greater emphasis on time as a factor will lead to a more stimulating investment environment in our cities, towns and villages. If we are able to improvise in the short term, while retaining a focus on long-term objectives, we can respond much more quickly to sudden changes, and simultaneously prepair larger structural changes and implement these in phases. That will make towns and cities future-proof and adaptable again.

Time-based Flexibility

The current system for spatial development is based on the idea of endless resources and a rigid plan that does not change over time. This strong focus on planning and long-term, fixed objectives removes time from the equation. For many years, the idea was that in case the future would not turn out as expected, related failure costs could be compensated by growing profits. But now that various environmental crises are causing major problems, failure costs are suddenly becoming an issue. This, too, stalls the implementation of circularity and climate adaptation.

Circularity and climate adaptability therefore require time-based flexibility. A new set of instruments is needed that enables adjustments to be made when the future is capricious or does not turn out as expected. In practice, time-based flexibility means working in steps, whereby results are always temporary and open to change. Interventions no longer just depend on large amounts of capital, on-off interventions or a large scale for their success. Modest steps that are well chosen can ultimately have major consequences.

2. The Flexible City

A circular and climate-adaptive city can easily be reused, enables its inhabitants to be responsible for their own environment and is future-proof. A circular and climate-adaptive city is a flexible city.

Changes are not standalone events; they are emphatically part of a process of continual transition. New developments do not lead to a fixed final position, they rather emerge from future-oriented, dynamic starting positions. Only then can truly circular and climate-adaptive solutions be found.

In this chapter, we explain what we mean by flexible area development and how it works.

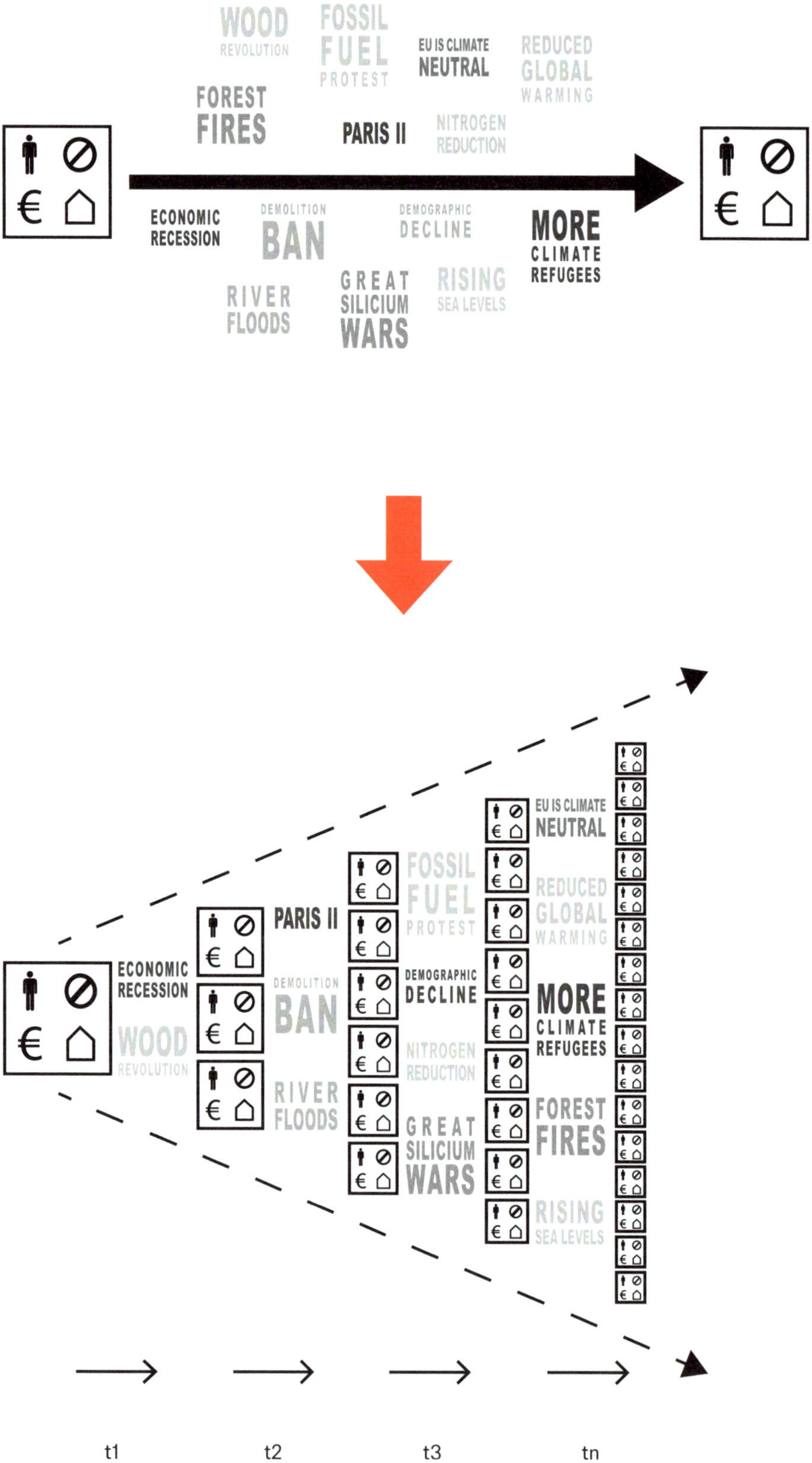
WOOD REVOLUTION
FOSSIL FUEL PROTEST
EU IS CLIMATE NEUTRAL
REDUCED GLOBAL WARMING
FOREST FIRES
PARIS II
NITROGEN REDUCTION
ECONOMIC RECESSION
DEMOLITION BAN
DEMOGRAPHIC DECLINE
MORE CLIMATE REFUGEES
RIVER FLOODS
GREAT SILICIUM WARS
RISING SEA LEVELS
€
€
ECONOMIC RECESSION
WOOD REVOLUTION
PARIS II
DEMOLITION BAN
RIVER FLOODS
FOSSIL FUEL PROTEST
DEMOGRAPHIC DECLINE
NITROGEN REDUCTION
GREAT SILICIUM WARS
EU IS CLIMATE NEUTRAL
REDUCED GLOBAL WARMING
MORE CLIMATE REFUGEES
FOREST FIRES
RISING SEA LEVELS
t1
t2
t3
tn

2.1 Flexible Area Development

In flexible area development, each individual development is explicitly part of a continual process of development.

If Europe's cities, towns and villages are to become more circular and climate-adaptive, an innovative approach is required that will enable a transformation that is more sensible to existing circumstances, is more focused on the inclusion and participation of users and is better able to cope with unpredictability. Our experience in our own projects, research and our analysis of the international case studies presented in Chapter 4 show that an approach in which each development is explicitly part of a continual process of developments is the one that best satisfies these requirements. If a development is seen as a stepwise process rather than a single event, it can gradually take shape on the basis of the existing qualities, while users and other stakeholders gain more influence and it becomes easier to respond to unforeseen and unforeseeable dynamics.

This stepwise approach to development contrasts sharply with the conventional approach to development, which assumes a single large step to a predefined situation or final position – what is known as blueprint planning. To emphasize the contrast with blueprint or final-position planning, we call the steps in the flexible development model *starting positions*. The stepwise approach with starting positions gives a development strategy that is far more pliable and flexible than in the case of blueprint planning.

In principle, this development strategy is scale-independent and can be used for a broad range of projects, from interiors to buildings, from streets to urban districts and from new buildings to conversions. Of course, the steps are relative and a step on the scale of an interior is not the same as a step on the scale of a city. From a temporal perspective too, small steps can be separated by months, years or even decades in some cases. The size, nature, duration and impact of the steps are determined on a project basis. A building that can temporarily be present, because it is built out of circular, demountable elements to satisfy peak demand and then be removed without leaving any traces can just as much be a step as a functionally neutral building designed for the long term that is constantly able to adapt to fluctuating forms of use. The essential element in development on the basis of starting positions is that there is always a follow-up step available.

As a result, spatial development no longer produces an outcome that is static and permanent. Instead, it produces something that is in a constant state of flux. Development is no longer about fixing a building or area according to a blueprint or final position; it is about taking steps in a continual process of gradual change.

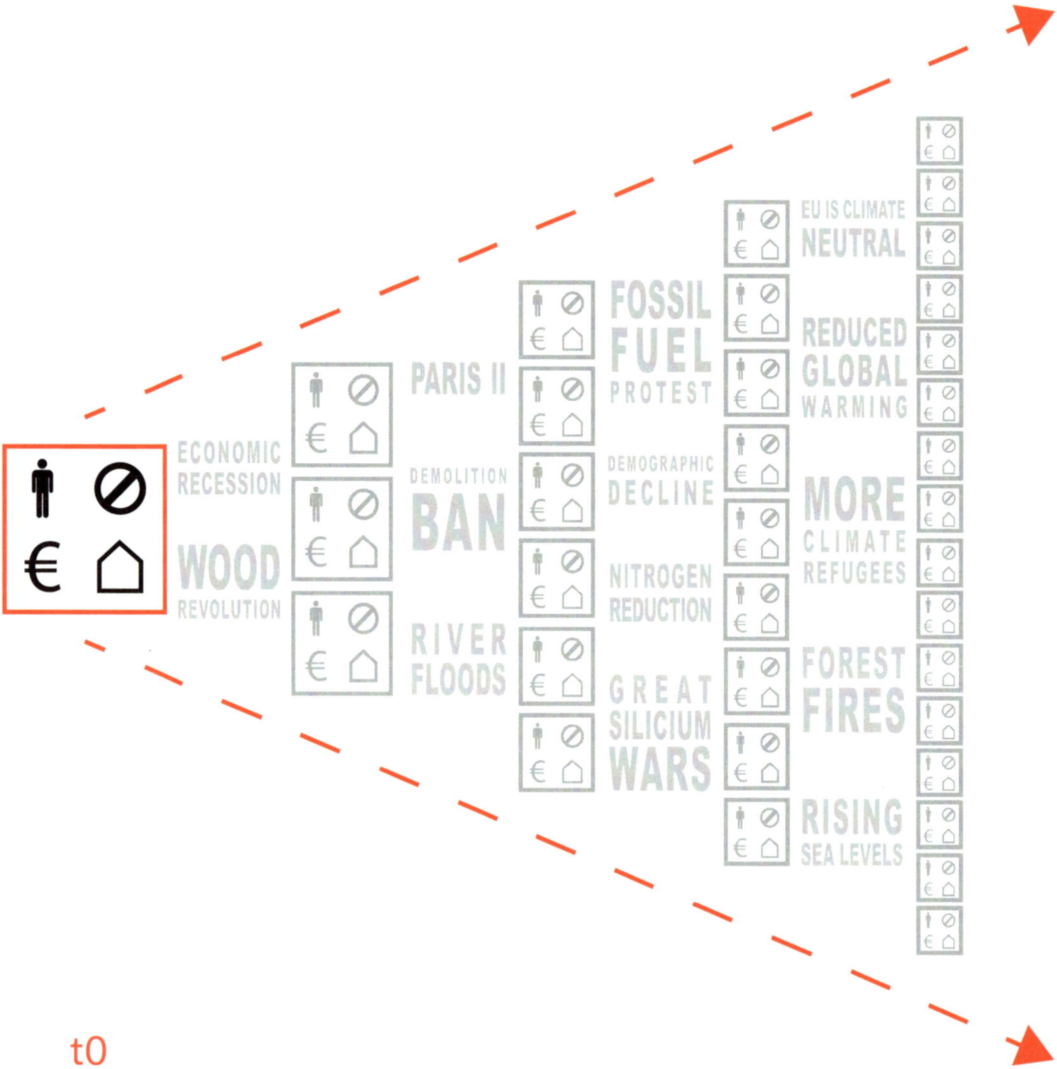
ECONOMIC RECESSION
WOOD REVOLUTION
PARIS II
DEMOLITION BAN
RIVER FLOODS
FOSSIL FUEL PROTEST
DEMOGRAPHIC DECLINE
NITROGEN REDUCTION
GREAT SILICIUM WARS
EU IS CLIMATE NEUTRAL
REDUCED GLOBAL WARMING
MORE CLIMATE REFUGEES
FOREST FIRES
RISING SEA LEVELS
t0

2.2 Local Flexibility

In blueprint planning, specific local conditions play a subordinate role in the drive for efficiency. In this development approach, it is standard practice to remove or simply ignore as many of the existing elements as possible when preparing the site for building in order to keep processes manageable. However, this practice is at odds with the drive for circularity and climate adaptation.

Flexible area development, on the other hand, enables specific local conditions to be taken as the starting point for redevelopment. Taking these conditions as the point of departure rather than eliminating them brings major benefits such as a better fit to the underlying landscape, more chances for the reuse of materials, shorter procedural and construction phases and broader support among stakeholders. In this way, flexible area development leads to tailored solutions, enabling existing parts of the city to become circular and climate-adaptive.

A qualitative and quantitative analysis beforehand of the specific local conditions shows what developments are possible based on the existing situation. Future situations therefore evolve from the characteristics of the current situation.

Limiting Conditions

The possibilities for incorporating circularity and climate adaptation are determined by the local process-related, legal, financial and spatial limiting conditions.

The process-related limiting conditions are set by the local stakeholders and the way in which they are organized. These stakeholders include not just the parties that are traditionally involved, such as the public authorities, developers, investors, consultants and builders, but also other parties that are locally engaged, such as maintenance managers, energy suppliers and, last but not least, the users. The organizational form determines who is able to exercise influence over a development, when and how.

The legal limiting conditions are determined by the rules that apply for the location, for example those laid down in structural concept documents, zoning plans and local by-laws, as well as generally applicable standards as defined in building decrees and legislation.

The financial limiting conditions are, for instance, the value of existing lands and properties related to the capitalization of environmental risks as well as any rental income and the opportunities for financiering or refinancing.

Finally, the spatial limiting conditions concern the physical characteristics of the location, such as the soil characteristics, the structure of existing buildings and the local availability of resources. The spatial analysis should include a survey of the technical and historical features of the location.

Development Framework

These limiting conditions give an understanding of all the available development or redevelopment options at a location. However, not all these options are desirable. All the undesirable development options can be excluded by drawing up a development framework with critical qualitative and quantitative upper and lower thresholds. Although such a development framework leaves much still open, it helps to clarify the prospects for a location. It seems logical that the development framework should primarily be determined by the owner in consultation with the governmental authorities, which would be responsible for checks. But in principle any party can draw up a development framework.

Because it is easier to map out the near future than the more distant future, this results in an overview of prospects that fans out from a few identifiable options in the short term that could in the longer term lead to many possible follow-up steps, whereby the more distant steps cannot yet be predicted in detail.

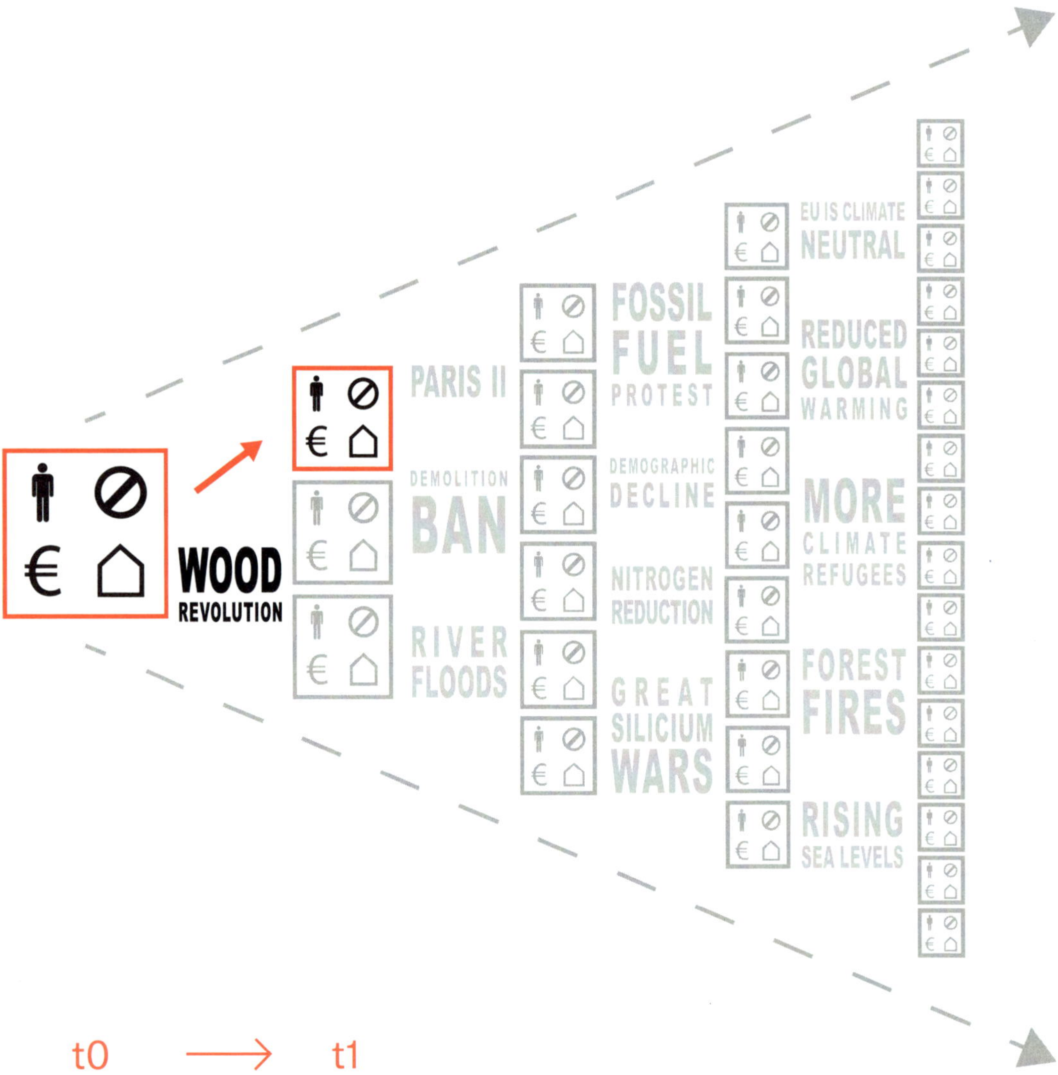

WOOD
REVOLUTION
PARIS II
DEMOLITION
BAN
RIVER
FLOODS
FOSSIL
FUEL
PROTEST
DEMOGRAPHIC
DECLINE
NITROGEN
REDUCTION
GREAT
SILICIUM
WARS
EU IS CLIMATE
NEUTRAL
REDUCED
GLOBAL
WARMING
MORE
CLIMATE
REFUGEES
FOREST
FIRES
RISING
SEA LEVELS
t0
t1

2.3 Use-driven Flexibility

In blueprint planning, a small team of professionals decides on the cubic content of the buildings, the land values and the designated use of new developments beforehand. However good the market research is, any development that is fixed in advance in this way is bound to be speculative. This means that there is a risk of new developments disregarding the actual needs of local communities. This approach can lead to neglected environments, social segregation and waste.

Flexible area development enables users and local communities to take responsibility for their own environment; as a result, developments are based on concrete requirements rather than being speculative. Having all parties that are relevant to the success of the new development take decisions jointly, rather than restricting this to a small team of professionals, ensures that only developments for which there is a demonstrable demand are realized. This reduces investment risks and makes it more likely that residents get involved in the project.

This approach to decision-making requires different forms of collaboration with different decision-making structures and different hierarchies.

Decision-making

Flexible area development permits input from local communities of users, but also from financers and the parties charged with maintaining and running the properties, from owners to government bodies such as city districts, municipalities and provinces, and other relevant parties. This does not mean that all parties automatically have equal influence in the decision-making process. The extent of their say depends on the project. It is reasonable to expect the owner and perhaps the initiator too to have the most influence on the setup for the decision-making process. They determine what decisions have to be made, by whom, when and how. It also seems likely that stakeholders will have less of an influence in decisions where the impact is on a larger scale and for a longer period, as the public interest will be greater then. On the other hand, self-determination is a more obvious choice for smaller-scale decisions.

The role of advisors such as architects, urban planners and construction cost experts is an interesting question. Within the project's development framework, they list all the possible first steps based on the wishes of the stakeholders. The parties involved take good note of this information and then make a joint decision. Because they make the decision together, all those involved are committing themselves to the decision and confirming their own tasks and responsibilities, such as letting out the space, carrying out maintenance tasks, providing permits or financing the plan. Once a decision has been taken, it is irrevocable for a limited period, and the impact on the future remains limited.

Starting Positions

The series of possible next steps as identified by the advisors are termed starting positions. The starting positions form a comprehensive description of the options in the short term. Each of these shows the interactions between the process-related, legal, financial and spatial consequences. The selection of one specific starting position implies the rejection of all other starting positions and automatically alters the development framework.

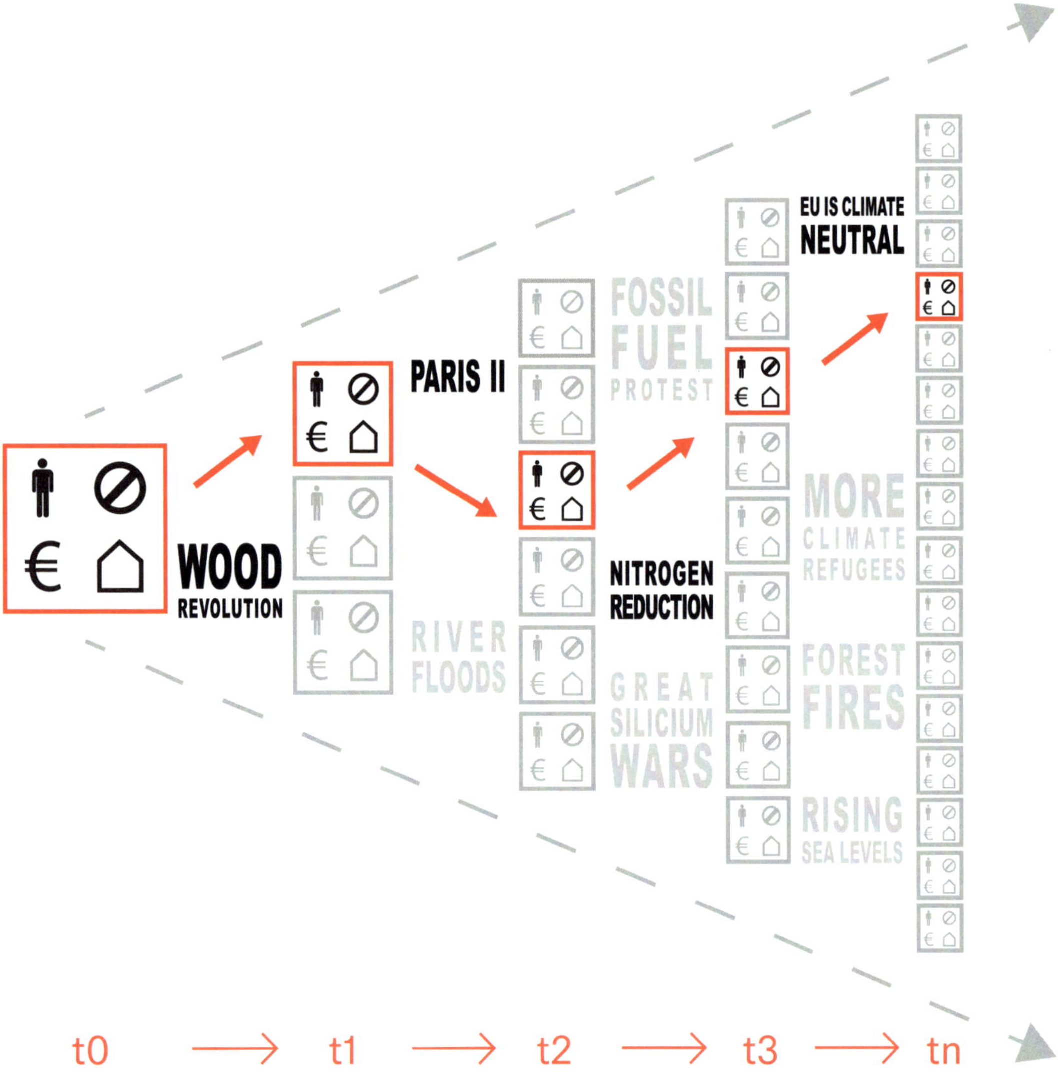
WOOD
REVOLUTION
PARIS II
RIVER
FLOODS
FOSSIL
FUEL
PROTEST
NITROGEN
REDUCTION
GREAT
SILICIUM
WARS
EU IS CLIMATE
NEUTRAL
MORE
CLIMATE
REFUGEES
FOREST
FIRES
RISING
SEA LEVELS
t0
t1
t2
t3
tn

2.4 Time-based Flexibility

In blueprint planning, the development process is kept manageable by keeping the final position fixed with no further alterations after it has been calculated, checked, adopted by administrators and communicated to others. Time and time again, though, it turns out that actual situation develops in a way not envisaged in this final position. As a result, this approach leads to high costs of failure, which are increasingly difficult to earn back elsewhere.

The stepwise approach used in flexible area development means that it is still possible to work on a development during the project execution. Changing availability of resources or other new insights can still be taken on board once the project is in progress. Parties that join later can still have a say rather than being faced with definitive plans. It is possible to experiment during the development process and to incorporate the conclusions in the decision-making. Investments are made in phases rather than all in one go, which spreads the risks.

In this way, all kinds of unforeseen events can be taken into account during the development process.

Events

Project-related conditions can change, with the threat of budget overruns and shifts in the number or category of users as a result. External factors can also change. Examples are an increase in energy costs, changes in the political climate or a deterioration in the economic situation. The consequences of both project-related events and external events can be allowed for in flexible area development.

Such events have an impact on the number and size of the steps in the flexible development model. If the economy is going through a tough time, the investments and therefore the steps are small; if the economy is flourishing, the steps can be bigger. If there are many unexpected events, many extra steps are needed; if there are few unexpected events, fewer extra steps are required.

Recalibrating

Because of the stepwise approach, plans can be recalibrated within the development framework if there are unexpected events or new insights. An assessment based on the latest insights is made as to what forms of optimization are necessary, desirable and possible. A series of new starting positions gives an understanding of the consequences of these optimizations. This enables a new development course to be set based on sound considerations. Each subsequent step is treated as a new starting position.

During the development process, it may transpire that the development framework (containing all desirable future scenarios) itself needs to be modified or shifted. What are termed 'reflective sessions' can be used for the recalibration. In these sessions, stakeholders reflect on the development process and discuss the consequences of recent events with one another. The decision-making model as described above, which is designed specifically for a particular project and in which other stakeholders in addition to the initiator and the owner are also able to exercise influence, shows how the recalibration takes place exactly.

Thus, the factor time plays a key part in *Flexible area development.*

Flexible Ecosystem Restoration

Unintentionally, green networks in our cities have in the last decades been interrupted by roads and buildings, breaking up ecosystems, isolating species and decreasing biodiversity. These connections can partly be restored by carefully reconnecting the isolated green areas with chains of trees, plants or unpaved land strips.

As significant quantities of our cities are privately owned, the strategy to reconnect these green parts should contain tools of different kinds, both public and private, both large-scaled and small-scaled, both temporary and permanent. Close analysis of each possible casus should lead to the right combination of tools. Eventually, time will tell how fruitful the green reconnection can become.

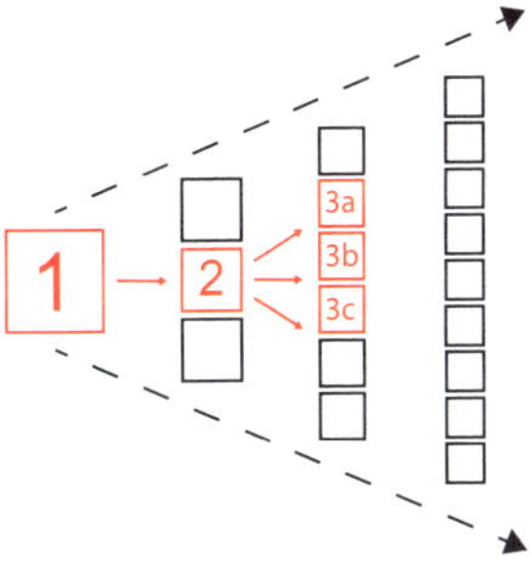

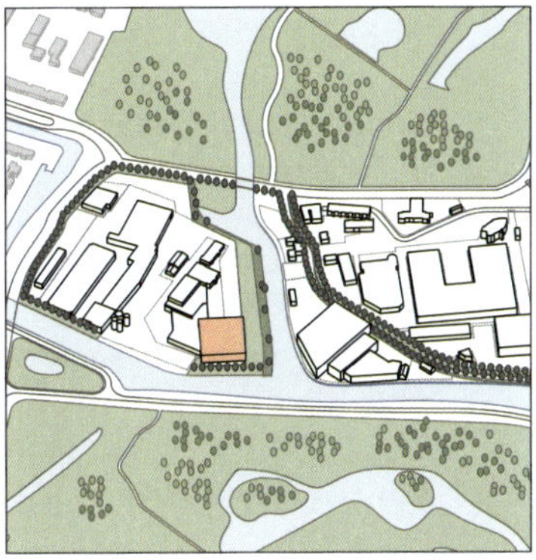

3a. Furthermore, only municipality-owned parts like the verges of public roads are transformed into green belts of plants and trees.

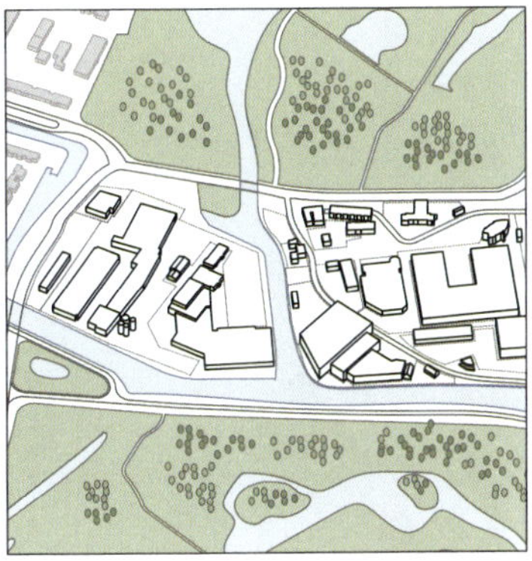

1. An unfortunately positioned business park breaks up an ecosystem, isolating green areas on both sides.

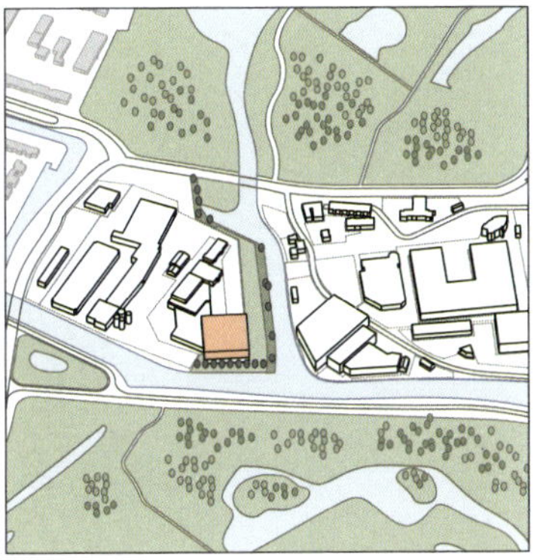

2. With smart land politics, good timing and a bit of luck, some private owners are encouraged to introduce green to their properties.

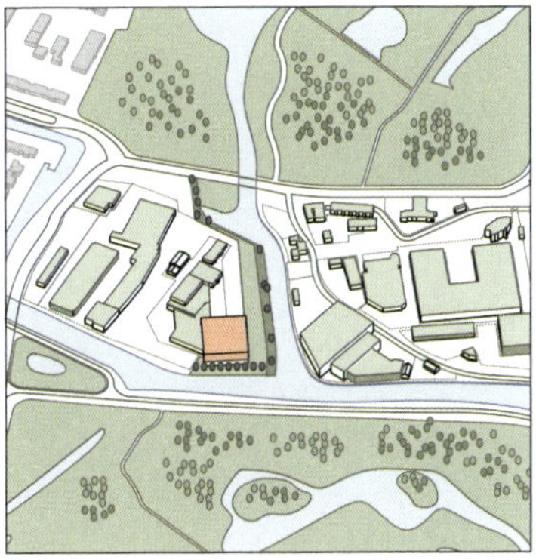

3b. More private owners are stimulated to have green facades and roofs and plant trees in their borders.

3c. More private owners are encouraged to densify their building volumes, creating space for green.

Flexible Heat Island Attenuation

It is widely known that the introduction of green in our urban environments reduces the heat island effects on sunny days. Not in all city districts, however, additional plants and trees are easily imaginable. Especially the monumental parts of our cities - in a way the most problematic parts because of their mostly stony pavements and brick or marble facades - are considered to be unchangeable.

By carefully following and emphasizing the monumental structures of building volumes, facades and pavements and by avoiding any irreversible losses, it should be possible to introduce green in our monumental streets and facades. Based on the specific context, the amount of local support and the exact legislation, experiments should lead to new possibilities.

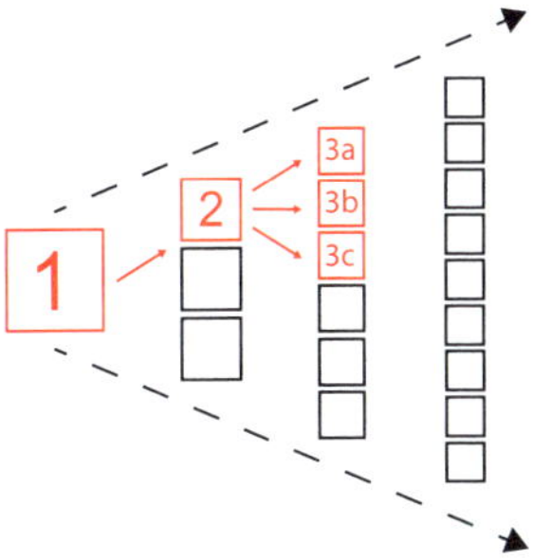

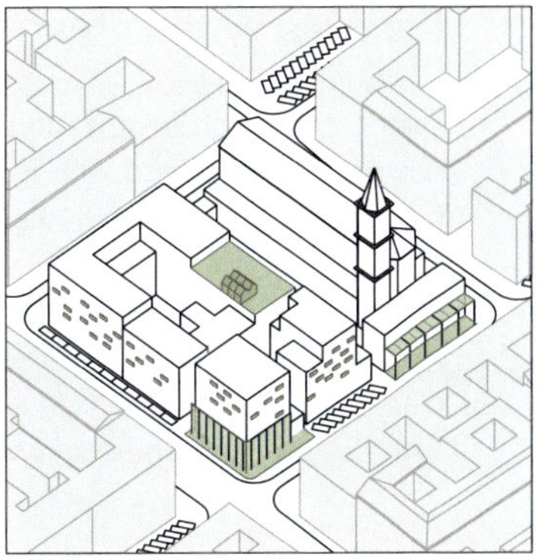

3a. Individual residents discover added value of green, filling their private balconies with plants.

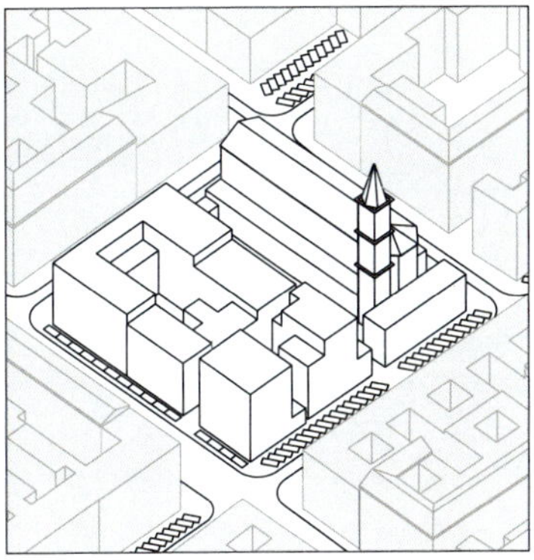

1. A monumental part of the city, characterized by its stony materials, suffers from heat on sunny days.

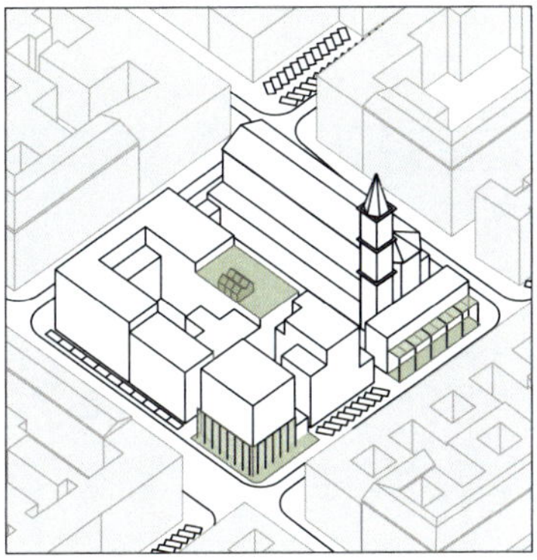

2. Experiments introducing green reveal which of the interventions are the most promising.

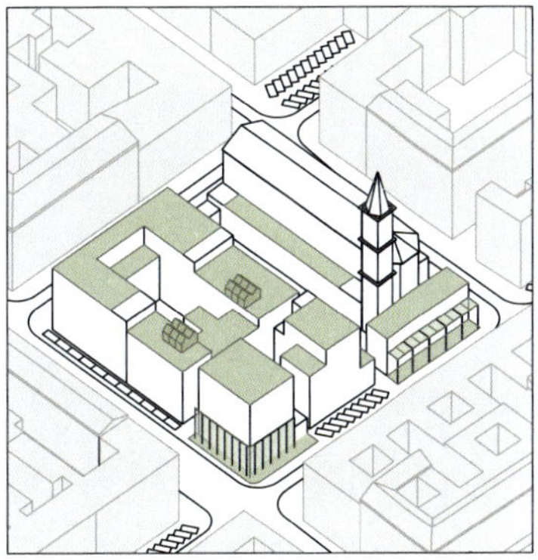

3b. Private building owners discover the added value of green, transforming their roofs into green terraces.

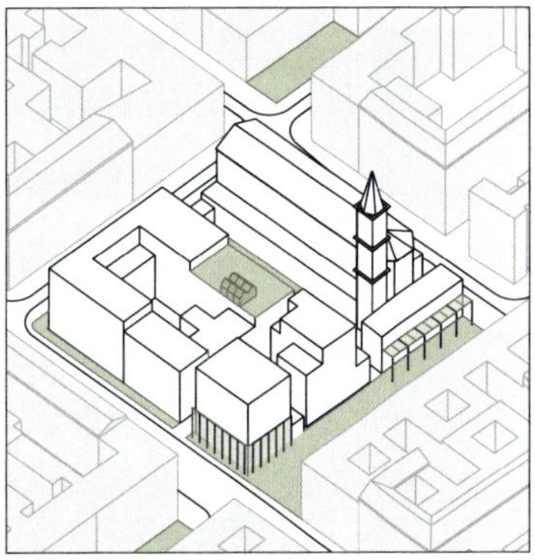

3c. Reducing car traffic leads to possibilities for more green.

Flexible Water Responsivity

Water stress will become more apparent in the future due to climate change. This might be stormwater accumulation in depressed areas, inundation from polder systems or even flooding when dykes break.

This plan shows that the right flexibility can be reached by a strong accidentation of the ground level combined with smart basements for all buildings, introducing the possibility of a second ground floor.

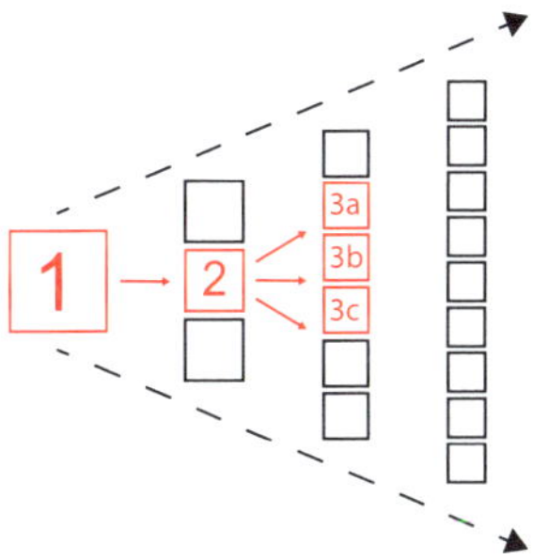

3a. Small fluctuations and surplus water can be stored in the lower parts of the accidented terrain. Traffic and daily life are unaffected.

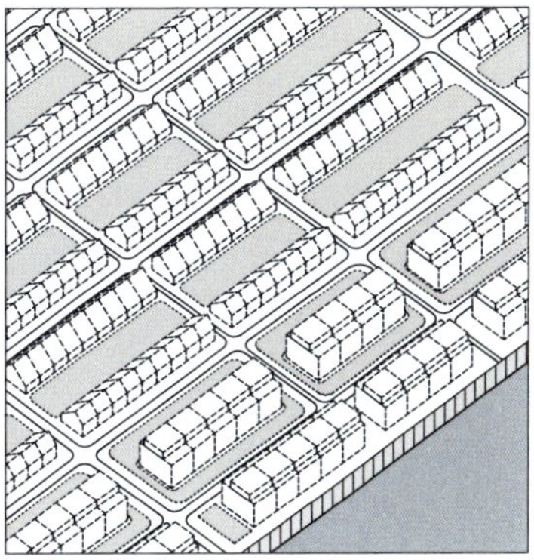

1. A generic housing plan is assessed as being too vulnerable to floods and is cancelled.

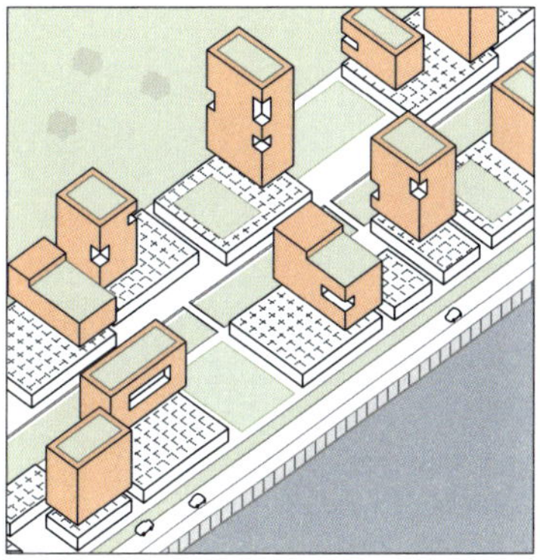

2. An alternative housing plan is realized with a strongly accidented ground level and smart basement storeys, offering the future possibility of a raised urban ground level.

3b. Bigger fluctuations are blocked by the introduction of a massive dyke along the waterside.

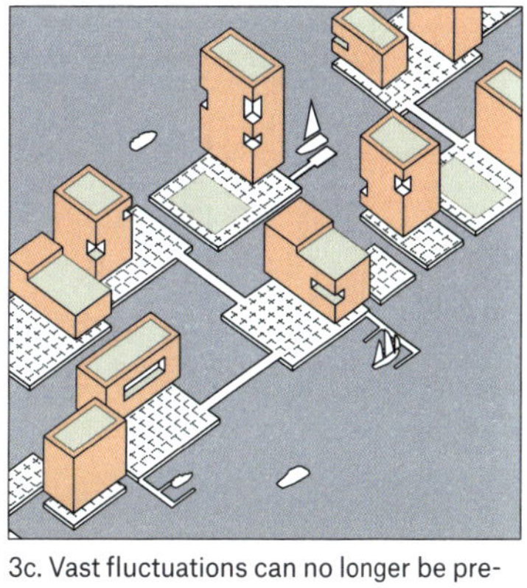

3c. Vast fluctuations can no longer be prevented. The basements are dismantled, building materials are reused elsewhere and basement roofs become the urban ground level.

Flexible Reuse of Circular Materials

The finiteness of building materials will lead to a serious scarcity of resources in the near future. Deliveries will become increasingly insecure and prices for materials will rise, so we will have to develop alternative building methods, in which existing building structures form the base for new developments and reused building materials are highly sought-after.

Having reuse as a central principle, future architecture will have an element of improvisation. The availability of material resources is one of the key factors determining future perspectives for a location.

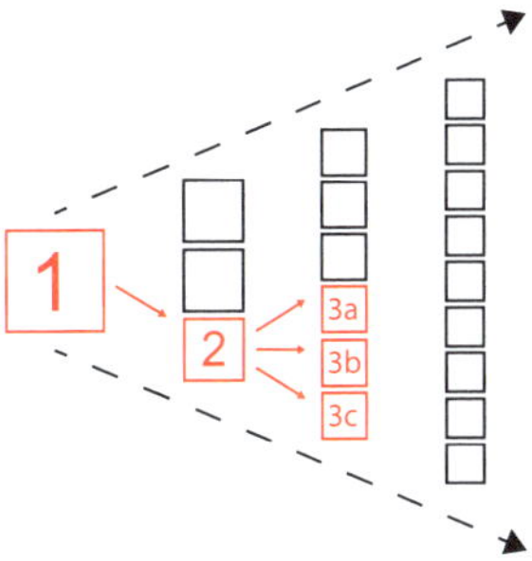

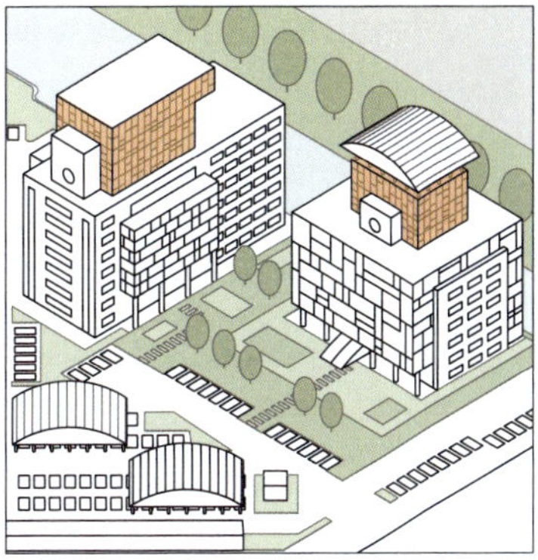

3a. As the circular transformation of the first building was successful, other buildings follow.

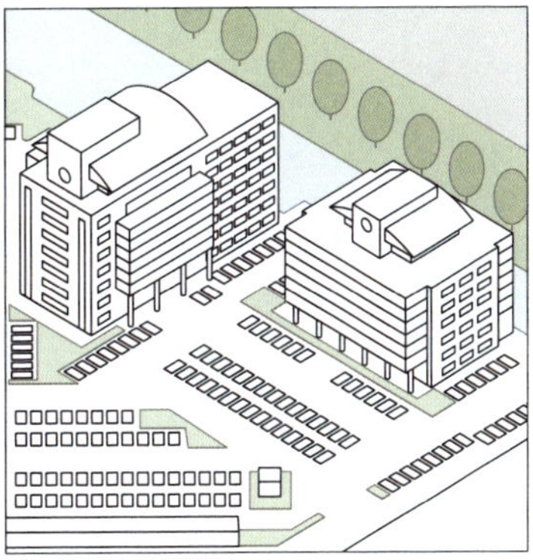

1. An office area is suffering from vacancy, while the city is particularly in need of residential space.

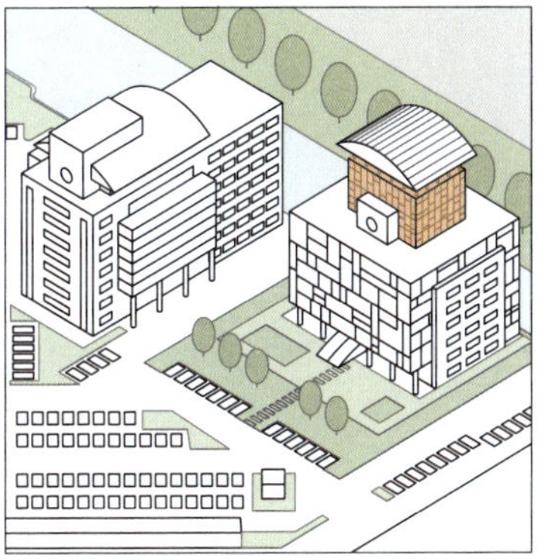

2. One of the buildings is transformed into a residential building, reusing its casco.

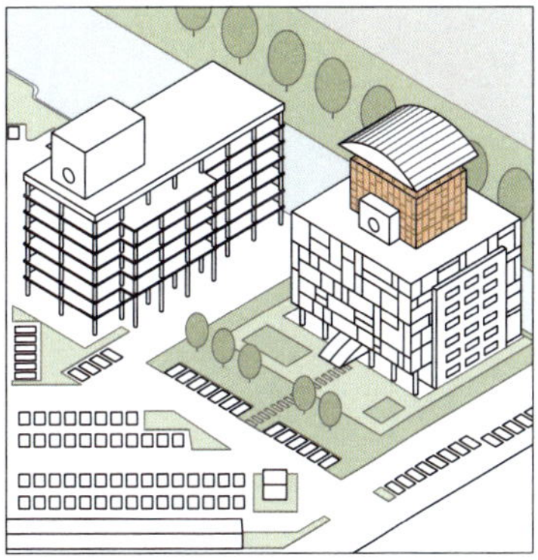

3b. Transformation of other vacant buildings is not possible anymore; all demountable materials are stolen.

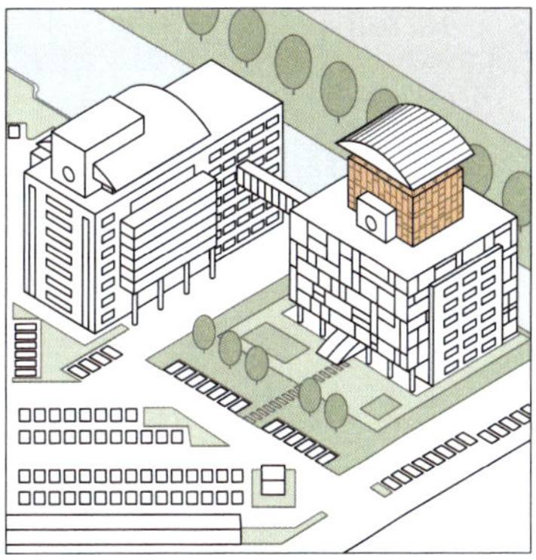

3c. Now that the residents get to know the place, they appreciate the office building and connect it to their own property with a bridge.

Flexible Suburban Mixing

Many suburban parts of our cities are monocultures. Quickly built in the rush of twentieth-century urban expansion, they are monofunctional, mostly car-based and barely green. These areas are increasingly problematic as their monofunctional housing stock ages and needs a thorough renovation. Counteracting a growing social segregation, the existing suburban housing stock should be diversified, so that not only families, but also single and elderly people can live here. The addition of green and reduction of car-based traffic make these areas contribute to a healthier suburban population.

Changing existing urban tissue, however, asks for a careful strategy that allows stakeholders to have their say and that can adjust to various outcomes.

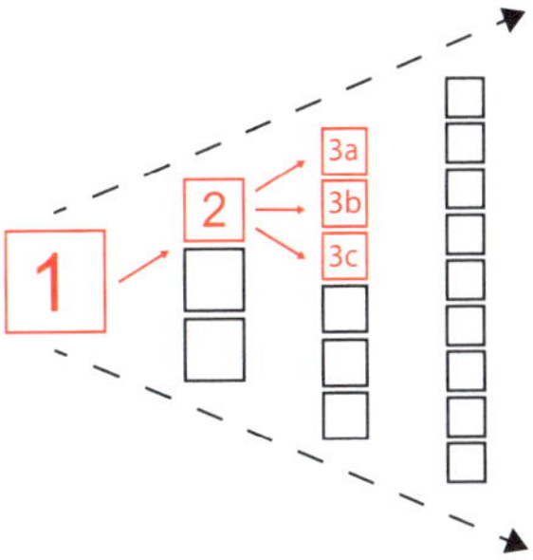

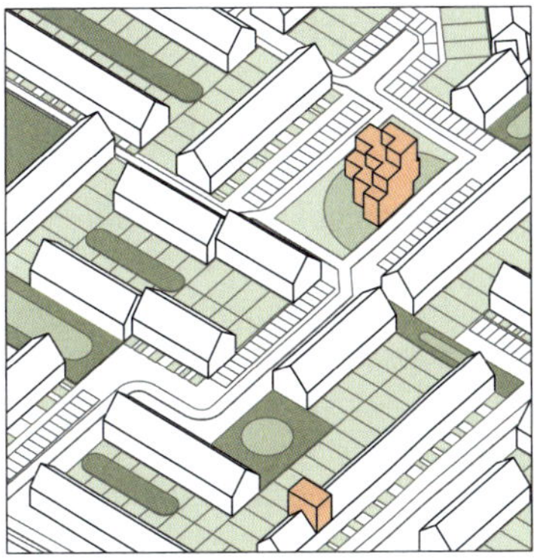

3a. Adding green and reducing the car-based infrastructure appears to get the most local support.

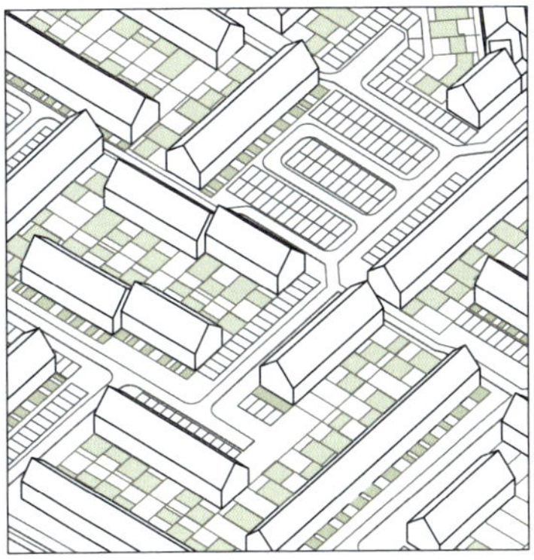

1. Many suburban parts of our cities are car-based, monofunctional, barely green, and therefore not future-proof.

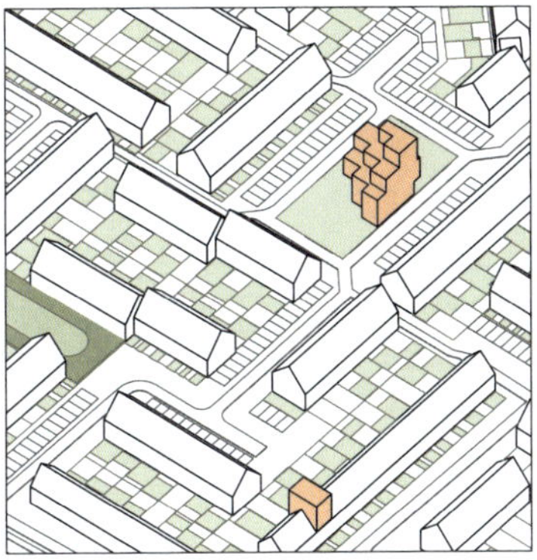

2. Experiments are done to add vegetation, reduce car-dominance and diversify housing types.

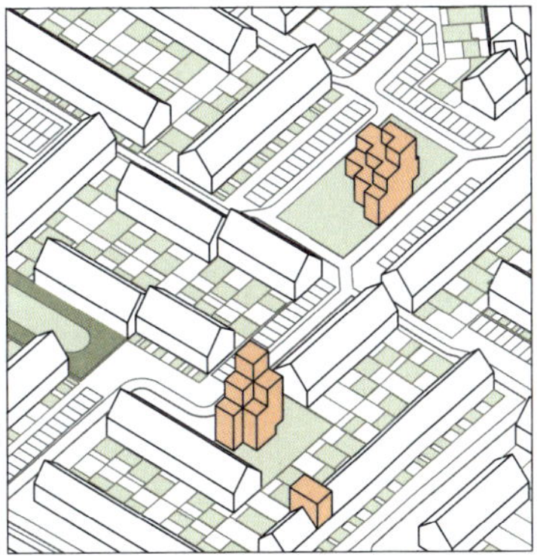

3b. Diversifying the housing stock by adding new buildings appears to be the best future option.

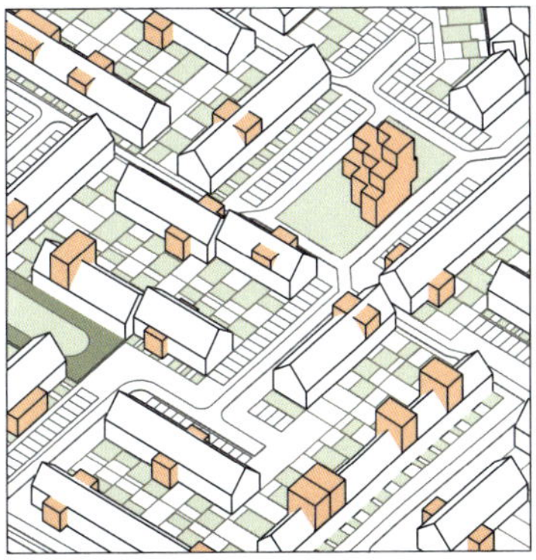

3c. Diversifying the housing stock by adjusting, splitting or enlarging existing residential buildings appears to be most popular.

Flexible Food Production

The ecologic footprint of our current food consumption is too large. We must look for ways to reduce its consequential negative effects such as greenhouse gas emissions and waste. Locally producing food helps to counteract these negative effects and has unexpected benefits, such as healthier food and social inclusion.

Local stakeholders think it is practical to link the introduction of urban farming to other sustainability-related challenges in the neighbourhood, such as renovating apartment buildings, greening the neighbourhood or maintaining public gardens. After the linked introduction, an evaluation should tell if urban farming would be appreciated, if residents would participate and in what way it would work the best.

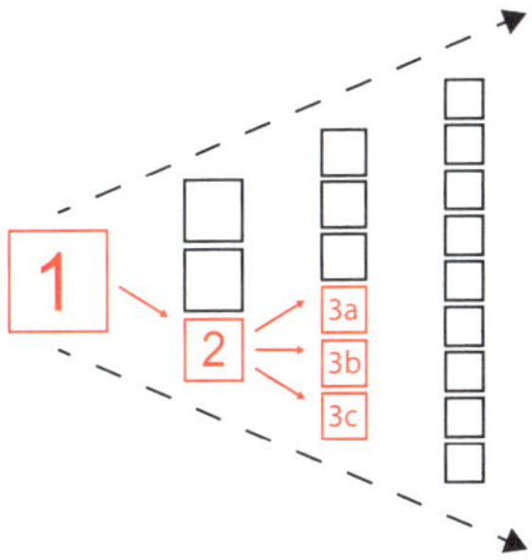

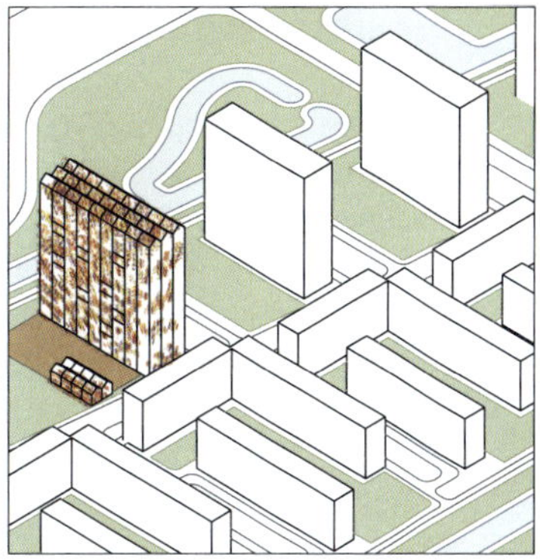

3a. Urban farming turned out to be a temporary fad. Only the residents of the renovated apartment building grow their own food.

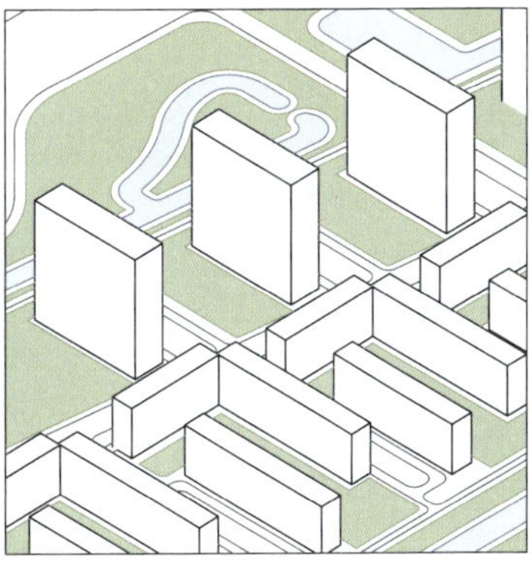

1. A 1960s suburban residential area is facing big challenges, among which the bad eating habits of its inhabitants.

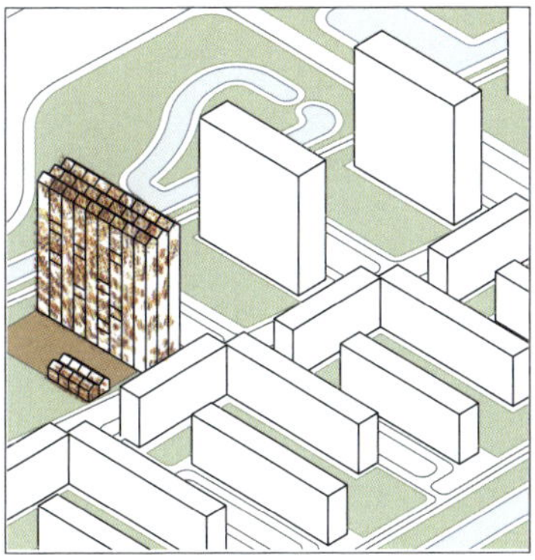

2. Private food production, both within and next to the building, is part of the renovation of a huge apartment building.

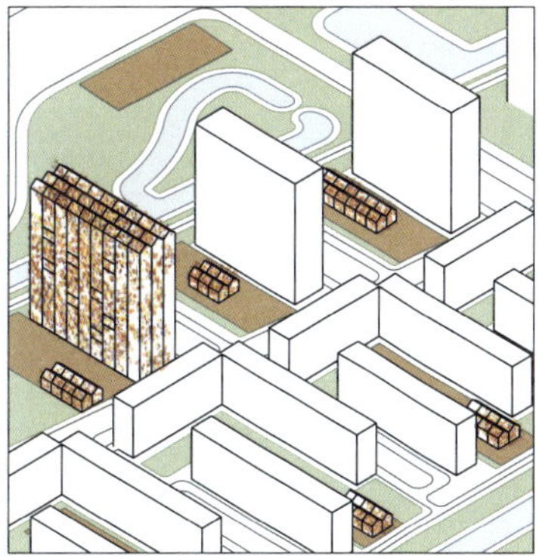

3b. Urban farming is appreciated in the area, but only outside of the buildings.

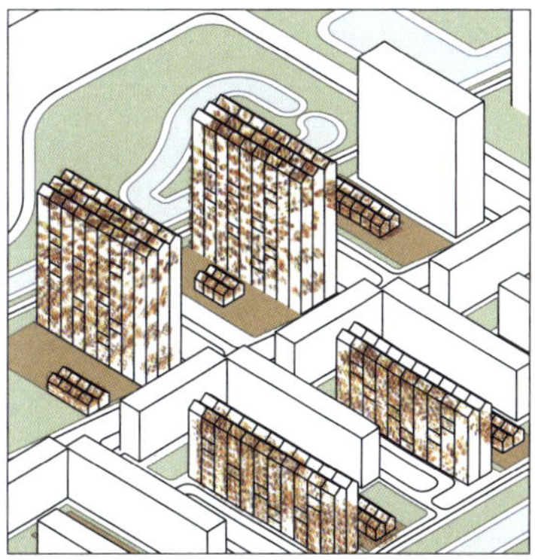

3c. Due to societal circumstances such as inflation, inhabitants embrace private urban farming.

Flexible Elimination of Pollution

While transforming the city, sites with heavy industry or waste management become available for more vulnerable functions such as housing or public space. Cleaning the polluted underground is expensive and often done chemically or by means of excavation, causing lots of unrest in the soil.

It is about time to experiment with new ways of dealing with polluted sites, embracing the principles of circularity. When soil remains untouched, existing infrastructure can be kept. New temporary buildings are lifted and don't touch the ground so that phytoremediation plants can decontaminate the soil in a natural way.

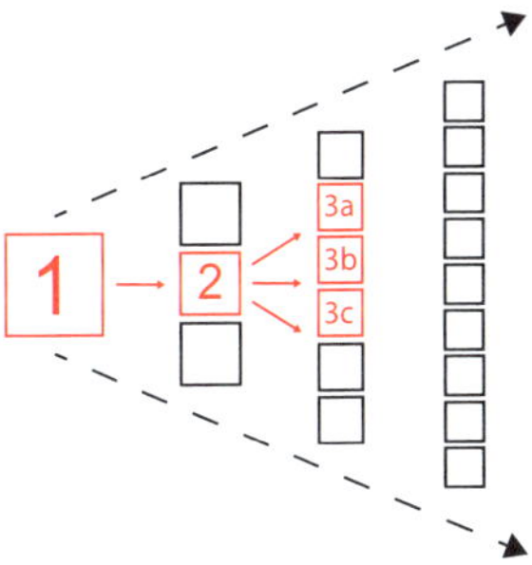

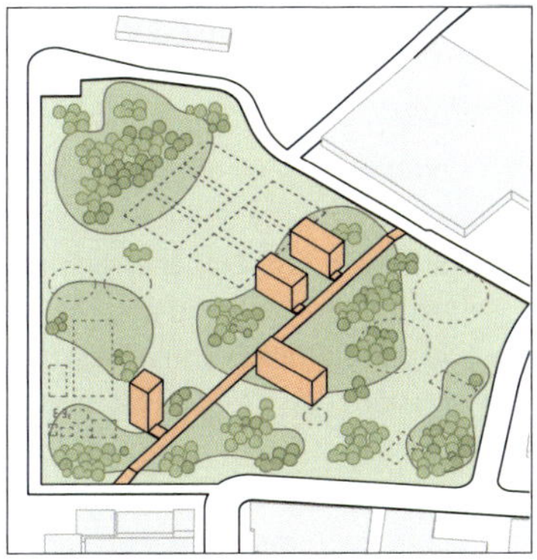

3a. Next to some temporary buildings, plants clean up the soil in a biological way and with a slow pace.

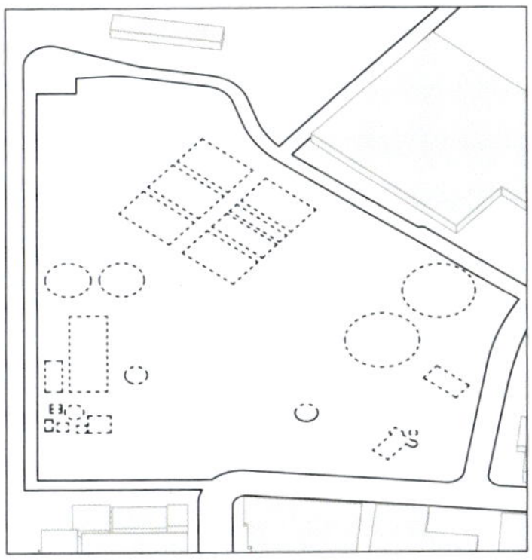

1. Devices for water purification and garbage collection are dismantled, leaving a site that is heavily polluted.

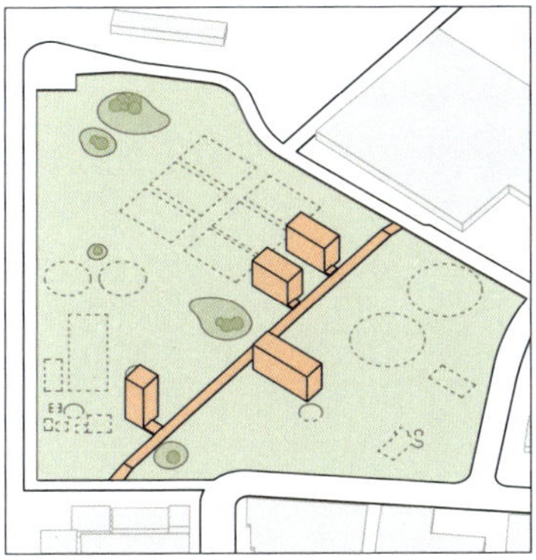

2. Avoiding chemical purification and high cleaning costs, a lifted deck offers possibilities for temporary buildings.

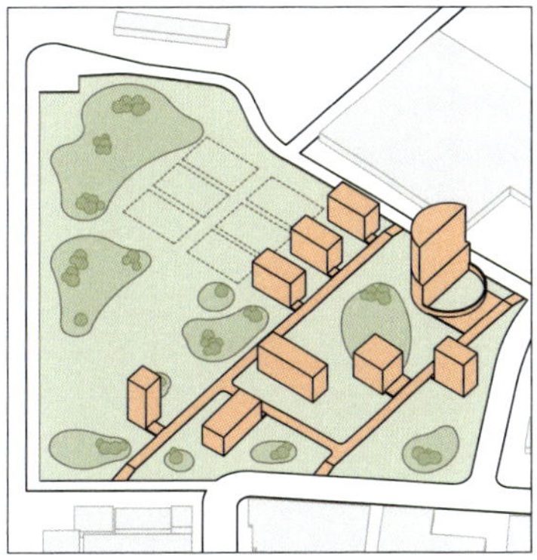

3b. Plants decontaminate the soil while the temporary city grows a bit.

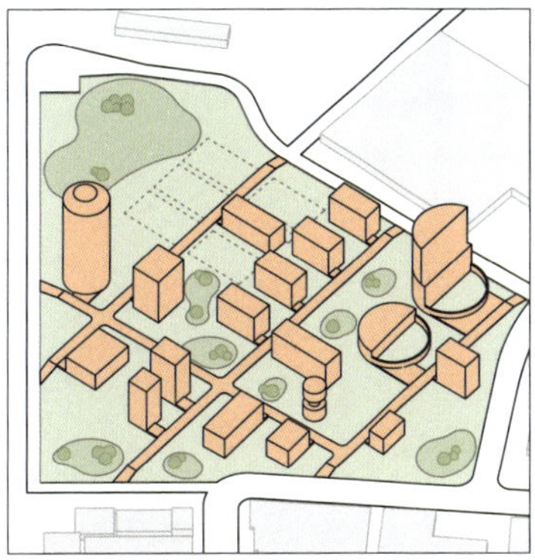

3c. The temporary city grows quickly, while on the ground, plants decontaminate the soil.

Flexible Energy Transition

Reducing our greenhouse gas emissions means, amongst other things, using renewable sources of energy. As the energy supply is of vital importance to our buildings, this energy transition cannot be underestimated. It should not only lead to physical changes in our buildings and infrastructure, but also to organizational and legal alternatives in order to make the transition of our complete energy system work.

There are several ways to make this transition happen. For consumers, it can be an opportunity to gain more independence and strengthen social inclusion. Aspects such as scale, ownership and the type of resource can all be reconsidered.

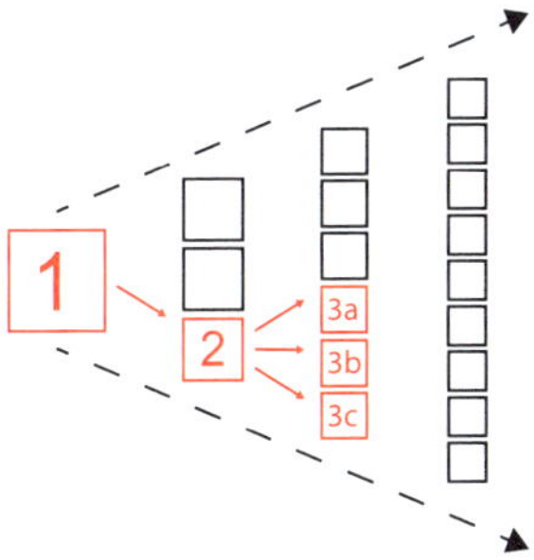

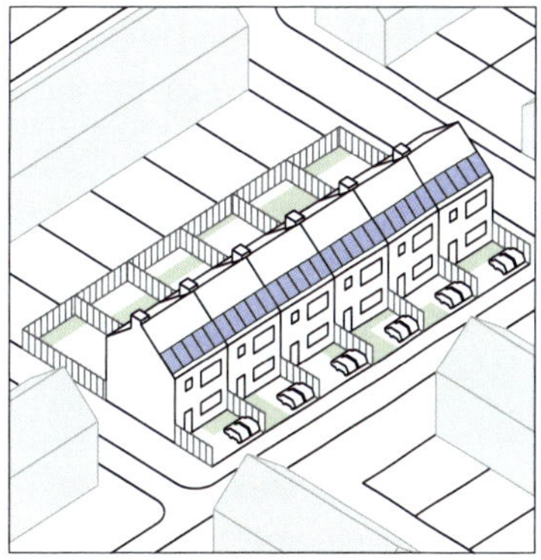

3a. Residents struggle with implementing additional measures for renewable energy and stop making additional investments.

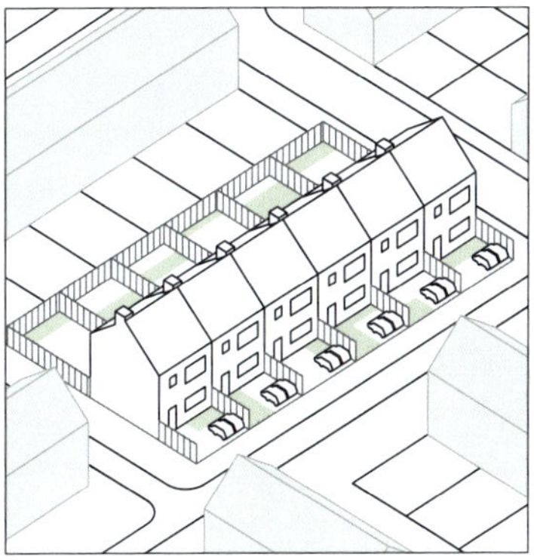

1. A generic housing block should be connected to renewable energy sources.

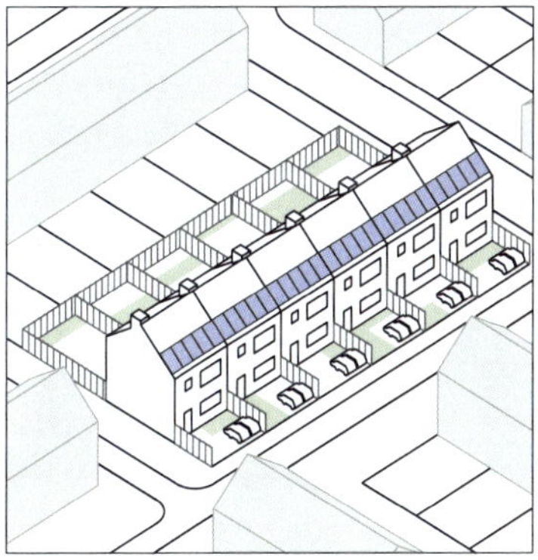

2. A collective investment leads to collective solar panels on the common roofs.

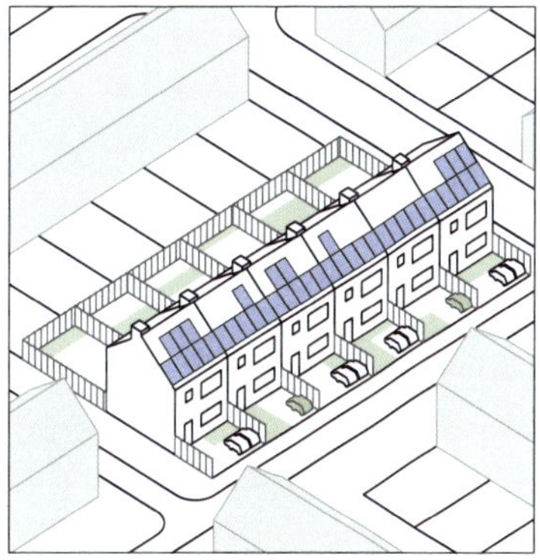

3b. The energy transition is continued, but only with private investments.

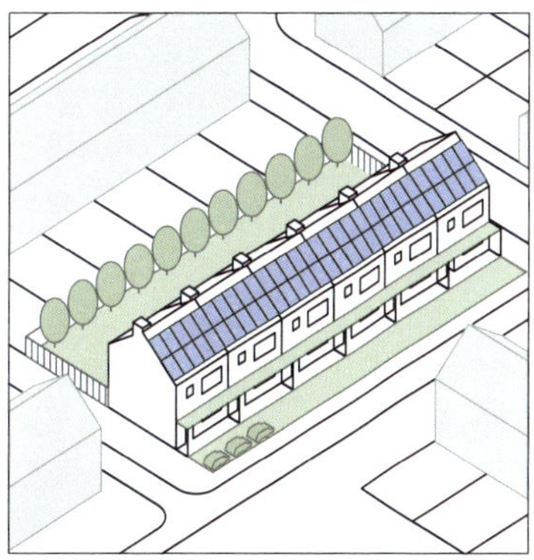

3c. The collective investment leads to more collectivity, such as shared cars, bicycles and a communal garden.

Flexible Car Reduction

Though in our cities, an increasing group of citizens embraces alternative means of transportation, such as walking, electric bicycles or public transport, many public spaces are still mainly equipped for cars. Politicians may have difficulties transforming these spaces, afraid of complaints of the remaining car users about the car accessibility of their neighbourhood.

With a stepwise transformation, citizens and entrepreneurs can slowly get used to a new balance between car accessibility and other qualities of life in the city. When the first transformation step turns out well, more car-based public space could be transformed. If the remaining car-based areas become more crowded, only a few car-accessible roads or parking spaces are lost.

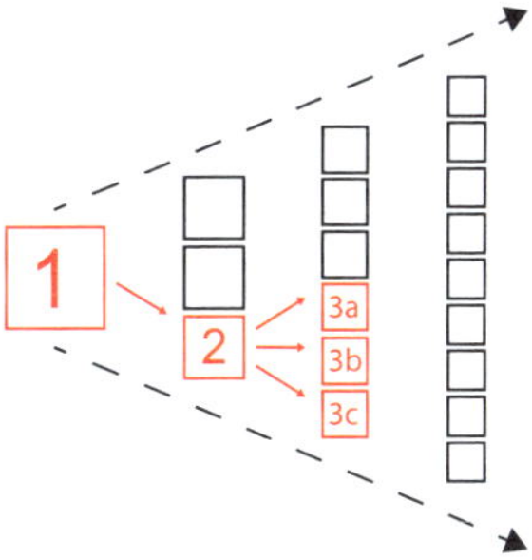

3a. The other part of the parking strip is better used and remains unchanged.

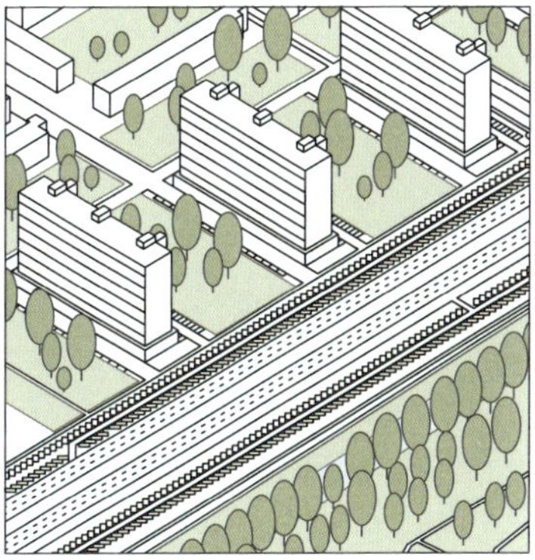

1. A wide strip between an urban quarter and a city park, destined for large-scaled car parking, is barely used any more.

2. In the part closest to the urban quarter, the car parking is transformed into housing blocks with gardens.

3b. The other part of the parking strip is transformed into a park-like strip, linking the city quarter and the park.

3c. The other part of the parking strip is also transformed into housing blocks with gardens.

3. Instruments for a Flexible City

Different instruments are needed to create more circularity in our cities and adapt them to the changing climate. Together with experts in organizational, legal, financial and spatial affairs, we have compiled a set of 36 instruments that can give shape to the flexible city. The instruments in this chapter offer more flexibility by focusing more on existing structures, usage and timing.

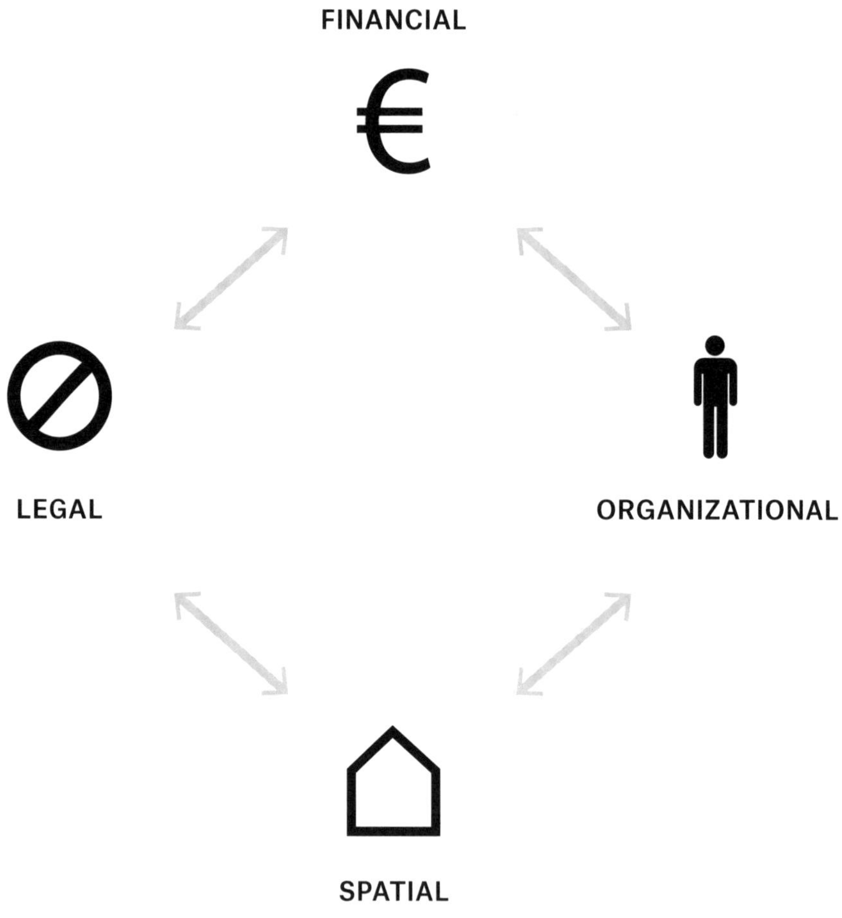
FINANCIAL
LEGAL
ORGANIZATIONAL
SPATIAL

3.1 The Key Domains Determining Spatial Development

Spatial development is traditionally subject to four limiting conditions, namely the process, the regulations, the financing and the spatial design. There are instruments for each of these limiting conditions. Spatial development takes shape through the interplay of these different instruments. Specialists in each of the four domains collaborate and coordinate their own input with that of other specialists.

Now that spatial development needs to become more circular and climate-adaptive, the conventional instruments are being called into question. Are they helping European cities to become more circular and climate-adaptive or are they in fact hindering that process? Our analyses and studies show that different instruments are required – sometimes to replace the usual instruments, sometimes in combination with them – in order to arrive at a more flexible kind of spatial development.

Together with experts in organizational, legal, financial and spatial affairs, we have drawn up a list of the instruments that enable flexible spatial development. In this chapter, we present nine flexible instruments for each of the four domains.

Not all the instruments presented here are instruments in the literal sense of the word. You could also call the instruments described here *conditions for success*. Some deal with the necessary change in attitudes or describe a generally applicable principle.

In line with the structure of the previous chapters, the instruments relating to each domain are subdivided into instruments for local flexibility, use-driven flexibility and time-based flexibility.

3.2 Organizational Flexibility

The 'process' is the way in which the relevant parties collaborate in the development of the space. Process-related instruments facilitate this collaboration.

Creating a more circular and climate-adaptive living environment requires forms of collaboration that involve more parties than perhaps was customary in decision-making in the past. If this decision-making process becomes continuous rather than a one-off event, a neighbourhood, village, town or city becomes more future-proof as a result. Parties should therefore be enabled to continue to exercise influence in the longer term too.

Local Organizational Flexibility

Because new developments tend to be located within the existing urban fabric, many stakeholders are already settled there, and many different interests play a role. It is best to get these local stakeholders involved early on in the decision-making process in order to ensure sufficient support. To achieve this, local processes need to be tailored to requirements.

Use-driven Organizational Flexibility

Getting users and other stakeholders more involved in decision-making from an earlier stage ensures that the supply of space is shaped by their actual needs. This prevents consumerism and does more justice to users' requirements. But it does demand a new, more flexible approach from established players such as public authorities, housing corporations and institutional developers who are used to working top-down.

Time-based Organizational Flexibility

Now that processes can be subject to big changes in the conditions during the development period, resulting in new process-related dynamics, it has to be possible to make adjustments to the collaborative form and the decision-making model during the process.

3.3 Organizational Instruments

Local Organizational Flexibility

DYNAMIC BIODIVERSITY MANAGEMENT

DATA-BASED POLICIES

HOLISTIC APPROACH

Use-driven Organizational Flexibility

REUSED MATERIALS MEDIATOR

EMPOWERING LOCAL COMMUNITIES

DESIGN OUTPUT MONITOR

Time-based Organizational Flexibility

INNOVATION BOOSTER

INFRASTRUCTURE REARRANGEMENT

CIRCULAR SUPPLY CHAINS

DYNAMIC BIODIVERSITY MANAGEMENT

Local Organizational Flexibility

Degraded ecologic conditions are considered as a new base from where conditions for plants and animals can be improved in order to boost biodiversity.

Why

Human activity induces the transformation of natural land conditions and often harms nature. The main direct cause of biodiversity loss is land use change which drives an estimated 30 per cent of biodiversity decline globally, the second is overexploitation which drives around 20 per cent.

Growing awareness of this negative impact may, in the end, lead to projects that clear away all human activities at a certain area and restore its original land condition. Though used as an antidote to anthropogenic environmental degradation, these land-restoration projects are often met with criticism and are cost-intensive. In addition, the restoration of land requires another disruption of the environment, which can again disturb wildlife, alter the soil structure, and change the landscape. Therefore, our approach to thoroughly manipulated land conditions is worth reconsidering. Destroyed landscapes might unintentionally contain positive conditions for new species. Being aware of these conditions and improving their quality could foster biodiversity or let new ecosystems arise.

How Does It Work?

Changing natural landscapes into agricultural lands, mines, industrial sites or cities usually means a reduction or even destruction of its original biodiversity. However, it also leads to new conditions that can be attractive to both some of the original species and to new ones. The main focus of people then is the introduced economic activity such as farming, mining, producing or living. The renewed balance in biodiversity is often not seen, nor recognized or appreciated.

Dynamic biodiversity management accepts the changed local biodiversity and starts by analysing it. How varied, stable and balanced is it? How is it related to the original biodiversity and to surrounding biotopes? What species could be added or should be suppressed, in order to improve balance and variety? Did native species that were originally not familiar with this specific site, discover it? Wherever possible, native species should be encouraged and exotic species – when threatening local biodiversity – should be eliminated. Using the changed land use as a basis for further development of local biodiversity is in most cases more realistic and promising than trying to return to original conditions.

Example: Life in Quarries, Belgium

The Life in Quarries is an initiative by EU, regional and industry actors focusing on the hosting capacity of biodiversity in active quarries in Wallonia, Belgium. The work of 'dynamic management' consists of implementing biodiversity management measures during and after the operation of the mines. Creating a network of active quarries that function as biodiversity protection sites is achieved through a range of measures, such as creating and maintaining new habitats, monitoring species, as well as education and outreach. This can involve the creation of temporary ponds or the protection of scree sites. Monitoring the plant and animal species that inhabit the quarries guide management decisions to ensure that the quarries continue to provide suitable habitats. The Life in Quarries project has achieved significant successes, proving the validity of this unique approach. In addition, the project has helped to change the perception of quarries, from problematic to being an asset for biodiversity conservation. The Life in Quarries project shows how mining sites can be used for both economic and environmental purposes, with the right balance between the exploitation of natural resources and the protection of biodiversity.

DATA-BASED POLICIES
Local Organizational Flexibility

Policies are based not on assumptions, but on detailed data that clearly identify our challenges in space and time.

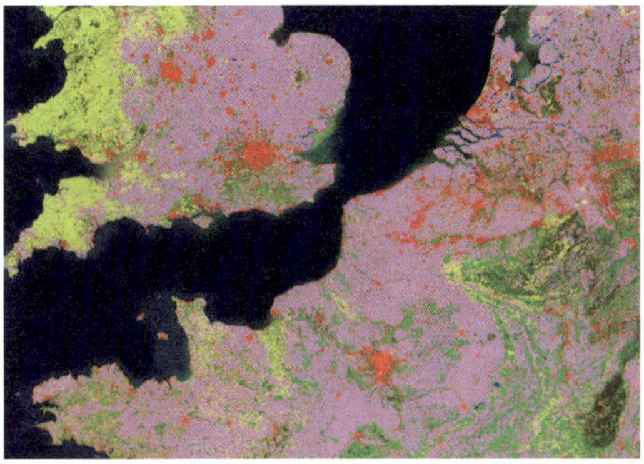

Why?
When policy, leading to legislation, is based on intuitive assumptions, political convictions or rhetoric phrases, it is hard to predict if the legislation will be effective. Recently however, artificial intelligence has reached a level at which all kinds of data can easily be collected, analysed and extrapolated on a large scale and with a high level of precision. Climate change related phenomena such as greenhouse gas emissions, heat stress, subsoil drought or rainwater floods can be easily localized and determined, so that exceedances can be detected, patterns can be discovered and chances can be formulated. This makes it much easier to define the kind of regulation needed and the scale at which this regulation should apply. For example, collected data may indicate that a specific local ordinance is most effective for one issue, while national-level legislation is necessary for another.

How Does It Work?
Data identifying problems related to climate change can be gathered in many ways. One effective method includes placing measuring equipment at strategic spots within the urban network, to collect site-specific real-time data about air quality, traffic movements or for instance noise levels. Satellites are instruments that detect varying values in, for example, carbon dioxide emissions or variations in temperature on a bigger scale, leading to a better insight in patterns over time. Urban services for waste management or electricity suppliers can also collect data for more efficient policies. By providing them with data-collecting devices, patterns can be detected and solutions can be found leading to more precise and effective local legislation.

A particular example is the so-called smart city, an urban area that is made 'smart' through computerized technology and artificial intelligence. By automatically connecting data from various sources such as local income, store sales and public transport, public services can be optimized and legislation can be customized. Depending on the topic, legislations and optimalizations can be scaled up.

By making data publicly available, there is an automatic supervision by the public and stakeholders. Transparency in decision-making and action control leads to more pressure to achieve existing goals effectively. Additionally, companies and individuals with sustainability goals can understand what exactly is needed for the right measures, and can thus respond in the most productive way.

Example: Copernicus Land Monitoring Service
Copernicus is a European programme for monitoring the Earth and collecting data using Earth observation satellites. It combines these with observation data from sensor networks on the Earth's surface. The processed data is then made publicly accessible and serves to provide reliable and up-to-date information. Copernicus focuses on six thematic areas: land, marine, atmosphere, climate change, emergency management and security. The aim is to provide information that supports spatial and urban planning, forest management, water management, agriculture and food security, nature conservation and restoration, ecosystem accounting, mitigation and climate change.

The programme delivers information openly to policymakers, researchers, commercial and private users, as well as the global scientific community. It is known to have world-wide influence in political decisions and most effectively informs the European Union's policymaking.

HOLISTIC APPROACH

Local Organizational Flexibility

Measures are combined so that the outcome is not a one-issue solution, but an integral solution in which various measures amplify each other.

Why?

Projects promoting a more sustainable, circular or climate-adaptive urban development are often complex, because lots of aspects inside and outside the project are interconnected and influence one another. However, many instruments applied in current urban development processes focus on solving only one issue or one single problem. Interconnections between aspects within the project or with external social, economic and ecological factors are often underestimated and lead to implementations in projects that, despite single-issue solutions, cause the amplification of problems elsewhere in the project or in other areas.

A holistic approach, on the other hand, considers the complexity of urban challenges and recognizes the far-reaching impacts of individual urban development projects. This requires a perspective that is explicitly not limited to one sector but is open to a balanced mix of solutions for more than one sector, enabling sustainable, integrated and equitable outcomes. Because the numerous challenges related to climate adaptation and the circular economy are characterized by a high degree of complexity, holistic, multidimensional problem-solving strategies are best equipped to lead to real solutions.

How Does It Work?

Holistic approaches require open collaboration between different stakeholders and professionals from the public and private sectors. It works best when these stakeholders, despite their different specialties, understand each other's interests and look for ways to help each other. Key issues such as land and material use, transportation, energy and waste management cannot be neglected, but must be considered in an integrated manner, together with aspects such as economic efficiency and social structure. Different interests must also be balanced in the planning process.

In general, holistic approaches require a vision that extends beyond a specific scope of a particular project. When individual actors who are linked to the same project work together, they can make an effective assessment of potential impacts and pool resources. When decisions are made jointly by different actors, these decisions can positively influence and reinforce each other.

Example: Alnatura Campus, Darmstadt, Germany

Before they opened the Alanatura Campus in Darmstadt in 2019, they assessed all aspects, effects and impacts to come to an integrally balanced mix, from production to transport and assembling of building materials, from maintenance and programming to the future value of the building and its surroundings.

All building materials used were examined and selected according to their durability, also considering the possible need for recycling if the building were to be demolished in the future. For the stamped clay walls, which were produced on site to minimize transportation routes, excavated soil from the Stuttgart main train station construction site was used. Natural ventilation, lighting and cooling as well as the use of energy from renewable sources are central elements of a resource-saving and environmentally friendly building operation. In addition to flexible workspace for 500 employees, the site is home to a kindergarten with a nature-based education concept, as well as school and adventure gardens designed as public learning spaces. A public restaurant offering organic vegetarian food serves as a public meeting place and strengthens the social orientation of the complex.

REUSED MATERIALS MEDIATOR

Use-driven Organizational Flexibility

Mediator between available materials, coming from demolition or renovation projects, and initiators of building activities.

Why?

Circular building materials are those that are repurposed, reused, or recycled. These materials can include everything from reclaimed wood and bricks to recycled steel and concrete. By reusing these materials, builders need fewer new materials and therefore reduce the environmental impact of construction.

The first implementation of building materials and products, right after they are newly produced, is easy, because the products are delivered straight from the factory to the building site in exactly the right quantity and quality and at exactly the right time. Reusing these materials, however, is harder. Re-implementation of products and materials in large building projects comes with the problem that the demanded materials should be available at the right moment and with the right quality. Mostly, there is a mismatch between the supply and demand of these second-hand materials. As building processes are strict in both planning and quality, these mismatches are problematic. A mediator can match supply and demand for circular building, so that construction can progress according to plan and stay within budget. They can use their expertise and network to identify suppliers who can provide the required materials and negotiate fair prices.

How Does It Work?

Circular building material mediators play a vital role in promoting the reuse and recycling of building materials in projects. By facilitating the adoption of circular materials, these mediators can help reduce waste, minimize environmental impact and support sustainable building practices.

Mediators can build a network of suppliers, builders and other stakeholders in the construction industry who are interested in using circular materials. By bringing these stakeholders together, mediators can help identify potential sources of materials and create a marketplace for buying and selling these materials. Databases can include information on the quality and availability of materials, as well as their price and location. Opening these databases to potential project partners increases the chance for a match. The closer the old location is situated to the new building project; the smaller the impact of transport on emissions and costs. An effective mediator has access to sufficient storage space, so that the period between disassembly and reuse can easily be bridged. Mediators can offer consulting services to builders and architects to help them identify the most suitable circular materials for their projects by providing organizational, legal or technical guidance on how to integrate these materials into the building process.

Example: Zinneke, Brussels, Belgium

The socio-cultural organization Zinneke in Brussels was accommodated in a historic building that used to be a printing workshop. Instead of using new materials for the renovation, the architects of Ouest Architecture chose to reuse as many building materials as possible, including doors, windows and flooring, which were all cleaned and refurbished for use in the new design. Building materials coming from other buildings and sites were reused too. Rotor, a specialized Brussels-based organization played a crucial role as a mediator between the architects and the suppliers of reclaimed materials. Rotor helped identify potential sources of materials, negotiate prices, and coordinate the transportation and delivery of materials to the construction site. They also provided technical assistance to the architects, helping them identify the most suitable materials for their design.

EMPOWERING LOCAL COMMUNITIES

Use-driven Organizational Flexibility

Local communities are supported in their role in improving the conditions of their own habitat.

Why?

Cities across Europe face a wide range of environmental crises. Addressing such complex issues requires a collaborative effort that involves both bottom-up and top-down approaches. However, many European countries' currently have a top-down governance structure, often not sufficiently equipped to support with bottom-up initiatives effectively. This frustrates progress because local people and their communities have great knowledge about both problems and possible solutions in their own neighbourhood. As they inherit local property and raise children, have businesses to run and maintain local networks, they are highly invested in the wellbeing of their neighbourhood. Solutions have more precision when their knowledge is taken into account and solutions are more effective when they are understood, accepted and incorporated in their daily lives. Measures stimulating circularity and climate adaptation should lead to a stronger sense of ownership by local communities. To bridge the gap in the system between top-own and bottom-up approaches, organizations have arisen (sometimes private initiatives, but mostly NGOs: non-governmental organizations) that work towards resolving local challenges through community engagement and cooperation.

How Does It Work?

Engaging and empowering local communities in a participatory process to cocreate sustainable solutions for their direct environment requires a well-structured approach. This process starts by identifying the interests, ambitions and abilities of local communities through thorough research and analysis of the specific area, often including interviews and data collection from scratch.

The next step is to activate the local community and raise awareness. The community members are key to defining appropriate solutions. Potential solutions are explored by facilitating brainstorming sessions, community meetings and partnering with local networks. Ongoing encouragement and guidance are necessary to support citizens. Additionally, it is important to reflect on implemented changes. The balance between top-down and bottom-up powers should be a dynamic one and managed carefully.

Example: Innovative Communities Onwards (InCommOn), Thessaloniki, Greece

InCommOn is a Greek civil non-profit organization (NGO), established in 2016, that promotes the circular economy through the activation of citizens. Its main objective is to offer solutions to environmental and social problems through interactive and creative cooperation with local communities. It specializes in a multi-disciplinary, participatory approach.

Kyklos, InCommOn's Lab, is a participatory project in the Ano Poli neighbourhood in Thessaloniki, testing in practice how a neighbourhood could become more circular. Kyklos, meaning 'circle' in Greek, refers with its motto 'no-one left out, no-one left behind', to the circularity of ecosystems, where all parts play a role and nothing is wasted. To bring the community together and facilitate a dialogue about adopting circular practices in their daily lives, a physical space was created that is equipped for cultural, educative and creative activities. The space has become a reference point for the neighbourhood, attracting both local residents, including local refugee and migrant integration groups, and people from other parts of the city. By organizing workshops and events on sharing and reusing products, the local circular economy is stimulated and social inclusion is fostered. The installation of a community composter in the nearby square has been a great success, bringing together different stakeholders, including the municipality.

DESIGN OUTPUT MONITOR

Use-driven Organizational Flexibility

Measurable output criteria set at the beginning of a process, stimulating fine-tuning between stakeholders such as clients, designers, contractors and regulators, to achieve optimal circular output.

Theme	Topic
environmental impact & material use	environmental impact
	embodied carbon
	construction stored carbon
	material use
	reuse potential
flexibility	adaptivity
	disassembly
use of waste materials	waste materials (demolition)
	waste materials (construction)
material health	toxicity

Why?

Building processes are complex chains of proceedings and decisions, starting with the definition of the assignment, followed by subsequent design and construction phases, finally ending in the delivery of a project. In these processes, many stakeholders are involved, both sequentially and parallel, all with their own speciality and responsibility.

As building processes are usually based on conventions that have been shaped by lessons learned during the years, it is hard to implement sudden big changes. Now that we want to turn our linear take-make-consume-dispose processes into circular ones – closing building material loops by reusing, sharing, leasing, repairing, refurbishing, upcycling or recycling – significant changes are needed though. When all parties involved, from clients to designers and from contractors to regulators, agree beforehand on clear and measurable output criteria, each of them can recalibrate their specific part of the process. Based on clear design output criteria, parties can easily understand what part of the project they are accountable for and how to change their output so that it meets the criteria. By monitoring the output during the process, possible failures can be detected quickly and replaced before it is too late.

How Does It Work?

At the very beginning of the design process, it is important to determine which (often generic) circular principles and criteria apply to the project. The chosen circular principles determine the design process and the technical design choices. Criteria can be set in advance, for example, regarding the maximum carbon dioxide emission, the lifespan of the building or the detachability of it parts. It is often difficult to add these criteria later in the construction process, because this requires interim changes. Furthermore, parties should be involved at an early stage, so that it becomes possible to explore what a choice for potential materials would mean for legal matters (warranties and liability) and management (maintenance required). This allows them to tailor their specific output to the specifications of the materials that become available. When this is taken into account early on in the process, it can be done relatively efficiently.

As selecting and contracting all parties in the beginning of a project is unusual, working with a design output monitor asks for different legal forms of collaboration.

Example: The New Normal for Circular Construction, the Netherlands

The New Normal is an innovative Dutch 'standard' with ambitious, but achievable performance output on circular design and construction. Making the circular ambition tangible beforehand, by describing what has to be delivered is both helpful for clients, designers, contractors and regulators. For this purpose, a toolbox has been developed that can be used to determine what participating parties may be held accountable for. Within four main themes, such as 'flexibility' or 'environmental impact', ten topics have been defined that all can be given a certain ambition at the beginning of a project. By expressing these ambitions in clear units, for example kg CO2-eq / square metres for embodied carbon or the ratio between new and reused materials, a concrete, measurable output can be defined and monitored.

The New Normal is a product of a Dutch network called *Cirkelstad* ('Circular City'), a cooperation of both private and public members that share the ambition of accelerating circular building. Being developed carefully and integrally, the New Normal has the potential to become a building standard on a European level, meeting future European regulation regarding emission reduction, green investments and circularity.

INNOVATION BOOSTER

Time-based Organizational Flexibility

Encouragement of experiments leading to a building culture that is more circular and climate-adaptive.

Why?

In order to deal with the current challenges for circularity and climate adaptiveness, the way we work should change. To speed up this change, innovation should be accelerated. The complexity and urgency of the issues require 'out-of-the-box' solutions that go beyond the standard market products and processes. To do so, a better link needs to be found between research and theory on one hand, and the implementation of it on the other. While many public and private organizations invest significant resources in research, adapting those findings to the market remains a slow process, particularly in the construction industry, which is conservative by nature because of the high investments and big interests building is associated with. Keeping up-to-date with the latest research and innovations and finding ways to make them feasible and implementable, is a prerequisite for speeding up the adaptation process.

How Does It Work?

Innovation can be stimulated in many ways, from small-scale experiments to design competitions, from subsidies to legal exemptions. Pilot projects – realized experiments in which the latest knowledge is implemented, whereafter the performances are analysed – can be key in accelerating innovation. Both good and bad performances of the realized experiment help further innovation. When lessons learned are spread widely, pilot projects are most effective.

Education is a crucial element in this process, with universities and other educational institutions playing a key role in sharing best practises and proven successful approaches. Also making innovative knowledge accessible to less obvious stakeholders in the supply chain – for instance older or less educated employees – is essential for implementing innovative solutions on a mass scale. In an innovative and fast-changing construction market, commercial companies should not only focus on making profits on the short term, but also take care of the education and long-term development of their employees. Innovation is not always a smooth ride, as existing financial and legislative frameworks not automatically match with innovative building practices. Therefore, implementing innovative processes preferably happens in close collaboration with policymakers, business developers, and other stakeholders.

Example: Habiter2030, Hauts-de-France, France

Habiter2030 was established in 2016 by a group of universities, researchers and construction professionals from Hauts-de-France with the aim of designing and building the house of the future. The organization developed a proposal to renovate the typical 1930s houses that are abundant in the region, representing the last vestiges of the industrial era. The team showcased their solution in the Solar Decathlon Europe 2019, an international competition for university teams focused on highlighting innovations in sustainable housing.

Habiter2030 sought to respond to the social, economic, energy and environmental issues of the coming decades in order to sustainably improve the living quality of residents and make the renovation method of those 1930s homes accessible to all. Through their innovative approach, they combined low-tech strategies and energy-efficient systems to transform the low-performing brick houses, including a glass extension towards the garden for pre-heating the air in winter and preventing overheating in summer, thermal curtains for space modulation, and biobased hemp plasters for interior walls. The facade walls and roof were insulated with recycled cotton to give the textile tradition of the region a boost as well.

INFRASTRUCTURE REARRANGEMENT

Time-based Organizational Flexibility

Reorganization process, defining an optimized balance between above- and below-ground interests such as biodiversity, water retention, public space and (sustainable) infrastructure.

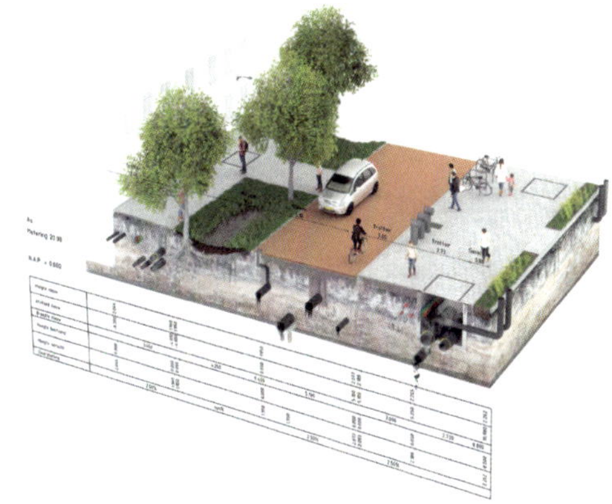

Why?

The ambition to make our cities circular and climate-adaptive is claiming more of our underground space than we are used to. Infrastructure supporting circular supply chains, such as local networks for heat or rainwater, requires additional space on top of the conventional infrastructure for electricity and sewage. Additionally, the subsoil can significantly contribute to biodiversity and climate adaptation in our public realm if more of it is used to improve soil ecosystems and for water retention.

As it is not only scarce, but also key to solving our problems, the way we use, subdivide and organize the space available in the soil requires reconsideration. Traditionally, above-ground functions, such as roads and infrastructure serving our buildings, determine the occupation of the underground. Vegetation and rainwater permeability are only possible there where the soil happens to be free of other needs. By taking into account other interests, related to biodiversity, health, circular supply chains or the public space, other balances can be found, reducing traffic and creating more space for plants, trees and water retention.

How Does It Work?

When these balances are defined together with stakeholders such as property owners, the companies responsible for infrastructure and the keepers of urban green, the different interests will be rearranged. Furthermore, cross-sectoral agreements can be made about responsibilities and procedures avoiding potential conflicts.

In 2021, the city council of Groningen adopted their Design Guideline for the Quality of Life in Public Space. The core of this guideline was an alternative process to come to an optimal balance between all stakeholders involved in designing, realizing and maintaining the city's public space. Instead of focusing first on car accessibility, the aspects of safety, experience, health, slow mobility, social interaction, ecology, climate adaptation, economy and cultural history are all integrally considered to come to the right contextual balance. For various types of areas and neighbourhoods, the Guideline defines principles and starting points for a participative process. While in Groningen, the Guideline mainly focusses on organizational aspects, the integral design principles from the municipality of Amsterdam forms a technical and spatial basis for rearranging urban streetscapes and what's underneath them. Together, the Groningen and Amsterdam principles would be a good basis for the massive assignment of rearranging our underground urban infrastructure, in order to contribute to integrated, transition-based organization.

Example: Integral Design Method Public Space (I.O.O.R.), Amsterdam, the Netherlands

The municipality of Amsterdam has developed a new method for public infrastructure planning. The Integral Design Method Public Space (I.O.O.R.: Integrale Ontwerpmethode Openbare Ruimte) is a comprehensive strategy that involves stakeholders from different sectors. The method divides public space into three parts – underground soil, ground level, and buildings & roofs.

Making underground soil as important as buildings, makes it possible to reserve space underground for measures that contribute to a green, attractive and high-quality public space. By analysing soil composition, conducting water-runoff stress tests and modelling climate scenarios before an area is developed, better contextual goals for sustainable design can be defined across sectors. This allows stakeholders to co-ordinate efforts to optimize underground services infrastructure and maintain the quality of public space. It is paramount that solutions at the network level, such as energy infrastructure, water systems or cycling infrastructure, are integrated in 3D-modular design solutions at the street level.

CIRCULAR SUPPLY CHAINS

Time-based Organizational Flexibility

Production processes in which residuals are not turned into waste, but are somehow brought back into the process, reducing or even abolishing toxic emissions and pollution.

Why?

Our current economy is largely run by systems that convert raw materials into waste, be it energy, water, consumer goods or construction. In contrast to such linear processes, the circular economy makes these systems circular. Resources left over at the end of a process are no longer considered to be waste, but are reused and fed back into the system, with the goal of building circular supply chains.

By reusing and recycling resources in circular systems, the demand for resources can be significantly reduced, as it is no longer necessary to constantly add new resources to the system. Circular supply chains can thus ease the burden on existing infrastructure and help reduce harmful emissions by lowering the need for fossil fuels. In a circular food system, for example, food waste can be converted into renewable energy sources and fertilizer.

Circular supply chains often are realistic and viable when implemented in small-scale geographic units such as neighbourhoods or blocks. Such decentralized systems often provide better solutions to local challenges than large-scale systems. Citizens can more easily connect to and benefit from such systems, helping to build (partly) self-sufficient and resilient communities.

How Does It Work?

The implementation of circular supply chains requires the restructuring of processes providing energy, water, food, (building) materials and waste-collection. In order to successfully transform such systems, it is necessary to understand conventional flows and the role stakeholders play.

Only based on this knowledge can existing infrastructures be adapted accordingly. A circular supply chain for energy might include, for example, solar cells or an underground heat and cold storage. A circular supply chain for water will surely include the sufficient collection of rainwater, perhaps combined with a system that splits grey water from dirty water. A circular system for food might imply the introduction of local collective gardens and possibilities for interchange. Recycling (building) materials requires a materials mediator and recycling facilities and repair shops. Purely circular supply chains might differ radically from what we are used to. However, a mix of conventional and circular supply chains is quite conceivable as well.

Since the restructuring of production processes is often initially associated with high costs that only pay off in the medium to long term, government financial incentives make sense in order to encourage private actors to make corresponding investments. However, equally important as the actions of public and private institutions is the behaviour of consumers. They determine whether they use recyclable products or repair services, or even take action themselves and implement small-scale circular systems in private.

Example: Garden Streets, Antwerp, Belgium

The garden streets in Antwerp are minor roads in which circular water cycles have been established. The streets are traffic-calmed and largely unsealed with the help of water-permeable paving. Rainwater from the roofs of the buildings is channelled into the numerous green spaces along the streets or collected in underground infiltration systems.

The collected water can be reused by all residents with the help of pumps and no more rainwater has to be discharged into the sewage system, which reduces the load on the corresponding infrastructure. The greened and calmed climate streets also serve as new meeting places for social interaction.

3.4 Legal Flexibility

Regulations determine the legal framework within which spatial development takes place. Legal instruments enable initiatives to be executed within this legal framework.

The current legal framework in most European countries is not sufficient enough for facilitating the process of implementing circularity and climate adaptation. The reuse of structures or materials is sometimes made unnecessarily difficult, new initiatives face unintentional delays and future opportunities are nipped in the bud. Implementing circularity and climate adaptation therefore demands a more flexible legal framework.

It is difficult to give a detailed description of legal instruments that could be used in all European countries, as each country has its own specific legislation. The instruments described in the following pages are therefore chiefly general legal principles that enable or foster the enhancement of sustainability in various ways. Each section explains how the principle works and then describes how this translates into specific legal instruments in the case of various European countries. The descriptions can therefore serve partly as a manual, partly as a source of inspiration for a modified legal framework and partly as a plea for the further harmonization of European regulations.

Local Legal Flexibility

New developments mainly take place in an existing, complex urban context. Each site in the existing city has its own unique set of conditions. In some cases, generic regulations can inadvertently hinder desirable new developments. Local flexibility can offer relief in such cases.

Use-driven Legal Flexibility

As users gain influence over the layout of their own living environment, supply and demand will become more aligned. Use-driven flexibility contributes to a more sustainable society through its social impact. Use-driven legal flexibility makes it possible to make more space available for initiatives and programmes that do not fit neatly within generic legal frameworks.

Time-based Legal Flexibility

The increasing unpredictability of climate change and the availability of resources requires either more tailored solutions in terms of timing or a wider legal framework. Temporary provisions or exemptions can be solutions too.

3.5 Legal Instruments

Local Legal Flexibility

- CAR BAN
- PURPOSE-SPECIFIC FREEZONE
- SUSTAINABILITY PROTOCOL

Use-driven Legal Flexibility

- LAW CHANGE MOTIVATION
- GUERRILLA GARDENING
- CUSTOMIZATION

Time-based Legal Flexibility

- MATERIAL PASSPORT
- EMISSION LIMITATION
- DEMOLITION BAN

CAR BAN

Local Legal Flexibility

Legal intervention that reduces or even blocks car traffic in favour of other urban functions such as pedestrian traffic, bicycle traffic, greenery or public space.

Why?

Cars enable citizens to get to a wide variety of places in cities at flexible times. As a popular means of transport, it is hard to imagine most European cities without them, even though they have numerous negative consequences for the cities' residents and the environment. In response to such effects, however, a trend towards banning cars from parts of cities to make them more liveable and environmentally friendly can be seen in more and more cities.

In particular, banning cars with internal combustion engines means a significant reduction in air pollutant emissions. This is not only essential to achieve climate protection goals, but also has a positive impact on the health of the people living in the city, who benefit from better air quality and less noise pollution. Additionally, land use by roads and car parks can be significantly reduced by banning cars from cities. Space can thus be freed up for more sustainable modes of transportation such as bicycle paths or be used to solve pressing challenges such as housing shortages and the protection of biodiversity.

How Does It Work?

Banning cars from cities can be implemented as a temporary or permanent measure. In some cases, it may make sense to close off selected areas from car traffic only at certain times of the day, on selected days, or at certain times of the year, while in other places, long-term banishment is the right choice. Individual car traffic can also be reduced through measures such as car sharing. In this way, people are still free to use cars, but the vehicles are used more effectively.

A car ban should be accompanied by a preceding or parallel expansion of alternative mobility solutions. Banning private car traffic can otherwise lead to significant reduction of mobility for the citizens, whose habits often remain shaped by the long-lasting paradigm of a car-friendly city.

Sometimes, however, car bans can also be stimulated through civil society engagement. The short distances in cities compared to rural regions and a well-developed public transport system can facilitate a switch to other modes of transport. In this case, it is the responsibility of policymakers to have the courage to use more resources to implement this and to ensure that the transformation of the selected areas is carried out in such a way that broad segments of the population benefit from the intervention.

Example: Siegtreppe, Siegen, Germany

The Siegtreppe in the city of Siegen are an example of the consistent banishment of cars from a section of the city centre that had been heavily dominated by car traffic since the 1960s. In response to the poor structural condition of the so-called Siegplatte – a concrete overhang of the urban river that provided space for 230 car parking spaces – as well as increasing decline in the adjacent downtown area, the city government decided to remove the Siegplatte and replace it with a pedestrian area and a large-scale progression of steps along the riverbank. The demolition was followed by the renaturalization of the river below, which was restored as an inner-city natural habitat. The newly created public area can be flexibly used and is completely car-free. The overall quality of the area had a positive impact on local business, contrary to initial reservations among retailers.

ZONE

PURPOSE-SPECIFIC FREEZONE

Local Legal Flexibility

General regulations are set aside to experiment with alternative regulations in order to find out what legal arrangement enforces circularity or climate adaptation best.

Why?

The societal changes regarding circularity and climate adaptivity are urgent, while changing the legal framework that is needed to enforce these changes takes time. This is because in Europe, changing the law is a democratic and sometimes time-consuming process. Moreover, it is also not always immediately clear what arrangement of new rules is the best route to the desired changes.

A certain flexibility in law-making can facilitate rapid sustainable change by allowing actors to adapt and respond quickly to changing circumstances, new technologies and emerging challenges. Overall, the possibility to establish legal freezones can be a powerful tool for finding out how rapid and sustainable change can legally be promoted. By providing a supportive legal framework that encourages innovation, experimentation and continuous improvement, new laws and regulations can help realize a more sustainable future.

Purpose Specific Freezones (PSF) help define an effective set of adjusted rules. By introducing some specific regulations in a limited area, an alternative legal framework can be used for purpose-specific experiments. Careful analysis of the experiment should tell how effective the change of the regulations is. If the results of the experiment are positive, changes in regulation can be implemented on a larger scale or in general statutes. Including exceptions in a generally valid legal framework should be done with the highest care to avoid unclarity, exclude the risk of clientelism and to make sure authority is not undermined.

How Does It Work?

A Purpose Specific Freezone (PSF) is a designated area that is established to promote system experimentation. These zones can generate rapid and sustainable changes by creating a legally supportive environment for various sustainable goals, such as attracting sustainable investment, fostering green innovation, encouraging sustainable production-practices, developing local knowledge or promoting international cooperation. Ideally, PSFs are set up through a collaboration between national governments, local municipalities, industry and civilians. PSFs can be used as an experiment to help regulatory bodies and policymakers make the adjustments needed for localized changes. If it is possible to embed the PSF in an existing legal framework, a PSF can be established relatively quickly and thus accelerate the defining and implementing of the right set of new regulations.

Example: Fossil Free Energy District (FED), Gothenburg, Sweden

The goal of the Fossil Free Energy District (FED) in Gothenburg is to reduce energy consumption by establishing a local market place for electricity, heating and cooling. The area is exempted from the law of concession for electricity distribution, so that a local energy market can be tested and validated. This purpose-specific legal exception prevents monopolies of production or network-management. It also makes it possible to work with multiple energy-sources and producers, and allows parties to simultaneously be consumer, distributor and producer.

One of the key features of the FED system is its use of geothermal energy. The energy plant uses water from the nearby Göta River, which is heated by the earth's natural heat, to generate energy. Additionally, the roofs of many buildings in the district are equipped with solar panels, which generate electricity that is used to power the energy plant and other buildings in the district. This solar energy is also used to power electric vehicles in the area, further reducing the district's carbon footprint.

SUSTAINABILITY PROTOCOL

Local Legal Flexibility

An internal policy framework that can guide both public and private organizations towards more circular and climate-adaptive output or processes.

Why?

In Europe, sustainability is increasingly translated into regulations and laws. Making new laws and regulations, however, is a slow process and as a result legislation is always a few steps behind on current insights. Therefore, more and more governments, NGOs and large commercial organizations want to pursue additional ambitions on top of current legislation. This urge to do more can be driven by new governmental policies that are not yet formalized in laws and regulations. Moreover, governments and NGOs are role models, given their social position. Due to the increased public interest in sustainability, sustainable values have also become more important and widely embraced in the private sector. Having an ambitious company policy in relation to sustainability is a great way to stand out from competitors.

To be able to be more ambitious than official legislation or to shift the emphasis, both the public and the private sector can single-handedly decide to introduce a sustainability protocol: a set of rules and agreements that has to be followed in a predefined area or context.

How Does It Work?

Due to the impact and size of most governmental organizations using a protocol to change internal behaviour is an important sustainability goal in itself. Being permit issuers, governments can also place additional demands on urban redevelopments. For governments, internal protocols can function as a precursor of new legislation. The Sustainability Protocol from the Àrea Metropolitana de Barcelona, for example, contains 18 environmental criteria that projects in the area have to meet, regarding water usage, circular materials, sustainable energy, comfort and health. The protocol is considered as an experimental tool with which policies are tested, possibly leading to new legislation in the long run.

Many companies in the private sector have policies for tenders, obtaining for example a minimum of three price offers or a minimal annual revenue of the sub-contractor. More and more of these companies also include ethic or sustainable requirements in their request for quotes by contractors. When governments and NGOs operate as a contracting authority, they can add specific requirements regarding sustainability in their tender documents too.

Example: Action Plan for Socially Responsible Procurement, Municipality of Leiden, the Netherlands

With the ambition to be fully circular by 2050, the municipality of Leiden made its first action plan for socially responsible procurement in 2016. However, it turned out to be quite difficult to turn good ambitions into good practice. The fear of requiring things that are too expensive or even impossible often prevailed over the courage to challenge the market and ask for something innovative.

In 2022, a thorough evaluation led to the action plan for socially responsible procurement 2.0, which turned the municipality of Leiden into one of the most sustainable procurers in the Netherlands. The sustainable ambitions in the complex process of procurement were limited to three: circularity, carbon dioxide emissions and social return. The evaluation made it clear that procuring processes should always start with these ambitions, instead of adding them in a later stage. Procurement based on demanded performances led to better results than procurement based on prescribed solutions. Civil servants struggling with the implementation of the sustainable ambitions were offered personal and customized assistance in their particular procurement processes.

LAW CHANGE MOTIVATION

Use-driven Legal Flexibility

In order to foster commitment, governments explain why strict laws regarding sustainability are in people's benefit.

Why?

The introduction of strict laws can pave the way for a more circular and climate-adaptive society by incentivizing sustainable practices, holding polluters accountable and fostering public awareness.

By mandating the use of renewable energy, promoting the recycling of waste and imposing fines on polluters, laws can encourage individuals and businesses to adopt sustainable practices that reduce their carbon footprint and promote circularity. Moreover, by raising public awareness about the importance of sustainability and the need for a circular and climate-adaptive society, laws can help educate us about the impacts of our actions on the planet. Ultimately, the creation of strict laws can help reduce our environmental impact and create a more sustainable future.

However, individuals and businesses tend to resist laws for a variety of reasons, including economic concerns, political opposition, lack of understanding, fear of change and regulatory fatigue. It is important for lawmakers to address these concerns and communicate the benefits of the new laws in order to gain support and ensure successful implementation.

How Does It Work?

Different platforms can play a crucial role in gathering, coordinating and supporting initiatives by individuals and businesses in the face of strict new laws. Platforms can facilitate communication and networking between individuals and businesses interested in promoting sustainable practices. This can help build a community of like-minded individuals who can share ideas, collaborate and support each other by providing a space for individuals and businesses to share best practices and success stories. By helping others learn from those who have successfully implemented sustainable practices, this can inspire people to take action. In addition, platforms can provide resources to support individuals and businesses in complying with new laws. This can include information about the laws, guidance on how to implement sustainable practices and access to funding and other resources. Finally, platforms also advocate for the adoption of new laws and policies that promote sustainability. By working with policymakers and other stakeholders, platforms can help shape the regulatory environment in a way that supports sustainable practices.

Example: Centre for Ecological Learning Luxembourg (CELL), Luxembourg

CELL is a non-profit organization that focuses on raising awareness and promoting sustainable living in Luxembourg, which was founded in 2009.

They provide an experimental platform for thinking, researching, disseminating and practicing alternative lifestyles. The platform offers a range of activities, including workshops and seminars, to encourage individuals and businesses to adopt more sustainable practices. As a driver of the ecological transition in Luxembourg, CELL works closely with other associations and government agencies.

The centre organizes events to give voice to new initiatives or bring citizens together so that they can join or implement projects. CELL uses specific pedagogical tools to anchor learning by experience, including permaculture design, agroecology, action research, radical and participatory pedagogy, deep ecology and various moderation techniques. Its work ranges from guidance on small interventions such as communal gardening to territorial strategies as for example regional planning policy.

GUERRILLA GARDENING

Use-driven Legal Flexibility

Neighbours turn underused or forgotten places within the public realm into pocket-parks – without legal permission.

Why?

Guerrilla gardening is a bottom-up practice commonly used by community gardeners who take over a piece of public land for the sole purpose of adding plants. The scale of the intervention can vary between an addition of a few decorative plants around a tree all the way to an urban community garden 'squatting' part of a park.

Guerrilla gardening can contribute to the mitigation of environmental challenges in the city. Newly planted greenery can help slow water runoff. Larger plants significantly reduce the heat island effect through water evaporation. If productive plants are planted, the neighbourhood can benefit even more. Sometimes guerrilla gardening projects also have a composting component, which eases the strain on public waste management.

The benefits and disadvantages of guerrilla gardening vastly vary from case to case. As it is a bottom-up strategy, it is inherently a community-building and -strengthening practice. Adding plants to places that are neglected or disused makes the city more beautiful and therefore more likely for people to care for it. Though guerrilla gardening generally is seen as a harmless civil disobedience, there are some possible disadvantages. If the wrong plants are chosen, exotic species can be introduced that are a threat to native species, for instance, or if maintenance is neglected, the new plants may attract vermin.

How Does It Work?

Guerrilla gardeners plant on property that does not belong to them, which is illegal. Some groups operate at night to avoid punishment, other groups look for cooperation with municipalities, depending on the political ecology of a given place.

Sometimes guerrilla gardening can be disruptive both politically and practically. Historically, groups have used this as a tool for peaceful protest and to demand direct action in the change of land rights and land reform, and even question the concept of land ownership itself. In practical terms, guerrilla gardening projects can be at odds with cities' regulations that demand that public space has certain characteristics – aesthetics, safety, historical value, et cetera. An intervention as small as placing a raised bed on a public pavement can break the regulations of safety by making the pavement narrower than deemed 'safe' by the city code.

Example: The Street Gardening Society, Prague, Czech Republic

The Street Gardening Society is a community organisation that operates in the Prague 3 neighbourhood, a residential part of Prague. The members are professional gardeners and teachers, who educate and support local street gardeners and give workshops. Their gardening efforts focus on beautifying spaces around trees with plants that will not harm the tree and are climate-appropriate.

Although the group operates illegally, the local government has turned a blind eye for a long time. But recently, it has launched several projects itself, some of which together with the Street Gardening Society. Community composting was introduced in 2020 to support an effective waste management of food scraps in the neighbourhood and use the compost as new soil for the area. The Street Gardening Society's practice of adopting trees as a way of beautifying public spaces was also recently formalized by the Prague 3 municipality, as it offered 7,000 flower plants to residents to plant in their neighbourhood.

CUSTOMIZATION
Use-driven Legal Flexibility

Tailor-made legal intervention based on existing legislation in order to achieve more sustainability.

Why?
Legislation always follows societal changes in a slow pace. However, sometimes needs for more sustainability are urgent and ask for a quick intervention. Innovative circular or climate-adaptive initiatives might therefore be hindered by existing law, which is not yet equipped for coping with these new challenges. Luckily, laws and regulations often only establish the outline of policy, offering civil servants room for interpretation. Legal facilitation, stimulation or approval of circular and climate-adaptive initiatives can thus be done quickly by customizing existing legislation, while updated new legislation is being prepared in a slower pace.

On the other hand, to get approval for their spatial initiatives, initiators are usually asked to prove that their initiative meets the legal requirements. In case innovative solutions do not comply with conventional laws, initiators can ask civil servants for a reasonable approach or to customize their burden of proof by for example adapting their way of calculation or demonstrating equivalence.

How Does It Work?
The success of customization stands or falls with the willingness of civil servant to look for solutions and not to automatically switch into the 'no that is not possible' mode. Besides motivation, this willingness of civil servants to investigate and stretch legal possibilities is also determined by the trust in and backing by policymakers. When there is both willingness and political backing, governments can already start putting their innovative sustainable ambitions into practice, while appropriate legislation is on its way. Sometimes, legislation contains opportunities for pilot projects or experiments within a certain bandwidth. Municipalities or governmental institutions might use these possibilities to permit innovative initiatives. To avoid complaints about favouritism or corruption, these institutions would do well to communicate clearly what they are allowing and why, and monitor the results of their legal experiment.

Example: Refurbishment of Private Homes in Pirineus Street, Santa Coloma de Gramenet, Spain
Because the density in the municipality of Santa Coloma de Gramenet, part of the Barcelona Metropolitan Region, increased dramatically between 1955 and 1975 (from 20.000 to 140.000 inhabitants) the area is now facing several problems concerning liveability. There is a lack of public space and public infrastructure, and many buildings are in a bad state. The ownership is fragmented, since all the houses are privately owned. Previous attempts by the majority of owners for collective renovations were blocked by only a small group of individual owners or their representatives, not willing to pay their share. These owners mostly appear to be slumlords who rent out apartments to new immigrants or banks who own expropriated houses.

Breaking this deadlock situation, the municipality of Santa Coloma de Gramenet, part of the Barcelona Metropolitan Region, set up a customized legal framework for the project by combining two laws, being the '3R act' (a planning act for new developments) and 'the right to housing act'. Within this legal framework, the municipality is able to define an area in which a feasible refurbishment can be enforced, sharing the burdens and benefits proportionally to the percentage of ownership.

Depending on their type of tenure, owners have different possibilities to pay for the refurbishment: landlords and banks have to pay everything in advance; owners who live in their property themselves can also pay their debt on a monthly basis or annotate their debt in the Housing Property Register.

MATERIAL PASSPORT

Time-based Legal Flexibility

Identifying certificate for building materials that helps understand their origin and possible future.

Why?

The building industry is currently based on a constant supply of new materials. As a result, the construction sector is accountable for the largest consumption of primary materials. Due to a lack of natural resources, however, it is increasingly important to reuse existing material goods.

Persistent, recurring problems regarding the reuse of building materials are their availability and questions about their origin and quality. When the intention is to reuse materials in a building project, how can it be ensured they arrive in time? What is their actual quality and how can the contracting company guarantee its condition and lifespan? Finding appropriate answers to these questions requires organizational systems that support and enable the reuse and recycling of materials.

By utilizing a centrally registered Material Passport (MP), available materials intended for reuse can be effectively traced and identified. When the passport includes comprehensive data on location, availability and age, contractors can easily plan their circular building projects and are able to make promises about the quality of the materials.

How Does It Work?

Ideally, the Passport is registered in an accessible database before the material is used in a building structure. The building then acts as a 'material bank' and once it is demounted, or altered, there is a detailed inventory of all the materials, components and resources in the building as well as their location. Thus, materials are not only to be part of a building, but also have an independent value outside of the current construction.

In theory, this system acts similarly to a library. By categorizing, documenting and identifying books, these can be lent out to different users. Every book is listed digitally in an organized system and, in its physical absence, is traceable to its current owner or location. Due to this system, books don't have to remain stationary but can be lent out to different users and locations. Like books, materials would remain accessible for generations. After the use of a resource in one construction, it could be repurposed, in another building or product. Again, the material would be registered, documented and saved digitally to trace its location and current owner.

Currently, the Material Passport is primarily used in individual projects, but it is promoted by the EU Horizon Europe Framework Programme. If a Passport is obliged for every single building element in future building legislation, circular building could easily become the starting point for all our building projects.

Example: Nest, Duebendorf, Switzerland

The Nest building, the flexible structure of which was designed by Gramazio Kohler Architects, is a building laboratory that demonstrates how to incorporate both recycled materials and flexibility into a new construction. The core of the building is made from a simple concrete backbone with three horizontal platforms, on which single modules are inserted that are demountable if the function of the building changes. The individual units have been designed for maximum sustainability; they are built from materials that are fully recyclable, reusable or compostable.

All materials used are stored in a material database and can be returned to the material cycle if the building unit chooses to change its function. This allows the structure to evolve with time without creating material waste.

EMISSION LIMITATION

Time-based Legal Flexibility

Legal limitation of the emission of pollutants such as carbon dioxide, nitrogen or waste.

Why?

Although the Paris goals clearly state the need to limit our greenhouse gas emissions, every European country tackles the path to that goal differently. Buildings – both in their realization and exploitation phase – generate 36 per cent of the EU's greenhouse gas emissions. While the necessary measures are widely known, it is difficult to guarantee the success of the sustainable approaches that individual parties use in their building projects.

By implementing legal restrictions for greenhouse gas emissions, initiators of building projects are obliged to develop their buildings with the necessary design and technology that meet the Paris goals from 2014. This way, the emissions are regulated and monitored through governmental legislation, ensuring the building's limited impact in terms of emissions no matter what users of the buildings do. Without these regulations, the efficiency of the building proposals is unreliable and difficult to track and control. As a result, governmental ambitions can be stated but, in their execution, remain unsupervised.

How Does It Work?

Controlling emissions through governmental regulations has already been an established tool in many areas such as public transport, energy production and many other aspects of the industry. In the building industry, the government has to identify the highest acceptable pollutant production in both the construction and use of a building, and then legally hold the developers of the building accountable.

In order to legally enforce limitations successfully regarding greenhouse gas emissions, the government has to define penalties for exceeding the limits. Setting a fine or legal consequence makes it inadvisable for building proposals to neglect the emissions regulations. An example of the effect of these implementations is seen in the Netherlands. Due to European legislation, the government is obliged to reduce the emission of nitrogen close to Natura2000-protected nature reserves. As a result, construction and farming in these regions are limited.

Controlling emissions of nitrogen, carbon dioxide and even waste with legal enactments, help in realizing higher ambitions and allows for a more effective way of tracking progress across different initiators and other stakeholders.

Example: Future Homes and Buildings Standard, United Kingdom

In 2021, the United Kingdom has implemented a national law that enforces new building projects to reduce carbon dioxide emissions during their exploitation phase. New homes and buildings in England will have to produce significantly less carbon dioxide under new rules. The government announced this initiative to help the country move towards net zero. This example is one of the first proactive government actions in Europe.

Under the new regulations, carbon dioxide emissions from new build homes must be around 30 per cent lower than current standards. The English government focuses on this as heating and powering buildings currently comprise 40 per cent of the UK's total energy use. It highlights the importance of improving the country's built environment and sets exemplary standards for other European countries to follow.

The UK government executed this legislation with very transparent and open communication. The department received a wide-ranging response from different individuals across organizations, representatives and trade bodies, industry professionals, academics and individual members of the public to their initial proposal. By reviewing these comments and concerns and carefully responding to such issues, the government's official limitations are responsible and reasonable.

DEMOLITION BAN

Time-based Legal Flexibility

Legislation that prevents existing building structures to be demolished, reducing the environmental impact of the building industry.

Why?

The construction and demolition industries are major contributors to global waste production and greenhouse gas emissions. In particular, the production of concrete skeletons, a commonly used building technique, generates significant emissions because of the chemical process involved. Furthermore, the demolition of such structures, especially those made as monolithic, poured concrete structures without demountable joints, results in a high energy consumption, high greenhouse gas emissions and an increase of landfill waste.

Moreover, the depletion of finite raw resources like chalkstone, pebbles and sand, crucial components in creating concrete, is another consequence of the construction and demolition process.

A possible solution to reduce waste production and conserve existing structures is implementing a demolition ban. Such legal limitations would help minimize the construction and demolition industries' environmental impacts while preserving structures that have already contributed significantly to emissions during construction.

How Does It Work?

Currently, no European country has a demolition ban yet, but the European Union is proposing to develop legislation that would prohibit the demolition of buildings with concrete structures. As opposed to being demolished, these structures would have to be thoroughly renovated. A future demolition ban could possibly follow the legal framework of monument-protecting legislation, that is already widely accepted in most European countries.

The effect would not only reduce waste production but also provide a greater incentive to design new concrete structures with a more serious focus on adaptability and flexibility. The proposed approach entails prioritizing building renovation over demolition and retrofitting new constructions to enhance their longevity and functionality.

By limiting the possibility of demolition, legislation would encourage the adoption of sustainable practices, ultimately leading to a more circular economy.

Example: Tour Bois-le-Prêtre, Paris, France

The Tour Bois-le-Prêtre is a 16-storey tower block located on the outskirts of Paris, originally designed by the French architect Raymond Lopez and constructed in the early 1960s. After decades of neglect and ageing, the building required significant efforts to bring its apartments up to modern standards. While the French government initially considered demolishing the tower, it ultimately organized a competition to solicit proposals for renovating the structure. The French Architects, Lacaton Vassal, won the competition with a proposal that had a cost lower than that of demolition and new construction and increased the living area of each apartment by approximately 40 per cent without raising rents. Their proposal was a radical transformation that involved adding new floors to the periphery of the existing building, creating additional living space, and enclosing balconies and terraces. The project also included replacing the small windows with large, transparent openings that offered stunning views of Paris.

Today the Tour Bois-le-Prêtre serves as a model for addressing the challenge of rehabilitating mass-produced housing developments across Europe from the 1960s and 1970s and as a testament to the value of clever thinking and ingenuity in revitalizing neglected urban areas. Jean-Philippe Vassal and Anne Lacaton's design demonstrates how renovations and modernizing existing structures can be a resourceful, sustainable and durable way to avoid demolitions and improve our built environment.

3.6 Financial Flexibility

In spatial development, the domain of financing concerns property values, investments, revenues and risk-assessment. Financial instruments make it possible to find the right balance between investments and revenue so that an initiative becomes financially viable.

Current planning models are mainly focused on urban expansion, but different financial models are needed if we want to implement circularity and climate adaptation in our existing villages, towns and cities. These new models need to be better at dealing with the existing tangible and intangible values, they should not depend solely on big players with plenty of capital, but should allow room for ownership by smaller parties too, and they have to be better at coping with unpredictability. To achieve this, financial instruments need to be more flexible.

Local Financial Flexibility
Implementing circularity and climate adaptation into existing parts of a city might lead to benefits on a much larger scale. Flexible instruments are in order to equalize costs and benefits between investors on the one side and all stakeholders on the other. These instruments are not based purely on generalizations, but take into account a location's specific values and possibilities.

Use-driven Financial Flexibility
The far-reaching institutionalization of spatial development has resulted in a huge gap between investors and users. Tenants, for example, might suffer financially when their landlords do not take circular or climate-adaptive measures, such as insulation or renewable energy resources. Use-driven financial flexibility enables a fair redistribution of investments and revenues in case cost-effective or risk-reducing investments have to be made.

Time-based Financial Flexibility
Investments for climate adaptation might mean substantial investments, with an increasingly high risk profile. The risks can be reduced by clever phasing, reducing the gap between the timing of the investments and the timing of the revenue flows. If financial instruments are more flexible, it becomes easier to initiate larger investments in circularity or climate adaptation.

3.7 Financial Instruments

Local Financial Flexibility

COMMUNITY SHARES

CAPITALIZED RISKS

PRIVATELY FINANCED PUBLIC ASSETS

Use-driven Financial Flexibility

FREE PUBLIC TRANSPORT

SOCIAL CURRENCY

SUBSIDY

Time-based Financial Flexibility

UPCYCLING

RECURRENT HOUSING FUND

LIFE CYCLE FINANCE

€ €
€ €
€ €

COMMUNITY SHARES

Local Financial Flexibility

Community shares are a way for community groups to raise money for a common investment.

Why?

Sustainable resources for people's need for energy, water or food may well be initiated, maintained, and financed by local communities. Advantages of these local initiatives include independence from large systems, big companies and their market power, and the absence of middlemen skimming off profits. In addition, it is possible to implement autonomous, off-grid systems in which active citizens can determine a community-based social or environmental focus.

Such projects are therefore characterized by a high level of acceptance and support from civil society and are usually tailored to local challenges and needs, which means they can provide more effective and meaningful solutions than large-scale systems.

Investing local communities, however, have to have a financial framework in which investments, profits, ownership, and the right to vote are well organized. Community shares offers such a structure. By investing in a project in the form of community shares, individuals and organizations can become co-owners of a project and benefit from the financial returns it generates. This means that the benefits of the project are not in the hands of a few private investors but are shared throughout the community – as are the financial and other risks associated with the project.

How Does It Work?

For the successful implementation of community shares, first a community must be formed. Then, a legal structure must be established that enables the issuance of community shares. In many countries, this can be done by establishing cooperatives that raise equity through the issuance of community shares. These are shares that can be purchased by individuals. With the share, a buyer not only receives a share in the cooperative, but also voting rights, whereby each person usually has one vote regardless of the number of shares they own.

If enough money is collected by issuing the community shares, the corresponding project can be implemented. The projects may include the installation of renewable energy systems, the development of green infrastructure or sustainable transportation. In the case of a cooperative, the voting members can run the project democratically after realization. Finally, it is important to establish mechanisms that distribute the financial return of the project in a fair way among the shareholders.

Example: Ballesteros de Calatrava, Ciudad Real, Spain

In the central Spanish village of Ballesteros de Calatrava, many of the 400 inhabitants have made a communal investment to install an intelligent electrical microgrid with the help of the municipality and private companies. In the long term, this will generate, and distribute the electricity for the community's residents through use of photovoltaic panels. After investing in the construction of the system, the village is almost self-sufficient in electricity production.

Already now, the residents who have joined the project save about 30 per cent of the electricity costs, which remain stable and are no longer exposed to price fluctuations of supra-regional electricity providers. Once the past investments have been refinanced, residents are expected to save 80 per cent of electricity costs and become the sole owners of the grid. The public sector also benefits from the system and passes the reduced electricity costs on to new residents in the form of property tax reductions.

Low electricity prices and tax reductions are intended to attract businesses and residents and ultimately help combat the rural exodus in the area.

€⚠

CAPITALIZED RISKS
Local Financial Flexibility

Estimated value loss through climate change, multiplied by its probability, expressed in an amount of money. Capitalized risks help owners to define the investments for making their property climate-adaptive.

Why?
In the European context, there have recently been increased occurrences of droughts, heatwaves, floods, wildfires, snowstorms and other natural disasters heavily affecting the value of land, infrastructure and property. As these disasters are likely to occur even more frequently in the near future, current property values and the stability of economies are seriously threatened by possible future climate disasters. These disasters may also negatively influence profitable exploitation, lower the value of the property, or even cause so much damage that premature demolition is warranted.

In the financial world, risks are calculated by multiplying the value by the chance that this value is destroyed. When risks are capitalized accurately in this way, people responsible for the value of a property can consider an upgrade or invest in order to retain a property's value. The sometimes large-seeming investments for climate-adaptive measures are put into perspective by the capitalization of the risks and the possible loss of value, in case these measures are not being invested in.

How Does It Work?
Investments in climate resilience of our cities are expensive, as they mostly concern large-scaled, structural changes like the enlargement of water basins or the reinforcement of dykes. For many of us, it is hard to imagine the necessity of these investments. Therefore, the willingness to invest is small. Capitalized risks, however, make an actual comparison possible between the needed investment and the possible losses. This can help convince people of the necessity of the investments.

Big climate-related investments that should be made by public authorities such as municipalities or provinces can meet public resistance because public money is to be spent. When governments are able to communicate what their intended investments are and what the estimated value loss as a result of a disaster would be if these investments are not made, it is easier to convince people that the investment is necessary.

An alternative to investing in climate-adaptive measures is an insurance covering the possible damage by climate disasters. Fees are based on an estimated financial coverage of damage. Recent cases show, however, that only the costs to rebuild the lost property are covered, without additional measures to protect the property from recurring disasters. Based on these recent cases, we may conclude that insurances don't seem to be an ideal means to come to future-proof solutions.

Example: Munich Re, Germany
Munich Re is a globally operating insurance company specialized in analysing and covering climate risks. Munich Re's NatCatSERVICE is one of the most comprehensive global natural loss databases with over 30,000 entries. Scientists have been collecting and analysing data since the 1980s in order to evaluate loss events worldwide. Based on this database, the insurance company offers tailor-made solutions for customers across the world, mostly businesses susceptible to climate change, such as in the sectors of agriculture or energy.

Worldwide, Munich Re is one of the few institutes that dares to estimate the costs of possible climate disasters. Though the insurance company is a commercial organization and their primary goal is to sell insurances, their ability to capitalize risks based on an extensive database contributes to a better awareness and understanding of these risks by owners and those financially responsible. By capitalizing their risks, the insurance company unintentionally stimulates parties to invest in climate-adaptive measures before it is too late.

PRIVATELY FINANCED PUBLIC ASSETS
Local Financial Flexibility

Private parties invest in the quality of the surrounding public realm with a percentage of their private investment, providing their private plot with a sustainable context.

Why?
Implementing a circular economy and a climate-resilient environment asks for big investments now, but will only lead to profits in the future. Ultimately, property owners benefit from this sustainable environment and see the value of their property stabilized or even grow. At the same time, in most cases, the public sector has tight limits to finance the much-needed transformations in such a short period of time. Therefore, it is reasonable to ask private parties to co-invest in the public space.

This addressing of private funds not only enables a fairer distribution of costs between the public sector and private parties, but also fosters a shared sense of responsibility in solving societal challenges. In addition, measures taken in the public realm can be easily supported by comparable measures on the private plots. These measures are then carefully integrated and cover a larger scale, which means the impact is bigger as well.

The collaborative approach fosters synergy effects, whereby experience and technical know-how of private actors can be transferred to the public sector and vice versa.

How Does It Work?
Local governments can impose site-specific requirements on private market actors in the planning process to contribute to climate-resilient public spaces and to establish a circular economy. These requirements can both concern a (financial) contribution to the redevelopment of the public realm or the implementation of measures on private plots, such as rainwater retention or incentives for more biodiversity.

In case of new construction, these requirements should best be formulated at the very beginning of the planning process, allowing private parties to align their plans accordingly. In case of transformation or renovation, the permission to change the private property should include a mandatory contribution to the public realm. In this way, initiators and investors understand their additional responsibilities before they create their business case. The conditions must be contractually signed off by both the local government and the private parties involved to ensure implementation in practice.

Example: VPOR Ensjø, Oslo, Norway
The Municipality of Oslo uses indicative plans for public spaces (VPORs) as strategic planning tools to provide guidelines for the development of public spaces. While they are not legally binding, they serve as a link between different planning documents and as a basis for further zoning and contractual agreements between the municipality and private developers, especially in areas where several private parties are active. VPORs thus provide both certainty and flexibility for developers, who are obliged to create specific plans for their properties including public space development based on the VPOR. Consequently, they carry out the relevant projects that include the public space at a reasonable price or provide (partial) financing.

The Ensjø neighbourhood in Oslo used to be dominated by car dealers before the municipality decided in 2004 to convert the area into a residential neighbourhood. For development in Ensjø, a VPOR formulates design principles for public spaces such as greenways, parks and a riverway. By 2021, some 52 hectares of public green space had been realized by private parties in the area based on this plan, in addition to some 6,000 housing units. Much of the public space is situated on formerly private land. By 2018 alone, 1 billion Norwegian kroner (about 850,000 euros) of private capital had been mobilized to create sustainable public space.

FREE PUBLIC TRANSPORT

Use-driven Financial Flexibility

By making public transport free, transport can become more efficient, less space-consuming, less polluting and socially more inclusive.

Why?

Car traffic and the infrastructure required for it take up a lot of space and generate harmful and disruptive emissions. The use of public transport on the other hand helps to reduce car traffic, which leads to a reduction in greenhouse gas emissions and other pollutants. Reducing car traffic also frees up inner-city space for other uses and can improve spatial quality. Despite these known positive aspects of public transport compared to private car use, many people still hesitate to use public transport, mainly for reasons of lower comfort, less flexibility and the price of services.

Zero-fare public transport is an effective way to make it more attractive. In addition to the above-mentioned positive effects on the environment, free public transport promotes social inclusiveness and equity. It enables low-income citizens to become more mobile and get to school, work or leisure activities more easily. The financial relief contributes to social emancipation as it stimulates education, increases purchasing power and encourages participating in society in general.

How Does It Work?

A loss of revenue from ticket sales makes it necessary for transport operators to find other financial sources to finance operation and maintenance. Private transport operators are therefore dependent on government subsidies. Publicly owned transport services can be made free of charge through financial redistribution of governmental costs and benefits. Funding can come, for example, from higher traffic taxes on the use of cars. As in the long term, empowering low-income residents plausibly leads to lower public costs for household depts, school dropouts or unemployment, it is reasonable to partly pay for free public transport from budgets of other social services.

When the capacity of the existing network is underused, zero-fare public transport leads to a better used system. When the capacity reaches its limits however, an expansion of the networks becomes crucial to meet the increasing demand. To estimate the effect of free access to the system it is also possible to gradually switch to free public transport in order to prevent sudden network overloads. To this end, the service can initially be made free of charge only for certain user groups, such as schoolchildren or pensioners, or at certain times of the day, for example outside the morning and evening rush hours.

Example: Free Public Transport, Malta

The government of the state of Malta has decided to make the Day Routes, Night Routes and Special Services of the nationwide public transport system, consisting of several bus lines, free of charge. Prerequisite for the free use of public transport is the use of a personalized Tallinja Card, which can be ordered by both Maltese and non-Maltese residents for a one-time fee of 15 euros. Previously, Malta had a fare system in which fares varied according to the length of the journey. The transition to free public transport was made possible by a change in the budget, which provided for an increase in government subsidies for the operation of public transportation. The decision to introduce zero-fare public transport was taken as part of the government's efforts to implement a greener transport policy, which aims to improve air quality and reduce traffic congestion.

SOCIAL CURRENCY

Use-driven Financial Flexibility

Investments and profits are not expressed in currency, but in goods, benefits, services or social returns.

Why?

The necessary shift towards a more circular and climate-adaptive society asks for great financial investments. Ideally, these investments are only done by our governments, enhancing the social inclusion in our society with equal benefits for everyone. But in reality, the investments will be partly private, not necessarily giving everyone a fair share. Commercial companies investing in sustainable infrastructure, for example, might only be in favour of their regularly paying customers. Private individuals might just not be wealthy enough to invest in solar panels or extra insulation for their private homes. So in the end, this shift might well lead to greater social segregation.

When the necessary sustainable measures are financially unattainable, alternative ways of funding can be defined. When people pay through knowledge, time or materials instead of through financial currency, this is called social currency. Paying with social currency can empower individuals and communities by giving them the means to purchase the resources and services that they need to deal with the societal changes regarding sustainability. By trading goods and services directly with others, they can bypass traditional economic intermediaries such as banks and create their own networks of exchange and support. In addition to that, by exchanging different skills and expertise individuals can learn from each other. Such models contribute to social cohesion by helping to integrate sensitive social groups, building strong and lasting relationships between individuals and organizations.

How Does It Work?

Social currency takes on various forms. Collaborative housing initiatives are one example, in which residents work together to design and build their own homes, while fostering a culture of solidarity and mutual assistance. Local governments can stimulate such initiatives by organizing markets that promote the exchange of construction materials that derive from demolition or renovation work in a certain neighbourhood.

In order to come to fair trades with social currency, payment preferably takes place in accordance with predefined agreements. In his book *The Future of Money*, the Belgian currency expert Bernard Lietaer advocates the introduction of complementary currencies alongside traditional money. Valuable things that are not so easy to express in monetary value, such as social capital or the care for the environment, can then become a fully-fledged part of the economy.

Example: Curing the Limbo, Athens, Greece

'Curing the Limbo' was launched in 2017, during the post-refugee crisis in Greece. The project aimed to assist refugees in breaking free from a state of inactivity by utilizing local forces, such as active citizen groups, that had helped Athens overcome its own inertia caused by the decade-long economic crisis. A range of services was supported by the programme, including psychosocial support, supervised by the National and Kapodistrian University of Athens, job counselling, language training and assistance in finding affordable housing.

In turn, refugees contributed to improving Athens' neighbourhoods by participating in various citizen-led actions, such as revitalizing public spaces and organizing business activities related to renewable energy and public facility construction. This exchange of services helped refugees build relationships with the locals who participated in the actions, practice the language, and develop both their social and professional skills. Together, refugees and the city emerged from the stage of inactivity, worked together and learned from each other.

€ ⌛

SUBSIDY

Use-driven Financial Flexibility

Project-based government contribution that facilitates developments towards more circularity or climate adaptation, but are not sufficiently profitable.

Why?

Investments for the transformation of cities towards circularity and climate adaptation are urgently needed and in the public interest, in the wake of the challenges posed by climate change, but are sometimes not profitable enough, too large, or simply too risky to be fully funded by the market. Subsidies are a tool that can be used to enable or stimulate the implementation of such projects.

While subsidies are government funds that can support the desired projects of private actors, governments can also use subsidies to encourage private actors to channel their financial resources into environmentally friendly measures by demanding a private investment basis for the projects that are subsidized. Implementing measures and projects that address climate resilience often requires trying out new techniques or methods, which conflicts with the desire for risk control among private companies. Subsidies provided to those experimental projects are an instrument to reduce financial risks and therefore specifically promote innovation.

Additionally, subsidies do not necessarily have to be financial, but can also be granted in the form of education, tools or tax benefits. These forms of subsidy are well equipped to provide subsidies to consumers on a large scale. Free trainings, for example, can teach city dwellers how to adapt their lifestyles to the challenges of climate change, leading to a large-scaled implementation of circular structures and climate resilience. Tax benefits favouring for example the private acquisition of solar panels or electrical bikes, can also accelerate lifestyle adjustments, such as the disconnection of fossil energy resources or changes in mobility behaviour.

How Does It Work?

Subsidies are usually implemented through targeted funding programmes by government bodies at the municipal, provincial, national or European level. Subsidy programmes specify which actors and projects are eligible, the conditions that must be met to receive a subsidy, the funding amount and how to apply for the subsidy.

To ensure an equal opportunity for all applicants, there are usually standard procedures and forms, which are often evaluated by independent expert committees appointed by the governments. Subsidies are usually awarded on a one-time basis rather than financing ongoing measures.

The implementation of subsidized projects is subject to strict monitoring to make sure that government funds are used appropriately and effectively. This also ensures that subsidy conditions are met. These include not only conditions during project implementation, but also afterwards, such as the public sharing of knowledge gained from subsidized projects.

Example: Poplar Works, London, United Kingdom

Under the Poplar Works project, disused garages in East London were transformed to create space for studios, workshops and event spaces. The project was based on the idea that the fashion industry, which once made a significant financial and cultural contribution to the economy of East London, would once again become an important part of the social and economic fabric of the city.

The project was realized with financial support from the Mayor of London and the London Economic Action Partnership through the London Regeneration Fund and the Good Growth Fund, which promotes growth and community development in the British capital. In association with similar developments in the surrounding area, the project received subsidies totalling approximately 2 million pounds.

€→€

UPCYCLING

Time-based Financial Instrument

By discovering uses that add value to poorly valued waste materials, circularity and reuse become a beneficial alternative for the conventional, linear way of producing materials.

Why?

The current economic production system is becoming increasingly problematic. Firstly, it relies heavily on the extraction of finite natural resources, which are being depleted at an unsustainable rate. This leads to a range of negative environmental impacts, including deforestation, water pollution, greenhouse gas emissions and climate change. Secondly, the current economic production system is based on a linear model of production and consumption, where resources are extracted, processed into goods, and then discarded as waste. This model generates enormous amounts of waste and pollution, which harms the environment and human health more and more.

Upcycling is a model of production and consumption that aims to minimize waste and resource depletion. Basically, the idea is that waste can be transformed into a valuable resource, creating a closed-loop system that reduces environmental impacts and creates new economic opportunities while fostering economic development and social equity.

How Does It Work?

One way to upcycle materials and products is to repair them when they are at the end of their 'first' lifespan. Good examples of this way of upcycling are the dismantling and reuse of components of buildings, vehicles or electronics. Another way of upcycling is by discovering uses that add value to poorly valued or waste materials. Instead of disposing of these materials, they can be repurposed or transformed into new products. Good examples of this are the use of rags as building insolation and the processing of scrap wood into furniture. The circular economy is critical for achieving sustainable development goals and ensuring a more resilient and equitable future for both the planet and its inhabitants. However, it must be said that many production systems are not suited yet for circularity and therefore consider circular production as an alternative that is more expensive.

Example: APPLAUSE, Ljubljana, Slovenia

Invasive alien plant species pose one of the greatest challenges to European ecosystems. They threaten native vegetation, destroy agricultural land and cost the European economy billions of euros every year. Many of them are removed on a daily basis, mainly by burning. In Slovenia, there are no special landfills for invasive alien plant species (IAPS), so all collected biomass is sent to incinerators.

The APPLAUSE project in Ljubljana brings a completely new approach to the challenge of waste biomass. IAPS are seen as a resource and the starting point for a new business model: through large-scale education and awareness campaigns, citizens are encouraged to participate in the harvesting and use of IAPS. Educational campaigns encourage and teach them how to harvest and collect alien plants, which can then be processed at home or at a processing centre. Collected IAPS are used in three main ways: at home (e.g., food, dyes), in guided workshops (e.g., to make wood or paper products) and in artisanal laboratories (e.g., to make innovative products with market potential in social enterprises, employing vulnerable groups).

As a Zero Waste City, Ljubljana has recognized the potential to establish a systematic participatory model that uses collected biomass to develop new sustainable products. Thanks to this platform, Ljubljana successfully employed circular production to control IAPS, instead of incinerating them. The project has trained at least 2,350 citizens and collected over 45,000 kilogrammes of alien plants to be used in wood and paper production.

RECURRENT HOUSING FUND

Time-based Financial Instrument

Fund with a seed capital, making it possible to buy vacant property, refurbish it and make it more sustainable. Renting or selling the sustainably renovated houses enables the fund to invest in new projects.

Why?

Access to housing is a fundamental right, yet it remains a major challenge for many people in Europe. Not only the limited availability of affordable housing is problematic, but also the fact that the affordable housing that is available often appears to be in a poor state, lacking energy-saving features and having poor, or even no access to sustainable energy sources. Tenants living in lower-quality homes might not pay high rents, but face serious maintenance costs and high energy bills.

The high cost of housing in urban centres makes it difficult for people to participate in society and build up a career, which contributes to social exclusion and inequality. The lack of affordable housing is mostly bigger when a local housing market is dominated by the private sector, while commercial landlords are more interested in making good profits than in providing affordable housing. In case commercially offered housing is affordable, sometimes the quality of it is relatively poor. Also privately owned homes can be in poor condition as the owners may not be able to afford to make their property more sustainable, which might eventually make it impossible for them to sell it. The issues around housing access are complex, and require a coordinated and comprehensive response from governments, policymakers and civil society.

How Does It Work?

Municipalities can incentivize private property owners to offer affordable housing. Tax incentives, such as reduced property tax rates, can be used to persuade landlords to rent out their properties at reduced rates. It is important that regulations are set for the quality and the level of sustainability, so that, for example, tenants are not confronted with unaffordable energy-bills. Another option is to offer rent subsidies to tenants who live in properties above the rental price index. This would allow property owners to receive market rent while still providing affordable housing options to renters. Public-private partnerships could also be established, where developers partner with the local government to build affordable housing units in exchange for tax incentives or other benefits. These subsidies or partnerships allow parties to engage in projects relating to sustainability, such as the use of renewable energy sources or a low carbon footprint.

Example: Yes we rent!, Mataró, Spain

The project 'Yes We Rent!' aims to increase the offer of affordable rental housing in the city of Mataró, Spain. Cooperatives of tenants offer favourable conditions to homeowners by generating an affordable and stable rental supply in the long term. In return, these cooperatives demand that the housing made available is in a good condition, so the energy bills won't be too high.

As an instrument of inclusion, 'Yes We Rent!' tackles a double challenge: 'people without flats, and flats without people' in a context where the housing market is highly deregulated, owner-dominated (75 per cent of the homes are owner-occupied) and highly volatile. There is a dramatic shortage of affordable housing in the city, and rents have risen by 27 per cent over the last three years, leaving the city's social housing sector totally incommensurate to demand. However, there are some 3,500 'flats without people' – properties sitting empty because their owners do not have the resources to renovate them or are afraid tenants won't pay their rents.

LIFE CYCLE FINANCE

Time-based Financial Flexibility

Linking the development accounts to the operational accounts.

Why?

Since the majority of construction projects are built by large development firms whose main interest lies in selling a building with the highest profit, the sustainability of a project is often neglected. The initial costs of investing in sustainable buildings are usually higher than conventional building costs. When developers sell their building projects directly after completion, the incentive to invest in sustainable measures is lost as there is no direct financial output.

However, the durability and longevity of the building eventually counterbalance these costs and often even result in lower costs overall.

The impacts of investing in sustainable and future-proof building methods only appear over time. Financial arrangements that combine the initial investment with the long-term exploitation of the property are life cycle financial arrangements. Life cycle finance is achieved by bringing the responsibilities of the development and the management phase in one hand. If the developers also profit from the long life cycle of a building, it would guarantee a stronger incentive to build sustainably. That higher initial investments in more building quality lead to a longer lifespan is proven by our monuments, which are still highly appreciated, sometimes even centuries after their completion.

How Does It Work?

Life cycle finance works best when development and maintenance are done by the same company. Investments in all kinds of quality, from durable materials to sustainable installations, from casco flexibility to extra insulation, lead to a higher appreciation of the property by the initiator itself. On a larger scale, companies that rent out property, such as housing corporations or real estate investors, are suited for life cycle finance. But also social institutions such as hospitals, libraries, townhouses and sports clubs could be developing their own property. Since a developer's trigger will mostly be financial, sustainability in a building should be financially profitable. Developers with 'green' ambitions or with sustainable goals are aware of this economic trigger and will focus on profitable, sustainable investments. Even when they sell their development directly after completion, they want to be sure that their sustainable promises to the user will come true.

Regular developers can also be encouraged – or even forced – to invest in sustainable buildings by banks, lenders and insurers that set restrictions for their loans or risk coverages. With a smart set of requirements, conditional loans or restricted insurance guarantees can very well lead to a sustainable exploitation period. Finally, governmental incentives or restrictions can stimulate a better life cycle finance. With subsidies or regulations regarding the basic quality of a development, profits made during the life span of the project can be spread out better between the initial and the successive phases of it.

Example: Hermann Miller Factory, Bath, United Kingdom

Factory buildings are often subject to change due to their company's needs. While this regularly leads to vacancy and relocation of the company, the Herman Miller factory in Bath was built to anticipate this change. Throughout the years the building accommodated a production rate that was six times higher than the initial plan. The modular building was so flexible that in 2020, after the closing of the industrial activities, it could be easily transformed and repurposed to become part of the Bath Spa University of Art and Design.

3.8 Spatial Flexibility

The spatial aspect concerns the physical elements of a development. Spatial instruments are used to give shape to the spatial structures and manifestations of a development.

In the quest for cost efficiency, the construction industry has been working on the standardization of building products and methods for decades. However, standardization is at odds with solutions tailored to local requirements, user-friendliness and adaptability.

If the building industry is to be successful in tackling the challenge of circularity and climate adaptation, the set of instruments available to architects, product suppliers and builders will need to become more flexible to enable more customization, allow more input from users and building structures that can be adapted more easily.

Local Spatial Flexibility
Unlike in new build projects, the pre-existing conditions implementing circularity and climate adaptation into existing structures are multi-facetted, complex and a key determining factor. This demands a more flexible set of spatial instruments that enable location-specific customization.

Use-driven Spatial Flexibility
First and foremost, buildings and structures should serve the interests of their users and enable them to take responsibility. This is not always limited to the interests of individuals; a communal interest can also be a determining factor. However, standardization tends to prioritize the interests of abstract entities such as public authorities, banks and developers at the expense of the actual users. Use-driven flexibility means that a careful balance is found between the interests of users and institutional interests on a project basis.

Time-based Spatial Flexibility
Spatial development without a blueprint requires flexible structures that are adaptable so that they can change over time. There are two extremes: either the structure has a very short life span and is designed for a very specific function, fulfilling a temporary requirement, or the structure remains in place for a long time and has functional neutrality, so it can be used for many different purposes.

3.9 Spatial Instruments

Local Spatial Flexibility

BIOBASED BUILDING

SOIL-SENSITIVITY

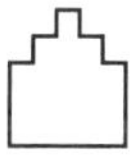
CONVERTING TRADITION

Use-driven Spatial Flexibility

MICROCLIMATE MODIFICATION

DENSIFICATION

ROOFTOP BENEFITS

Time-based Spatial Flexibility

MODULAR BUILDING

RE-INTERPRETATION

SEASONAL FLEXIBILITY

BIOBASED BUILDING

Local Spatial Flexibility

Building with materials that are organic, renewable and mostly plant-based such as wood, grass or hemp and therefore have a minimal carbon footprint.

Why?

Modern building materials are mostly stony (concrete, brick) or metallic (steel, aluminium). These raw materials have a large carbon footprint due to the energy-intensive production process involved in extracting them from non-renewable sources such as chalk, pebbles, bauxite or iron ore. In contrast, biobased materials are derived directly from organic resources and are renewable. Wood for example, under sustainable forest management, can be an endless resource. Such materials are intended to fully reintegrate back into the environment, creating zero waste. On top of that, biobased materials may have a positive carbon footprint because they can store carbon. Biobased buildings could therefore contribute to the reduction of carbon dioxide emissions instead of being only consumers of resources.

Besides their low environmental impact, biobased building materials can contribute to healthier indoor spaces. Certified materials made from natural resources do not emit harmful emissions and can furthermore regulate humidity and absorb pollutants, ultimately improving indoor air quality.

How Does It Work?

Although biobased building materials are getting more popular, their integration into the construction industry is not yet widespread. Designing and building with these materials often requires a creative and innovative approach that goes beyond traditional construction methods. As contractors, investors and building owners are not yet familiar with biobased materials, they often have doubts about their performances and qualities. Some also consider it a risk if biobased materials will meet legal building requirements.

Out of all the layers that make up a building, the structure has the most significant impact on carbon dioxide emissions. By creating a timber structure, we can greatly enhance its carbon storage potential. Building a demountable timber structure facilitates the future recycling of materials. Cross-laminated timber (CLT) has the technical possibilities for using wood as a structural material in complex or high-rise structures. Regarding the building's envelope, the most common biobased method is using prefabricated timber-framed elements or solid timber components, combined with biobased insulation such as cellulose, straw or cork. Such a method requires increased wall or roof thicknesses (compared to conventional insulation products) in order to achieve a highly insulated envelope.

Biobased cladding and interior finishing include wood, bamboo, straw, clay finishes and compressed-grass panels. If exposed to water, a protective coating may be required.

Example: House of Nature, Silkeborg, Denmark

Located next to a forested area, the building serves an educational purpose, for teaching about nature and outdoor life. Aiming to fully integrate the design with the natural environment around it and reflect its educational programme, the building was constructed using only biobased materials.

The foundation of the building is made of screw piles and a wooden deck, minimizing its impact on the ground. The wooden structure is visible both inside and outside, seamlessly blending in with the surrounding forest. The facade is inspired by traditional architecture, combining oak columns with cladding made of shingles from acacia wood. The structure is well-insulated with wood fibre boards used for thermal insulation and cardboard-based material used as a vapour barrier. By using demountable fixations only, a future disassembling of the building structure is easily imaginable.

The end result is a warm and inviting building that has a natural look and immersed in the surrounding landscape; an inspiration to its visitors.

SOIL-SENSITIVITY

Local Spatial Flexibility

Local soil conditions determine the risks caused by climate change. By carefully taking these soil conditions into account in the design, risks can be reduced.

Why?

Cities must anticipate climate change and respond with interventions to help them withstand future changing conditions. Understanding the role soils can play in supporting these interventions is key to determining effective measures.

Soil quality either stimulates or frustrates the way we can cope with challenges such as flooding, drought, heat stress, forest fires or decreasing biodiversity. For example, soil that is naturally water-impermeable needs adapted building methods to prevent ground floors from being flooded after heavy rains. Subsoil that hardly retains moisture is an easy basis for forest fires. Human interventions, such as building, excavation, paving or planting vegetation, seriously affects the capacities of the soil. Awareness of both its natural capabilities and the effects of human actions is dearly needed in order to develop climate-adaptive, future-proof cities.

How Does It Work?

Risk identification and mapping of the soil is the first step to adapting the built environment to environmental changes such as flood conditions and heat stress. Depending on the state of the ground, the next step is to identify implementable strategies that support resilience. A well thought-out, clever design of soil-related uses such as squares, parks, roads and private gardens can effectively suppress the impact of extreme weather conditions. In case buildings cover the ground, the role of the soil could be taken over by re-arranging rooftops as green spaces or gardens. Green roofs reduce heat stress and capture large amounts of rainwater. Otherwise, buildings can also secure stability in changing soilscapes by detaching the base of the building from the ground beneath it, such as stilt houses or floating cities.

Example: Floating University, Berlin, Germany

The 'Floating University' in Berlin is an ephemeral structure in the centre of Berlin, built onto a disused rainwater retention basin at Flughafen Tempelhof. The wooden construction is not actually floating but is planted into the concrete floor of the artificial lake. Throughout the years of disuse, the basin has developed its own ecosystem with a large variety of plants, species and different layers of soil. This is a vital component of the architect's design and style of building. By elevating the structure with stilts, the ecosystem can keep evolving beneath the platforms. Simultaneously, the structure is safe from the risks of high-water flooding and protects the building's materials from the water. The architects and builders from the collective use the months with low precipitation for the construction of new elements of the sustainable structure. During these months, the basin is drained and it is possible to continue the construction of new paths and platforms. Once the construction is completed, the floating university returns to hosting its interdisciplinary programme of activities. By adapting to the existing landscape and recognizing its benefits and risk factors, this construction successfully uses a landscape that would otherwise be uninhabitable.

The project describes itself as a 'unique ecosystem', a self-led collective, which invites the public to take part in educational and academic workshops, lectures and events. Founded in 2018, the architects of Raumlabor invited a collective of students, designers and neighbours to join the construction. The ever-evolving wooden structure is altered and upgraded every year. The site is a place to inform, challenge and create a discourse, all in the context of the risks, strains and chances of global warming.

CONVERTING TRADITION

Local Spatial Flexibility

Traditional building methods contain local knowledge about the optimal combination of available building materials, dealing with local climate risks and costs. Generic, industry-driven building systems lack this knowledge.

Why?

Twenty-first-century sustainable architecture aims to re-establish a harmonious relationship between humans and nature. This relationship is already evident in traditional building practice and architecture. For thousands of years, anonymous builders searched through trial and error for ways to create climate-adaptive buildings that provided indoor thermal comfort, by taking into account geographical and climate factors. Limited by the opportunities offered by their local environment, they came up with resourceful solutions using available materials and tools.

Despite significant differences between modern and past lifestyles and demands, the accumulated knowledge of the past can serve as a valuable resource for designing contemporary buildings that are both adaptable to local climates and incorporate sustainable practices.

How Does It Work?

Traditional architecture can be converted into contemporary sustainable designs by taking the local climatic and geographical knowledge and adapting to it using modern building techniques and materials. This can include using passive design strategies to provide natural heating, cooling and lighting, as well as utilizing environmentally friendly materials and incorporating circular design principles to reduce waste. A thorough analysis of the local climate and geography is crucial in determining the optimal placement, orientation and shape of the building, ensuring it's both comfortable and functional. Factors such as prevailing winds, sun exposure and daylight are key elements in the design process and can greatly impact the comfort and performance of the building. Furthermore, combining locally sourced materials and traditional building techniques with contemporary technologies and materials can result in buildings that are both sustainable and culturally and socially relevant.

Example: House of the Winds, Santorini, Greece

The Cyclades are a group of islands in Greece that have a Mediterranean climate with mild, windy winters and hot to warm summers with varying levels of humidity. With low rainfall and the nearby sea providing cooling breezes at night, the local vernacular architecture evolved in response to the climate, resulting in a unique, highly contextual style. The settlements feature an organic form with high density and repetitive building volumes in simple cubic shapes.

The 'House of the Winds' (2013) by Couvelas architects resonates traditional knowledge of positioning and designing buildings that successfully deal with local circumstances. For this house, which has a modern appearance, the north wind became the guiding design tool, determining the building's volumes and the location of its openings. Thick walls were constructed to provide protection against the wind and to ensure a stable indoor temperature during the hot summer months. Funnels formed within the mass of the thick exterior walls deflect the wind, thus creating a protective wind curtain in front of the corresponding openings. Part of the house is constructed underground, a common practice in Santorini's cliffs, contributing to passive cooling.

The materials, such as the coarse peach-coloured sand used for the coating of the exterior surfaces and the pumice stone used for roof insulation, have a direct link to the local environment, blending in with the surrounding earth and creating a harmonious, timeless and yet contemporary aesthetic.

MICROCLIMATE MODIFICATION

Use-driven Spatial Flexibility

Small-scale interventions in the public realm that diminish the negative effects of climate change such as heat stress, flooding or air pollution.

Why?

Reducing the negative impacts of climate change in urban areas usually requires large-scale climate-adaptive measures, for example strengthening urban green belts, redirecting traffic flows or mitigating river flooding. Small-scaled, easily integrable and cheap interventions, however, can also help increase a city's resilience to the impacts of climate change. Because such measures usually involve significantly less administrative effort and the decision-making processes are limited to the local level, such microclimatic modifications can usually be implemented quickly and inexpensively.

Well-positioned microclimatic modifications can improve the quality of life in cities, for example by helping to reduce noise, heat or pollution for residents or by improving air quality. The visibility of such measures in public spaces can also lead to increased awareness among city residents of the need for climate adaptation measures and of their effectiveness. Ideally, citizens are even encouraged to become active themselves and implement appropriate measures in their private sphere. Even if the effectiveness of single measures remains limited, synergetic effects can be achieved through the combination of many small measures or city-wide networks can be established, which contribute to increased resilience of a city to the impacts of climate change.

How Does It Work?

For a successful implementation of microclimatic modifications, local climatic challenges must first be identified to understand if and how they can be improved through small interventions. Local climate issues suitable for microclimate modification are for example heat stress, rainwater floods or bad air quality. Examples of measures that can improve microclimates are numerous. The most interesting ones are cheap, low-tech and easy to implement, such as planting a tree, removing tiles from gardens, greening roofs and installing nest boxes or so-called insect hotels. In some cases, it may be worthwhile to implement innovative or high-tech measures. Recently, for example, some cities have successfully tested moss walls that filter harmful particles from the air or water vapor sprays that cool the surroundings and help combat heat islands.

It is recommended to somehow monitor the results of the modification. If the small-scaled measures prove successful, they may be scaled up. Relatively easy, microclimatic measures could be subsidized by municipalities. In this respect, a city's resilience to the effects of climate change can be collectively addressed by many residents.

Example: Climate Shelters, Barcelona, Spain

The municipality of Barcelona, in collaboration with public and private entities, has established a network of climate shelters in the city. These help to counter the threat of heat waves that lead to increased health risks and mortality, especially among vulnerable groups such as elderly or chronically ill people. Such climate shelters are small, publicly accessible spaces, either in existing buildings or in new building structures, either with an indoor or an outdoor quality. The places offer good thermal comfort, free drinking water and comfortable furniture to rest. The shelters are located in school buildings, sports facilities, museums, public squares or parks. Outdoor areas operate during the preventive stage for heatwaves between 15 June and 15 September, while indoor areas are open all year round and can therefore also be used to protect from the cold. There is now a network of over two hundred climate shelters in the city, with 95 per cent of residents having to walk less than 10 minutes to the nearest one.

DENSIFICATION

Use-driven Spatial Flexibility

Adding more usable space to existing urban tissue.

Why?

Urban sprawl is a phenomenon that has characterized many cities around the world since the twentieth century. Due to population growth, the availability of cars, cheap gasoline and the popularity of suburban lifestyles, urbanization processes have increasingly focused on peri-urban and rural areas, while urban cores have been neglected. Since urban sprawl entails various negative consequences, densification of existing urban areas is strongly recommended.

Higher urban densities result in a better use of social and technical infrastructure, leading to lower infrastructure costs and lower resource consumption per capita. By concentrating new development in the existing urban fabric, nutrient-rich soils and natural landscapes outside of cities can be preserved, while further fragmentation and disturbance of habitats and ecosystems with high ecological value can be stopped.

Additionally, densification reduces emissions due to less traffic movements. Proximity also results in more opportunities to close material cycles. Producers can more easily find buyers for goods and a critical mass is reached at which it becomes worthwhile to share materials and services. In addition, higher density can have a positive impact on the social life of residents, who benefit from shorter distances to services and larger social networks.

How Does It Work?

The possibilities for densification essentially depend on the characteristics of the existing urban fabric and can vary greatly across different cities. In principle, densification can be aimed at the creation of new residential space, as well as commercial, cultural, social and other spaces.

Vacant lots, vast parking areas or brownfield sites can be used for densification. Densification can also be achieved by expanding existing buildings with additional storeys or building attachments. However, densification does not necessarily have to be accompanied by the creation of new building structures. If buildings (parts) are vacant or underutilized, retrofits and new use concepts can also lead to densification.

In any case, it is crucial that the surrounding infrastructure, such as public transportation or schools, is co-developed with the densification process to avoid overload of these infrastructures. Additionally, a balance must be achieved between densification and open space preservation, otherwise a loss of inner-city open space can negatively impact urban ecosystems and the health of city residents. Attention must also be paid to sensible zoning, so that different uses in a dense urban structure do not interfere with each other.

Example: K.118, Winterthur, Switzerland

Project K.118 is an extension project of an existing three-storey warehouse in a Winterthur business park. Without enlarging the footprint of the building, twelve studios and workspaces were created on three additional levels. The project is pioneering in the creation of much-needed production and studio spaces within the city. These spaces are increasingly being pushed to the outskirts of the city in the competition for inner-city space.

Key in this densification exercise is the structure of the warehouse, which was built for heavy merchandize. As the original warehouse building was also transformed into studios, the structural surplus could be used for the rooftop extension. The additional three storeys have a lightweight steel structure as a base, finished with lightweight facade elements and inner walls. The densification project is also characterized by its circular construction, with about 80 per cent of the building materials being reused from nearby donor buildings.

ROOFTOP BENEFITS
Use-driven Spatial Flexibility

Unused, empty rooftops in towns and cities can easily contribute to urban needs such as circular energy, biodiversity, food-production or rainwater retention.

Why?
Rooftops represent huge surfaces in our cities, which are often overlooked and undervalued. When suitably covered, rooftops can significantly contribute to various environmental challenges. Biodiversity suffers from our growing cities – animals and plants are replaced by buildings and urban infrastructure. By covering empty rooftops with indigenous vegetation, urban biodiversity is enhanced and wildlife habitats are created. This supports the well-being of people as well, as they get access to local nature again and air quality is improved.

Generally, our buildings are waterproof and surrounded by water-resistant surfaces such as streets and squares. This makes our cities vulnerable to floodings, as rainwater cannot easily be absorbed by the underground anymore. By capturing rainwater, rooftops can help mitigate the risk of flooding in urban areas when heavy downpours occur. Urban environments face higher surface and air temperatures than their rural counterparts, a phenomenon known as the urban heat island. A significant number of buildings are not designed to cope with the increased temperatures during longer and more frequent periods. Blue-green (BG) roofs can increase the insulation capacity of buildings, stimulate evaporation with the available water and in that way contribute to urban resilience to heat stress. Consisting of an additional water-management layer underneath a green, planted layer, BG roofs enlarge the albedo effect (the ability of surfaces to reflect sunlight). In the event of long droughts, maximum water availability is created through the blue layer and supports the survival of the upper plant layer.

In search of circular, renewable energy sources, our roofs also offer chances. Rooftops are sunlit and literally on top of energy-consuming functions. Finally, rooftops allow for more efficient use of existing space in overcrowded urban areas. Considering existing roofs as a base for new developments, building programme can be added while avoiding new land developments.

How Does It Work?
Adding qualities to existing rooftops – either vegetation, water storage, solar panels or building programme – starts with an analysis of the structure of the underlying building. What additional bearing load can the foundation carry? Once the structural possibilities are understood, the quality most beneficial to the existing building or its surroundings can be determined. Financial implications might be decisive. Adding programme can help finance more sustainability for the existing building as a whole. Solar panels make the building independent from fossil energy. Many governments subsidize both solar panels and roof covering. Possible complicating factors should be taken into account before starting, like ownership issues or restrictions concerning safety (wind, fire, earthquakes) and privacy.

Example: RESILIO, Amsterdam, the Netherlands
As part of the 'Resilience nEtwork of Smart Innovative cLImate-adapative rOoftops' (RESILIO), a blue-green roof cover was tested at several places in Amsterdam. RESILIO used an interdisciplinary approach with public and private stakeholders to repurpose over 10,000 square metres of roofs in different neighbourhoods. A network of smart BG roofs was created on top of social housing complexes and properties in the city. The roofs were fitted with smart valves that can micro-manage the collected rainwater based on real-time weather forecasts and relevant local water management data.

RESILIO aims to optimize the city's water management and reduce climate risks such as flooding, biodiversity loss and heat stress.

MODULAR BUILDING

Time-based Spatial Flexibility

Building with repetitive, easily transportable and combinable modules.

Why?

Conventional building tends to be a bit impracticable. Raw building products are transported to a building site where they have to be stored, waiting for the right moment to get assembled in unpredictable weather circumstances. This traditional process produces lots of greenhouse gases, has a negative impact on the immediate surroundings of the building site and its quality depends on local circumstances.

Modular buildings, on the other hand, offer several advantages over conventional building types. The production of modular building elements takes place in factories, where it is easier to collect and store building products. Since circumstances in the factories can be better controlled, the precision and quality of the building element is usually higher than building elements that are manufactured on site. Furthermore, this type of manufacturing offers better control over waste and emissions. Working conditions for builders are better too.

The use of prefabricated building elements can also increase cost-effectiveness. Especially when manufactured in large quantities, savings in materials, energy, and labour costs can be made. In addition, shorter development and construction times offer the advantage of being able to respond quickly to changing space requirements. It is easy to imagine the modules being moved to another location after some time for reuse, representing a form of circular use of building materials.

How Does It Work?

The development and construction process of modular buildings begins with the planning phase. In this step, the customer's demands are determined, and a design is made. Once the decision for a final design has been made, the building elements are prefabricated in factories, either in series or customized. However, it should be noted that modular construction requires more permanent building facilities, such as factories and warehouses, than traditional construction, which is mostly done on temporary sites. Therefore, modular construction is more cost-effective when the flow of production is regular and unceasing.

Prefabricated modules are transported as finished products to the construction site where they are assembled. This shortened and cleaner construction process impacts the environment less than conventional construction. If renovations become necessary after some time or if the spatial requirements change, the buildings can be dismantled into their individual elements and taken away. In the factories, the individual elements can be disassembled or renewed and adjusted before being reassembled elsewhere.

Example: Modular School Buildings, Berlin, Germany

To address the shortage of classroom capacity, Berlin's education and housing authorities collaborated with private architects to design a modular building type that can be used to extend existing school buildings. On ready-to-build spaces of school sites, these buildings can be constructed within six to ten months and have a service life of at least 50 years.

The assembly of the off-site prefabricated building elements is accomplished according to individual demand in four standard sizes with 12, 16, 22 or 24 classrooms, associated group workrooms and an optional cafeteria. Since 2013, the Berlin administration has completed approximately 80 of these modular school buildings, and 60 more are in the planning stages, with newer models consisting of wooden building elements. In case student numbers decline in the future, the buildings can be dismantled at short notice and the individual modules used for other purposes. The students can then be accommodated in the existing main school buildings.

RE-INTERPRETATION

Time-based Spatial Flexibility

A different interpretation of an existing building structure.

Why?

Challenges related to climate change often require innovative solutions that seem to run counter to conventional structures and practices. When implementing such innovations, the potentials of existing structures are often neglected. In urban development in particular, it is even a widespread practice to eliminate already existing structures to enable the creation of new solutions.

Re-interpretation, on the other hand, aims at integrating existing structures as an elementary part of problem-solving rather than as an obstacle in finding solutions. Successful forms of re-interpretation are often inspiring examples of circularity, showing how existing structures can be used for a purpose other than their original one.

Successful re-interpretations can contribute to the creation of climate-resilient cities by significantly reducing the need for new construction and thus resource consumption compared to demolition and new construction, thereby minimizing environmental impacts. Re-interpretations often lead to the revitalization of neglected structures, in which diverse social functions can be housed without taking up more space. The creation of newly interpreted spaces can also result in the emergence of innovative places that have an identity-giving character for residents and can have a lasting positive impact on a neighbourhood.

How Does It Work?

Re-interpretations require a high degree of creativity and usually relate to building structures that no longer meet the contemporary requirements of a changed environment. In order to develop successful concepts, therefore, precisely such spaces or objects must first be identified, and their building structure examined in detail in terms of its strengths for possible alternative uses.

Setting circularity as a standard for future redevelopment asks for innovative concepts for new building structures, anticipating their re-interpretation once they become outdated in the future due to changing circumstances. Examples of structures that should already include possibilities for future re-interpretation are underground parking facilities in urban areas that are introducing traffic-reducing measures, or office spaces in locations that are witnessing changing work patterns and require new functions.

Example: Energy Bunker, Hamburg, Germany

After the former flak bunker in Hamburg's Wilhelmsburg district stood empty for over 60 years following the end of the Second World War, a conversion and reuse concept was developed and implemented on behalf of the Hanseatic City of Hamburg as part of the International Building Exhibition, which took place in Hamburg from 2006 to 2013. The central challenge was to put a massive and inflexible building, built to be indestructible, to a new use after losing its original function of protecting residents from air raids.

In 2013, the remodelled building was opened as an energy bunker, producing clean energy from renewable energy sources for around 2,000 households in the neighbourhood. At the heart of the project is a two-million-litre water storage tank that serves as a large heat buffer in the energy bunker and as the heart of a local heating network. Complementing the technical functions, a café including a viewing platform was built at a height of 30 metres to attract visitors. The re-interpretation has succeeded in transforming a historic building that seemed obsolete into a centre that presents innovative and forward-looking solutions for energy supply.

SEASONAL FLEXIBILITY
Time-based Spatial Flexibility

Climate-adaptive device that has the flexibility to respond to changing circumstances, such as extreme weather or changing water levels, possibly leading to different programmatic uses over time.

Why?
Climate change will result in more extreme weather conditions, characterized by increasing peaks and troughs. Some cities have to deal with changing water levels over time, due to excessive rain or because they are in open connection to the sea. Other cities are completely covered in snow in winter or are threatened by drought and heat stress in summer. Becoming climate-resilient means incorporating measures that can counteract the negative consequences of these peaks and troughs. But as these negative consequences fluctuate, spatial demands for climate-resilient measures are preferably temporary. As the pressure on space in most cities is high, it makes sense that climate-resilient measures can change or even disappear when they are not acutely necessary, giving space to other urban programmes such as recreation.

How Does It Work?
Solutions can be high-tech such as automated flexible water barriers, for example using a wall that under normal circumstances is hidden in the quay but floats up at high tide. But also very down to earth and traditional solutions using rain gardens, green roof tops and green building walls that change over time to address heat waves and floods can be sufficient. In summer, when there is much heat stress, vegetation provides shade, while in winter, when it is cold, dark and rainy, the leafless plants let daylight and heat through. The rain gardens can be filled again.

In cities such as Copenhagen and Rotterdam, inspiring examples can be found of rainwater storage in stepped recessed squares that have a different function depending on the time of the year. In spring and summer, they can be used as recreational space, in fall as water buffers and in winter as ice skating rink. During a heavy rain storm, excess water is channelled into the square, turning it into a reservoir. In this way the public space can both help to prevent flood and still be used as recreational space.

Example: Reconstruction of the Scheldt Quays, Antwerp, Belgium
The Scheldt is the central river of Antwerp, which is in open connection with the sea. During heavy storm tides, the Scheldt quays are always flooded. After the 1976 storm surge, a flood defence was built: a concrete wall with a length of 5.5 kilometres and a height of 1.35 metres. This fixed wall protected the city from the river, but also made the river inaccessible for the city. The space between the river and the concrete walls was solely used to park cars when the water was not high.

Now the flood defences must be raised by 90 centimetres to protect the city against higher floods, there is a possibility to improve the arrangement of the quays over a length of almost 7 kilometres. Both the design of the public space and the position of the defence were reconsidered, connecting the quays and their direct environment in a much better way. Though the fixed water defence is still about 80 centimetres above the quay level this height transition is now softened using gentle slopes. At specific locations the connection between the city and the quay even is on the same continuous level now making use of mobile flood defences that most of the time open up the view to the river and can be closed when a storm surge occurs.

4. Examples of a Flexible City

In this chapter we show how circularity and climate adaptation is taking shape in Europe, using a number of completed projects as examples: they are illustrative of a new way of working and a new mentality, with a central emphasis on reuse, social inclusion and the time factor. A description is given of how each project was realized using the flexible instruments presented in earlier chapters.

Example Projects

Local Flexibility	**Les Berges du Rhône** Lyon, France **Klimatilpasning Kokkedal** Fredensborg, Denmark **Super Blocks Eixample** Barcelona, Spain **Sara Cultural Centre** Skellefteå, Sweden **Hospital Entrance Area Amsterdam UMC, location AMC** Amsterdam, the Netherlands **Cooperativa Agricoltura Nuova** Rome, Italy
Use-driven Flexibility	**IKEA Store** Vienna, Austria **Seestadt Aspern** Vienna, Austria **The People's Pavilion** Eindhoven, the Netherlands **Cité Maraîchère** Romainville, France **Atri** Sikhall Vänersborg, Sweden **Gent knapt op** Ghent, Belgium
Time-based Flexibility	**Resource Rows** Copenhagen, Denmark **Town Hall Extension** Korbach, Germany **Puukuokka Housing Block** Jyväskylä, Finland **The Triodos Bank** Driebergen-Rijsenburg, the Netherlands **Atelier LUMA** Arles, France **Crèche Justice** Paris, France

Les Berges du Rhône, Lyon, France

From open-air car park to climate-adaptive park

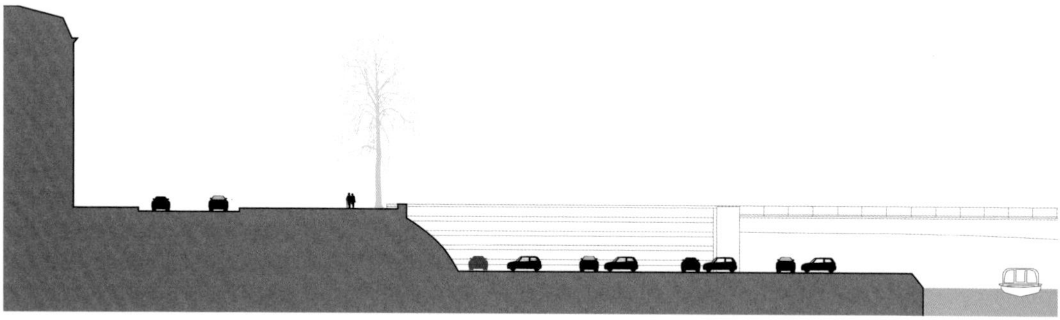

1. The banks of the Rhône river are only used for car parking and are regularly flooded.

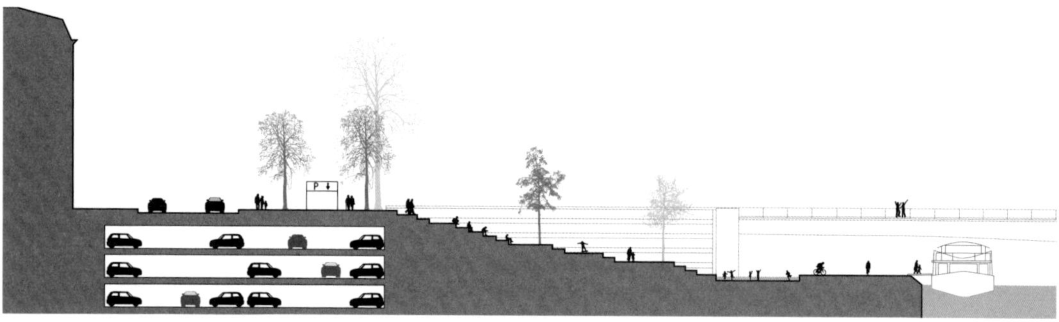

2. Restructuring the banks leads to better climate adaptation and highly appreciated public spaces.

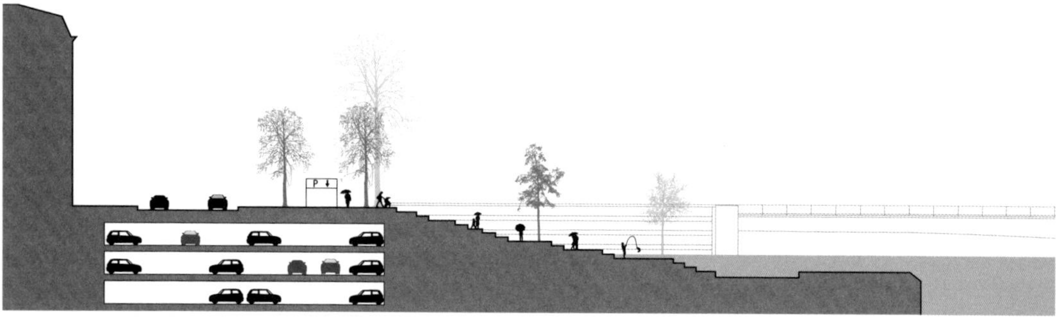

3. In case the river water rises, the banks of the river protect the city from floods.

Local Flexibility
Instruments: infrastructure rearrangement, car ban, capitalized risks, seasonal flexibility

Initiators: IN SITU, Françoise Jourda Architecte, Le Grand Lyon, Agence d'Urbanisme de Lyon, CNR
Completion: 2008
Programme: car-free, green promenade for pedestrians and slow mobility
Website: https://www.in-situ.fr/#/fr/projets/berges-rives/berges-du-rhone

The changing of our climate confuses our natural water systems on a large scale. Despite differences between European cities and regions, they all are facing the same challenge: the negative impact of alternating drought and flooding. The transformation of a huge industrial harbour area within the city of Lyon into a climate-adaptive park prevents flooding of the local rivers and offers residents shelter from the heat on a hot day. Seasonal variations lead to a public space with a variety of programmatic possibilities.

Lyon, the gastronomic capital of France, is crossed by two major rivers: the Saône and the Rhône. These rivers have characterized the city ever since the Roman settlement of Lugdunum was established along the banks of the Saône. The two rivers merge in the southern part of the city, a rare confluence of such large water streams. In the Middle Ages, housing was constructed directly along the river, like in Venice, where the facades would touch the water. At moments, the water level of the two rivers could change rapidly, often flooding the city and eroding the banks. After 1793, the riverbanks of the Saône were cleared up for better hygiene and to protect the city from flooding. The houses built right along the river were demolished, and large quays were built instead.

With time, Lyon's close relationship with the water was lost, as in the twentieth century, the quays were increasingly dedicated to traffic and parking.

In 2000, a national law came into effect, (SRU: Loi Solidarité et Renouvellement Urbain) aiming at more solidarity and sustainability, encouraging the redevelopment of cities, targeting urban renovation and housing in particular. This fostered many important urban undertakings, such as the redevelopment of the Confluence district in Lyon. This redevelopment focuses on bringing nature back into the district and reactivating the lost connection with the water. In the area, several projects emerged, like the development of a nautical plaza, the transformation of old boats into dwellings, the introduction of a water taxi system, the construction of the Musée des Confluences in 2014 and various housing projects. The redevelopment also recreates wild ecosystems in the humid and quiet zones of the river ('bertillod').

In line with this bigger redevelopment, the banks of the Saône and Rhône rivers are transformed and reactivated into large urban parks. The redevelopment of the Berges du Rhône ('berges' means 'riverbanks') is part of the larger ambition to reconnect Lyon with its waters and make the city more attractive and accessible for its inhabitants.

Organizational

Having accommodated a wide open-air car park lot for decades, the Berges du Rhône project started with the objective of removing cars from sight. Two car parks were therefore created underground, allowing 1,600 car parking spots to be removed from the riverbanks. Thanks to that, the quays could be given back to the citizens. Large parts of the previously widely paved areas (meant for parking), were unpaved and gave space to a green and water-permeable park. After two years, in 2007, the banks of the Rhône became a 10 hectares-wide public park dedicated to slow mobility, leisure and vegetation.

Legal
From 1991 onwards, the political and urban scene of Lyon talked about revitalizing the Rhône riverbanks: the 'Plan Bleu' was approved, with the reconnection to the Rhône in mind. The project initiators had the main ambition of removing car parking from the riverbanks to free-up this space for people, leisure and slow mobility, making the riverside more attractive. The municipality's decision to approve the 'Plan Bleu', was non-negotiable, and was criticized because of that. Especially residents living nearby rebelled against that decision, even though underground parking was planned to meet their needs for parking.

In 2002, the city of Lyon established a programme of requirements, which was used for a public tender to revitalize the riverbanks. This programme was first criticized because people thought a different parking situation would impact the commercial activities, but also because the project was judged not ambitious enough. To answer these critiques, several workshops were held in 2003, discussing slow mobility solutions and the landscape design. The removal of car parking and car-lanes on the riverbanks was balanced out with two large underground parking garages, slow mobility paths and the introduction of shared bicycles. After the workshop sessions, a consensus was found. Communication about the project turned out to be an important factor in the acceptance of the project by Lyon's inhabitants. All along the design process, meetings were held with stakeholders and inhabitants, and several placemaking programmes were carried out, such as the 'Quai des Guinguettes', a summer entertainment programme highlighting the potential of the aimed use of the riverbanks.

Financial
The Berges du Rhône project's objectives were to make the city more resilient to the natural effects of water movement and tides. The challenge was unique, since Lyon is subject to sudden and highly fluctuating water levels from two different rivers. The project aimed at easing the water discharge in case of floods, handling the rapidly rising water levels. At the same time, the Rhône river is of high importance to France since it produces one-quarter of its electrical energy, and 109,500,000 cubic metres of the rivers' water cater to the needs of the city's inhabitants each year. Interventions should improve the situation for the city without weakening the economy on a larger scale.

When the brief of the project was revisited in 2004, critics focused on the financial costs of the redevelopment, which gradually kept increasing. In fact, the construction works turned out more complex than imagined (difficulties with the removal of elements, damaged pavement that needed to be replaced), especially because the project site was so large.

However, the political decision to reactivate the river banks and the high environmental and social ambitions justified the higher costs. It could be stated that the Berges du Rhône project capitalized on the potential of the river proximity. In spite of the costs and the fact that there are fewer floods, but they do still occur, the 44+ million euro project of the Berges du Rhône enabled a profound transformation, making the city more resilient to its environment, while keeping its regional economic value and shaping a new, more attractive image of the city.

Spatial
The Berges du Rhône project enhances the aesthetic, environmental and social qualities of the area. The new city park and promenade connect the city with the river, as the design of the paths follows the natural rising rhythm of the Rhône. The paths change in width: from larger ones to narrower ones, with an urban character in the central part, and a more natural one in the northern and southern extremities of the promenade. Housing boats, cruise boats, catering, leisure and other seasonal and water-related activities emerged after the completion of the project. The Berges du Rhône became an attractive public space, hosting various programmes. For instance, the area became part of the bicycle tourism route from Genève du Léman to the Mediterranean Sea, attracting hikers and cyclists. A part of the 2008 marathon of Lyon was run on the riverbanks of the Rhône.

The large city park is very attractive during the summer period, but also functions well during winter times.

Since their opening in 2007, the Berges du Rhône are sometimes inaccessible to the public, because of floods, as in 2018 and 2021. These events haven't caused too much damage to the park so far, since the plant and tree species were chosen carefully to handle the floods.

The Berges du Rhône therefore function in accordance with the river, reconnecting the city to the water, and giving space to slow mobility and to the residents.

Klimatilpasning Kokkedal, Fredensborg, Denmark

From a public space at risk of flooding to a climate-adaptive and inclusive public space

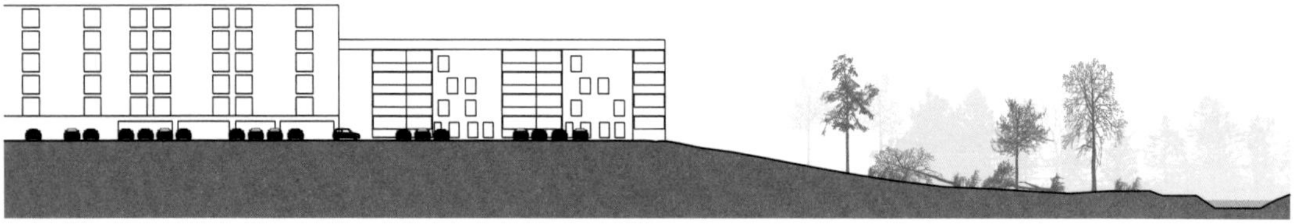

1. The suburban area of Fredensborg is facing both social and climate-related challenges.

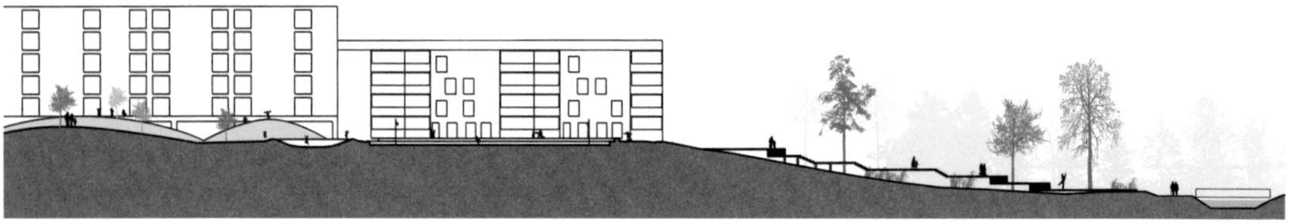

2. An intervention restructuring public spaces leads to better climate adaption and highly appreciated public spaces.

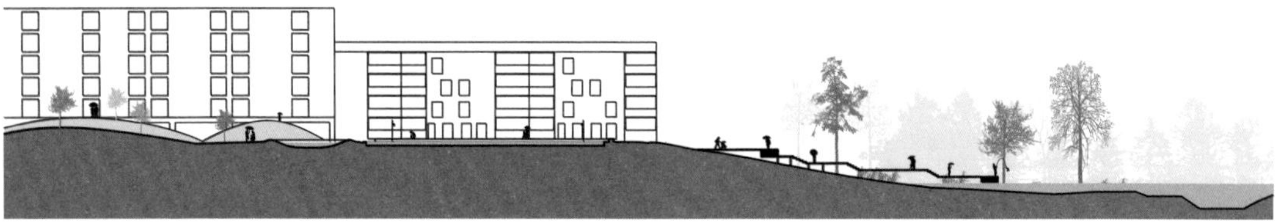

3. After heavy rainfalls, the public space retains the rainwater leading to alternative ways for using the public space.

Local Flexibility
Instruments: holistic approach, sustainability protocol, capitalized risks, soil-sensitivity

Initiators: municipality of Fredensborg, Fredensborg Utility Company, Boligforeningen 3B and Andelsboligforeningen Hørsholm
Completion: 2017
Design: BIG, Schønherr, Rambøll
Programme: drainage system, recreation, education
Website: https://www.realdania.org/whatwedo/grants-and-projects/climate-change-and-urban-development

The transformation of a densely populated area with affordable housing that is incidentally flooded into a climate-adaptive area not only prevents the area from flooding, but also forms a catalyst for social inclusion. Stormwater management has been coupled with other functions such as play, art and nature. The project consists of 35 contextual sub-projects, and is the result of a unique collaboration between local stakeholders including the municipality, the water company, homeowners and the local housing associations.

Kokkedal is a typical 1970s mono-functionally planned suburban area, part of the municipality of Fredensborg and 30 km north of Copenhagen. In 2007, central Kokkedal was facing both social and climate-related challenges. A massive cloudburst made the Usserød stream, which runs through the middle of the city, break its banks causing severe flooding in a residential area affecting thousands of people. Three years later it happened again, both times leading to significant repair costs.

At the same time social cohesion was challenged by an urban landscape divided along socio-economical lines. The urban spaces that were supposed to serve the community as meeting spots and for recreational use were worn-down, dominated by parking and in some cases perceived as unsafe.

The urgency of both coinciding challenges brought the municipality, the Utility company, homeowners and the local housing associations together with external parties such as Realdania and The Danish Foundation for Culture and Sports Facilities in one joint project. The Climate Adaptation Kokkedal project was conceived in 2012 when all ongoing sectoral projects and plans were merged into one shared vision to shape a climate-resilient urban landscape, while improving the quality of the built environment and supporting social and cultural activities and cohesion.

Climate Adaptation Kokkedal consists of 35 sub-projects spread over the entire neighbourhood, each of which enables the area's residents to meet, sport or play in the public realm. The water's flow through the urban landscape has been the overarching aesthetic inspiration and recreational theme. For example, garden rooms have been created that can function as green retainment basins and the local sports field has been walled in by a grass clad earth mound, so that it can hold back a lot of water during cloudbursts. The project includes gardens, activity grounds, exercise paths, nature playgrounds and areas that can be used for the schools' science teaching.

The formerly segregated urban Centre of Kokkedal is revitalized by reinforcing connections between major public functions, for instance the school and the shopping area, through a bright, open and inviting urban design. Shrubs, thickets and fences have been cleared, car parks have been transformed into places for play, learning and activities, a boardwalk creates a new-found access to nature, and paved areas have made way for blue and green infrastructure.

Affordable housing and communal areas have been renovated and upgraded integrating a comprehensive plan to manage excess local rainwater. Rainwater from roofs, car parks and green areas is retained in basins in the area to prevent flooding. Approximately half of all runoff rainwater from paved surfaces in the project area is retained in these basins before flowing towards the sewage system and, ultimately, towards Usserød Å, a local, natural waterway that runs through the area. Downwards, Usserød Å merges into another waterway and eventually leads the surplus of rainwater to the sea.

Organizational
Climate Adaptation Kokkedal is a pioneering project in the way that it has brought six different organizations to the table, each with their own purpose, interests and legal obligations: the utility company, municipality, housing associations and philanthropic associations. The inherent complexities and challenges were overcome by an extensive integral process and dialogue among project partners combined with a strong, shared narrative and vision for the project area playing a decisive part. Today, there is a shared acknowledgement among the parties that more has been achieved through a holistic approach and by working together than would have been possible if all parties had worked separately.

This holistic approach to climate change adaptation in the end enabled the designers to make stormwater management visible and to integrate recreational sites, including natural playgrounds, exercise tracks and green gardens, for both locals and visitors. Retention basins and rainwater reservoirs have become attractive urban spaces. For example, Bølgepladsen (wave square) collects rainwater but can also be used for basketball, skateboarding, parkour and other activities, and it is being used much better than before.

Legal
By organizing a design competition, the municipality and the other initiators turned their own ambitions into a framework for the designers. The large two-phase competition was won with an entry called 'The way of water is the way of the citizens'. The overall idea of this winning project was to use climate adaptation to connect the otherwise separate parts of the city to create new attractive meeting places and to bring nature closer to the citizens. This was exactly what was aimed for.

Financial
With a project area of 69 hectares, many subprojects and a total budget of 145 million DKK (19.5 million euros) the Climate Adaptation of Kokkedal is one of the largest and most complex projects of its kind in Denmark. The floods of 2007 and 2010 and its consequent costs were the main drivers for the willingness to invest in this project and it created momentum to bring about change. In order to reduce flooding and social costs in the long run, a coalition was created that was willing to do something about this situation and invest. Each of the joining parties enjoying the benefits in their own way, which is why it was so broadly supported.

Spatial
The driver for the new design was the local condition of the terrain. The river valley of the Usserød stream is the recipient of all surface water exceeding the existing sewer system capacity in the area and as such can only manage a water peak to a certain degree. The climate adaptation of Kokkedal is therefore based on a sustainable drainage system where the urban landscape is reshaped to optimize retention and water storage capacity. The main principle has been to manage and retain rainwater locally, upstream, and on the surface as much as possible to avoid bottlenecks and relieve both waterways and the sewage system on days with heavy rain or cloudburst.

On top of this it was the ambition to explore the possibilities of letting runoff rainwater lend aesthetic, recreational and even educational qualities to urban spaces. Where water was previously stored in pipes underground, water management is now visible in a way that also provides new recreational opportunities in the city. The retention of rainwater takes place within basins and volumes that have capacity for so-called 5-year rainstorm events. In addition, it is ensured that even when major rain events occur and the water basins overflow, it does not cause any serious damage. The rainwater is handled in a coherent system on terrain that makes it possible to follow it from landing until it runs to the smaller basins, on to trenches or ditches that lead into the large basins and finally to Usserød. All water is also led through purifying elements such as rain beds and basins.

Superblocks Eixample, Barcelona, Spain

From a car-oriented city to a cyclist- and pedestrian-orientated city

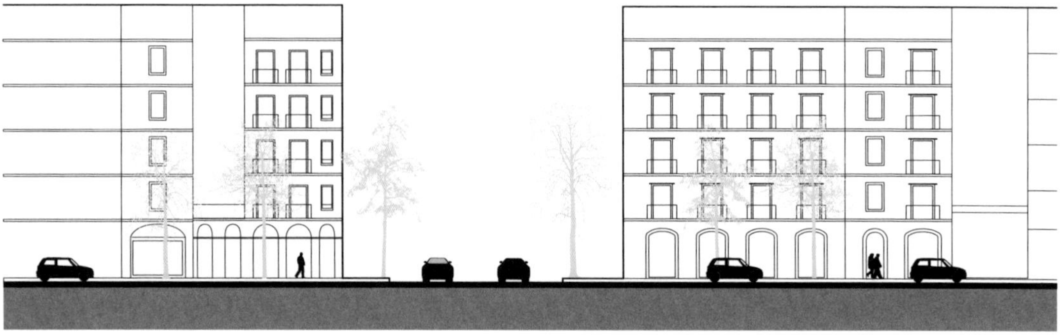

1. The Eixample district is suffering from an omnipresent car-based traffic.

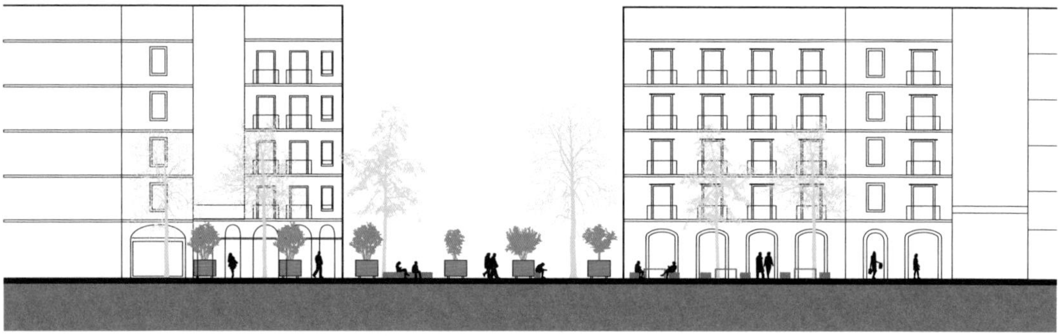

2. An experiment blocking off some of the street from car traffic leads to less pollution and improved social cohesion.

3. The temporary interventions blocking car traffic become permanent, leading to well-designed public spaces.

Local Flexibility
Instruments: empowering local communities, purpose-specific freezone, subsidy, re-interpretation

Initiators: Barcelona City Council
Completion: from 2016 onward
Programme: transformation of public space
Website: https://www.barcelona.cat/pla-superilla-barcelona/en

By reducing the speed and accessibility for cars, more space and safety is created for other modes of transportation such as cycling and walking. Furthermore, air pollution and noise are reduced and there is more room for recreation, encounters, relaxation and play in the city. By creating so called 'Superblocks' in its Eixample district, Barcelona shows that prioritizing people over cars leads to a variety of benefits that match well to various sustainable goals.

As omnipresent car traffic takes up much space and has other negative impacts on our cities, such as air pollution, cities have to reconsider their relationship with car traffic. On the other hand, many people see an unconditional access to their motorized vehicles as an unnegotiable asset. The Superblock model finds a new and intelligent balance between public space for bicycles and pedestrians on the one hand and car-accessibility on the other. The Superblock scheme emanates from the famous Eixample district, an iconic urban grid structure that is suitable for experiments with mobility because of its regularity and repetitiveness. Groups of mostly nine regular city blocks are put together to form one Superblock that is closed off for car traffic by planters and benches, introducing bicycle lanes, play areas and green spaces. Many of the parking spaces within the block are replaced by seating areas.

Barcelona introduced its first experimental Superblock in 1993 near the Basilica de Santa Maria del Mar in the historical neighbourhood of El Born. In 2005, two more Superblocks in Gràcia were realized. In 2014, it appeared that these pilot projects led to an increase of pedestrian trips by 10 per cent and of cyclist trips by 30 per cent. Based on these early pilot projects, in 2016 the so-called Superblocks-policy was introduced and Barcelona implemented another six fully functional Superblocks. In 2020, Barcelona has launched an ambitious 10-year plan that should finally lead to a total of 503 (!) Superblocks. This plan, estimated to cost 37.8 million euros, aims to reclaim the city's streets in the Eixample district from cars and cut down pollution with the creation of green spaces and public squares, resulting in 60 per cent of the streets that were previously used by cars now being available for other uses.

An inspiring example of a Superblock is the one in Sant Antoni. The intervention reconfigures the mobility and social uses in the streets, generating new places in the chamfer corners. This is done with a toolkit of urban furniture elements and a distinctive graphic style using yellow. As an affordable intervention, yellow patterns simply painted on the pavement redistribute the space and give it a new logic. Mobile wooden planters and lightweight benches function as adaptive urban furniture and can be moved around. The use of materials with an ecological certificate as well as the integration of water storage tanks in hydro-planters guarantee the sustainability and good maintenance of the new urban landscape. The intervention has generated a positive dynamic in the neighbourhood; residents and retailers now take care of the streets themselves in terms of use and maintenance. All this, together with significantly reduced pollution, and more room for green, pedestrians and cyclists, draws a new urban landscape of civic axes and plazas that make up a more people-oriented, healthy and green Eixample.

Process

Superblocks fosters urban transformation based on a maximum of participation and civic co-responsibility in all phases of the project. Stakeholders vary from residents, private companies, district organizations, non-governmental organizations, universities and expert institutions to the city council. New practices such as for example green roofs, water harvesting, rainwater management and tree planters are introduced in the neighbourhood in mutual consultation with local stakeholders. Together with local entrepreneurs, they are also considering new flexible uses for terrace space and a usage plan to safeguard against an excess concentration of similar establishments, trying to give room to diverse and multipurpose uses. Also, fewer vehicles and more people on the lanes is likely to be good for local retailers.

During the pilot run, however, there was major pushback from the local shop owners in the selected Superblock neighbourhoods. The shop owners argued that restricted car movement would affect business and their customer base would fall drastically. The city council counter-argued how recent databases showed that only 5 per cent of the customers came by car.

Legal

Banning cars from streets that are currently meant for car traffic asks for legal interventions that are tailored to specific areas and specific sustainable ambitions. In Barcelona, two types of purpose-specific freezones were introduced, the Low Emission Zones to reduce emissions in the areas the car is still allowed to enter and the Superblock Zones as pedestrian priority areas.

To be able to enter the Low Emission Zone, cars have to meet certain standards regarding, for example, the amount of carbon dioxide emitted by the vehicle. Drivers with vehicles meeting the standards are allowed to enter the zone only during daytime on weekdays and only with an environmental banner on their car.

For the pedestrian priority areas, the restrictions go even further. Here, the Superblocks are not accessible for non-residents by vehicle. Only public transport and emergency vehicles are allowed, plus those owned by local residents and disabled people. Several time slots allow deliveries and residents to enter the zone. The maximum speed is 10 kilometres per hour and the maximum weight of a vehicle is 5.5 tons. Motorized traffic is in only one direction. The roads thus become public spaces that are open and safe for pedestrians.

Financial

On the one hand the Superblocks do not involve major physical changes that require large budgets, but rather tactical urban interventions – soft measures that are often low-cost and easy to adapt. On the other hand, these light interventions have a huge sustainable and clearly visible impact on the city. This favourable cost-benefit ratio of the Superblocks increases the chance of realization and scaling up.

Even though costs are low, subsidies play a crucial role in implementing this innovative and experimental approach. A large part of the budget comes from various subsidies to stimulate climate adaptation. The European Investment Bank (EIB), for example, provides 95 million euros for forty projects in Barcelona to support climate change mitigation and adaptation, 25 per cent of which is explicitly earmarked for the Superblocks.

Spatial

Superblocks are a new twenty-first-century re-interpretation of the streets in the heavily polluted central Eixample district, famous for its urban grid devised by the engineer Ildefons Cerdà at the end of the nineteenth century. A more climate-adaptive urban environment for Barcelona is created by smartly identifying nine adjacent city blocks, restricting traffic to the perimeter, thus freeing up the interior for walking, cycling and green space. Here children can play, residents can drink coffee and chat on newly-made park benches. The result of this re-interpretation is that the streets become an extended living room.

The re-interpretation is not limited to rearranging space for leisure activities but includes the reconsidering of paving elements such as curbs, improving accessibility for wheelchairs and people with visual impairments. Furthermore, guidelines for redesigning the street pavements say that at least 20 per cent of the surface has to be rainwater permeable. Simultaneously, 80 per cent of the street should have tree cover and shade to avoid urban heat islands in summertime.

MORE

PEIXO
MARISC
GARN A LA BRASA
pa i trago
TAVERNA TIPICA
el pa i trago

Sara Cultural Centre, Skellefteå, Sweden

From a badly used car park to one of the largest wooden building structures in the world

1. The city of Skellefteå is suffering from economic and demographic decline.

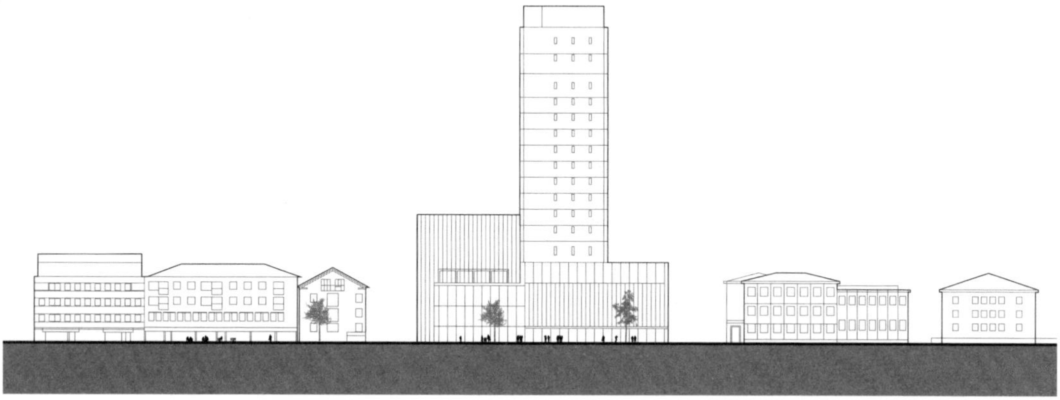

2. The construction of the Sara Cultural Centre makes people proud and stimulates the local economy.

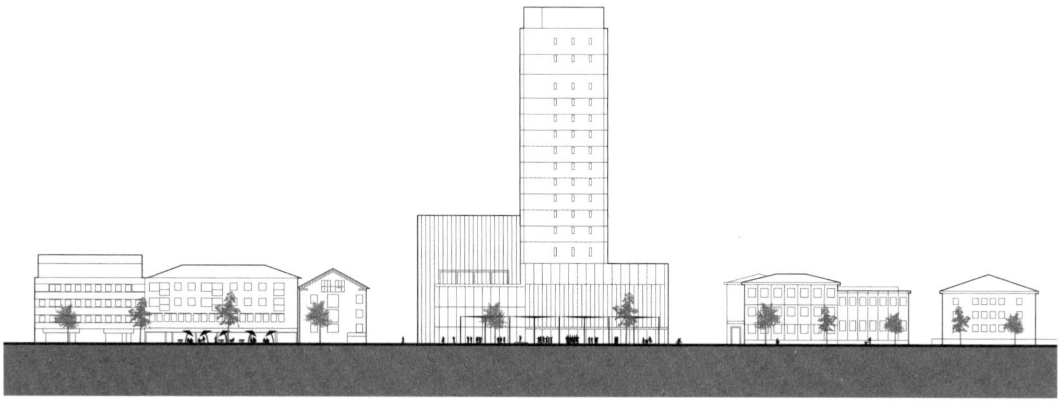

3. The local carpenter industry is revived; shops have re-opened.

Local Flexibility
Instruments: design output monitor, customization, life cycle finance, converting tradition

Initiators: Skellefteå Municipality
Designers: White Arkitekter
Completion: 2016-2021
Programme: cultural centre and hotel
Website: https://www.visitskelleftea.se/sv/sara-kulturhus/

The Sara Cultural Centre in the town of Skellefteå in northern Sweden is a landmark and a supra-regional attraction. The project, one of the tallest wooden building structures in the world, not only illustrates the future potential of timber as a construction material for all kinds of urban programmes, but also reactivates the local tradition of building in wood.

The Sara Cultural Centre, completed in 2021, is a venue for concerts, theatre performances and exhibitions, and also serves as a hub for local cultural activities and events. On top of the spaces for cultural use is a 20-storey hotel. The centre is notable for its beautiful and innovative timber construction, which reflects the region's rich history of wood manufacturing.

The timber construction industry has a long history in northern Sweden, dating back to the nineteenth century when the region's abundant forests and proximity to the coast made it an attractive location for a large-scale timber industry focused on neighbouring countries in Europe. Wood was harvested from forests and transported to the coast by rivers for processing and shipping to other parts of Sweden and Europe. The timber industry played a vital role in the region's economy, providing jobs and contributing to the growth of many northern-Swedish cities, including Skellefteå, Umeå and Luleå. Because twentieth-century building in Europe was often done in concrete, the local timber construction industry shrank and focused on the regional economy only. Recently, the industry started incorporating modern construction techniques and materials, such as cross-laminated timber (CLT), which is a strong and durable material that can be used for walls, floors, and roofs. Many experts consider CLT as the most promising circular material for large-scale sustainable construction in the near future. The use of CLT has helped to reposition northern Sweden as a leader in building materials, supporting sustainable and environmentally conscious construction practices.

The importance of timber in the region's history is reflected in the architecture of the Sara Cultural Centre, which also reflects modern construction techniques and environmental concerns. The Sara Cultural Centre was built using CLT. The wood used for the Kulturhaus comes from sustainable regional forestry; the production of the prefabricated components made of CLT and glued laminated timber (glulam) took place in a sawmill a mere 50 kilometres away. The building is a showroom for all kinds of applications of wood, as its exterior is clad in wooden shingles, which give it a warm and natural appearance. The interior features a variety of wooden finishes, including oak floors and birch panelling.

The Sara Cultural Centre has become a symbol for the city's economic and cultural revival and has won several awards for its design and construction, including the European Union Prize for Contemporary Architecture.

Organizational
Through innovative planning by the architects and engineers, the 75-metre-tall building was constructed without any concrete in the load-bearing structure. The lower four levels of the building host the cultural centre, which is constructed using columns and beams made of glulam. The hotel rooms in the tower are built using prefabricated modules made of solid CLT, which are stacked between two elevator cores also constructed using CLT. The efforts of the

engineering team to replace common concrete high-rise building solutions by wood, means that greenhouse gas emissions coming from the building process were reduced as much as possible.

The timber construction was partially pre-constructed, resulting in a shortened construction time of approximately 60 per cent and a significant reduction in the building's carbon footprint. The wooden construction of the Sara Cultural Centre embodies more than twice the amount of carbon dioxide emissions caused by the construction process, including the production of materials and transport. This means that the building, which is expected to last a hundred years, should be climate-neutral after half of this period.

Legal

Circular building means reconsidering traditional construction and the introduction of new, innovative building techniques. These new building techniques, however, do not automatically meet existing building regulations. To come to a new building culture that is both sustainable and meets restrictions for safety and comfort, it is necessary to either customize new building techniques or reconsider existing legislation.

In case of the Sara Cultural Centre, legal restrictions regarding ventilation and fire protection were contradictory at first sight. Rooms should be ventilated properly according to certain standards, whereas in case of fire, smoke should be kept outside the rooms to provide a safe escape. The combination of high-rise, the structural use of timber and the ambition to reduce the daily use of energy, made it hard to meet both restrictions at the same time. To comply with Swedish regulations, the architects and engineers worked closely with a leading supplier of ventilation and smoke extraction systems. Together, they developed a customized solution for this specific case. The solution included the implementation of smart sensors, designed to provide precise control over the building's windows, ensuring precise operation for both daily air supply and safety in case of fire.

The customized solution developed in collaboration with product suppliers, the building's architects and engineers, demonstrates the importance of close collaboration for the development of effective and efficient solutions.

Financial

The Sara Cultural Centre is an example of a building that incorporates financial lifecycle mechanisms to ensure its long-term sustainability. The building is powered entirely by renewable energy sources supported by a control system that regulates the demand for ventilation and heat. This allows for efficient use of energy, reducing exploitation costs and further minimizing the building's environmental impact. The building is equipped with a range of energy-efficient systems, including geothermal heating and cooling, solar panels and a heat recovery system.

In addition, a smart control system regulates the demand for ventilation and heat, which contributes to the financial sustainability of the Centre. Monitoring the indoor environment and adjusting the ventilation and heating systems accordingly ensures that energy is used efficiently. Generated energy that is not used can be stored, further reducing the building's energy costs. These requirements were part of the municipality's competition and they reinforce the Sara Cultural Centre's position as an icon of sustainable design.

Spatial

The Sara Cultural Centre is named after the prominent local author Sara Lidman, known for her powerful portrayals of working-class life and her strong political convictions. The centre was designed as an open-plan space to encourage the community to get involved. Residents got to choose where the building would come and, to an extent, how it was designed.

The cultural landmark is not only a modern, sustainable building, but it is also an homage to the region's rich timber tradition. With the construction of the Sara Cultural Centre, there is hope that the local timber industry can be revitalized and brought into the modern era. By incorporating timber into the design of the building, the architects and engineers sought to create a connection between the building and the local community. All the timber is sourced from within a 60-kilometre radius, and local workshops and people were engaged during the construction process, an investment in the regional economy. The Sara Cultural Centre is a testament to the importance of transforming local traditions and industries into modern design and sustainability.

Hospital Entrance Area Amsterdam UMC, location AMC, Amsterdam, the Netherlands

From a vast car park to a park for the neighbourhood

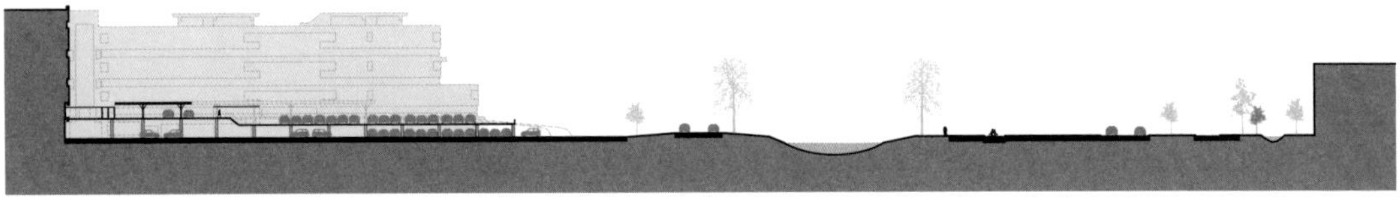

1. Though surrounded by city parts, the hospital building is isolated and gives a closed impression.

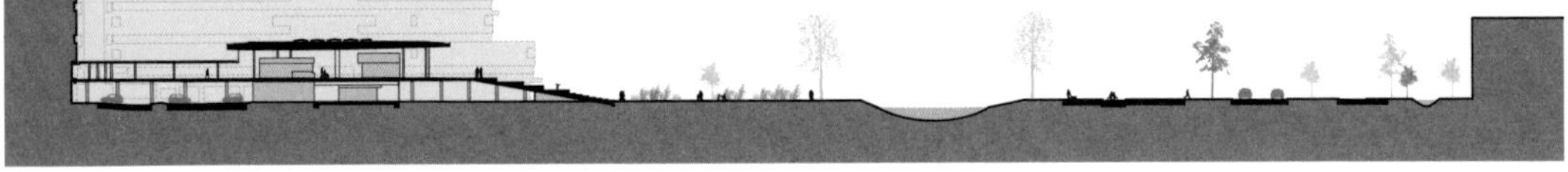

2. By redeveloping the entrance area of the hospital, the institute gets a clear and beautiful entrance area, offering a healthy and stimulating park for its neighbours.

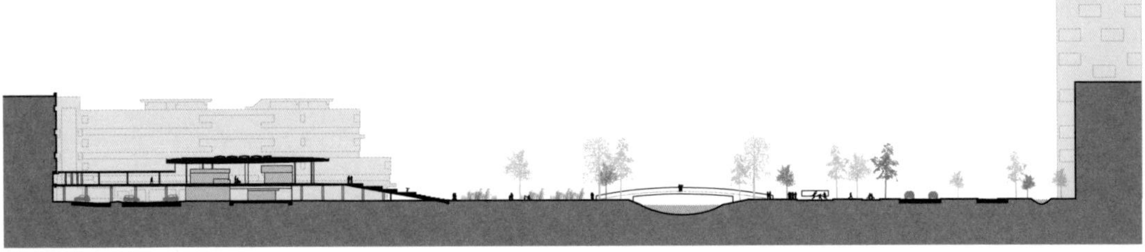

3. The relationship between hospital and its surroundings is improved even further, extending the park and adding bridges.

Local Flexibility
Instruments: circular supply chains, sustainability protocol, capitalized risks, soil-sensitivity

Initiators: Amsterdam UMC, City of Amsterdam, Architectuur Lokaal
Design: Temp.architecture & studio Nuy van Noort in cooperation with studio Blad
Completion: 2022
Programme: park, pedestrian decks and entry pavilion

Because of their size, large public building complexes such as hospitals can significantly contribute to their neighbourhoods when they become more circular and climate-adaptive. By transforming a vast parking lot into a green and hospitable entry area, the Amsterdam University Medical Centres (UMC) Hospital turned its AMC building complex into a social inclusive, climate-adaptive, circular and healthy environment: an upgrade and inspiration for the whole neighbourhood.

The approximately 500,000-square-metre AMC building complex in Amsterdam was completed in the period 1981-1985 as the largest hospital in the Netherlands. The building was located outside of the city, in one of the lowest polders near Amsterdam, as a solitary, efficient and introvert medical machine. There were no buildings in the immediate vicinity. In the following decades, the city moved towards the hospital. While new buildings surrounded the complex, the new urban environment did not establish a successful relationship with the hospital. Seen from the immediate vicinity, the entrance area was hidden behind a huge parking garage, giving an intimidating rather than a welcoming impression. As the entrance was mainly designed for handling car traffic, both pedestrians and cyclist felt lost.

In 2015, the parking building at the front of the AMC location was completely worn out and therefore demolished. This literally and figuratively gave space to rethink the entrance to the AMC on a more fundamental level. The real estate department of the hospital defined the ambition to create an entrance zone that no longer represents the hospital as an introverted medical machine, but as an open and hospitable meeting place in the heart of twenty-first-century society. The changing circumstances in the immediate vicinity offered the opportunity to review the impact of this redevelopment in a broader context, redefining the relationship with the immediate environment too. These ambitions and opportunities were base for a design competition, organized in 2017.

The winning design proposal was delivered in 2022. On the site of the large parking garage, there is now a park with green views and routes between the hospital and the surrounding neighbourhood, improving water drainage of the whole entrance area at the same time. The layout of the greenery offers a clear orientation and encourages time and time again to move and meet, so that the health and well-being of patients, employees, students and local residents are central. Centrally positioned in the entrance park, a pavilion offers a new, well-organized entry to the huge brutalist building complex, differing from it in size, form and materialization. A pedestrian deck, flanked by flowers and plants, links the entry to the nearby train station and offers pedestrians a safe walk to the entry without encountering cars.

Being the largest hospital in the area, the facility is key in case of regional calamities such as accidents or floods. Because the entrance zone, where all ambulances enter the complex, used to be one of the riskiest spots in Amsterdam in terms of rainwater floods, making the restructured entry zone climate-adaptive was an important part of the assignment.

Organizational
In this project, excessive rainwater and obsolete trees were not seen as waste, but as bases for a circular

supply chain. Using rainwater instead of tap water for irrigating plants means that the drinking water infrastructure is relieved. Rainwater that falls on the parking area, on the deck and on the roofs is led to and used for the green on the deck and in the park. The system collects, stores and releases rainwater, all depending on the varying climate conditions. This way, it is able to deal with extremes such as drought and excessive rainfall.

Carbon dioxide emissions were reduced by reusing trees that were felled for freestanding wooden benches and wooden seats in the auditorium. In this way, circularity was introduced into the project without requiring extra budget. Instead of ordering ready-made products from a supplier, the designers figured out how to turn the trees into benches and seats.

Legal

As a public organisation with over 14,000 employees, 2,650 students and hundreds of thousands of patients every year, the hospital is highly committed to corporate social responsibility. In its business operations they demonstrably take the impact of decisions for the environment into account by using a procurement governance and having an own energy and sustainability vision. The governance contains requirements in relation to sustainability, quality and social impact. Also for the new entrance area, these requirements were incorporated into the design and the execution tender.

Together with Architectuur Lokaal, a Dutch specialist in accessible tender procedures, the Amsterdam UMC organized a design competition in 2017 for the redevelopment of the entrance and forecourt of the AMC location. The jury, consisting of representatives of the hospital organization itself and also of the client council, the City of Amsterdam and the government architect, selected one design out of sixty entries: AMC Health Park by the design combination Temp.Architecture & studio Nuy van Noort in collaboration with studio BLAD. With the architect selection by means of a public competition, Amsterdam UMC has had the courage to look for the best plan without knowing in advance which architect it would end up with and what track record it would have.

Financial

Being one of the most important hospitals in the region, the potential consequences of flooding were difficult to oversee, but could even be life-threatening. Being aware of this, an additional budget was reserved for measures to improve flood prevention in the future.

In the realized plan, the park plays an important role improving water management around the building complex. Rainwater from impermeable areas such as the car park, the pedestrian deck and the roof of the pavilion is discharged into the waterways within the park, which acts as a sponge for the entire forecourt. The risk of accidents or injuries as a result of flooding is thus minimized.

Spatial

Situated below sea level in one of the lowest polders in the Netherlands, the relationship with water at the hospital site is precarious. First of all, the general groundwater level is relatively high. Groundwater easily pops up as seepage water, penetrating the layer of sand covering the original landscape. Furthermore, a large part of the entrance area was paved with impenetrable asphalt used for the original car park. Large puddles appeared when it rained. Therefore, rain- and groundwater management was a crucial part for the design assignment.

In the new situation, the roof of the entrance pavilion got a green roof for water retention, countering heat stress. The parking area is reduced and the asphalt is replaced by a small-tiles paving with water-permissive joints. The car park slopes from the edge of building to the park, so rainwater will automatically drain from the building to the park via this underground system. The park is arranged in such a way that the rainwater is retained for a long time by both the soft subsoil and the wadis. Wadis are water basins in which an excess of rainwater can be collected and retained. After a shower, the wadis fill up with rainwater descending from the parking area, the pedestrian deck and the pavilion. The park thus functions as a sponge for the entrance area.

Cooperativa Agricoltura Nuova, Rome, Italy

From a planned urban expansion area to an area of peri-urban agriculture

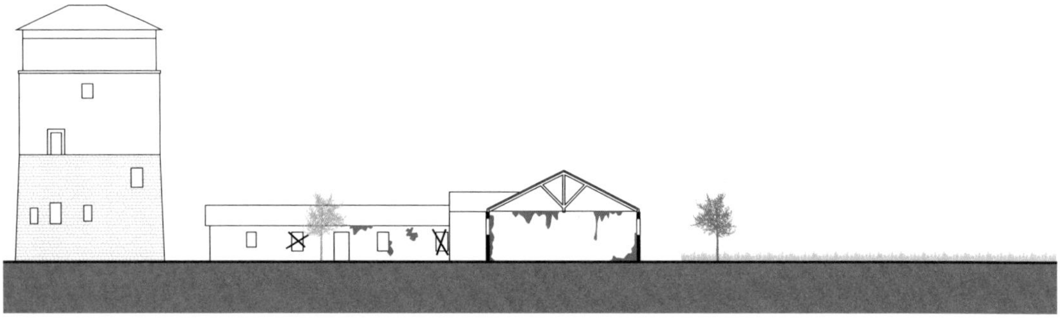

1. A new residential area is planned on a farmer's plot in Rome that has been vacant for 25 years.

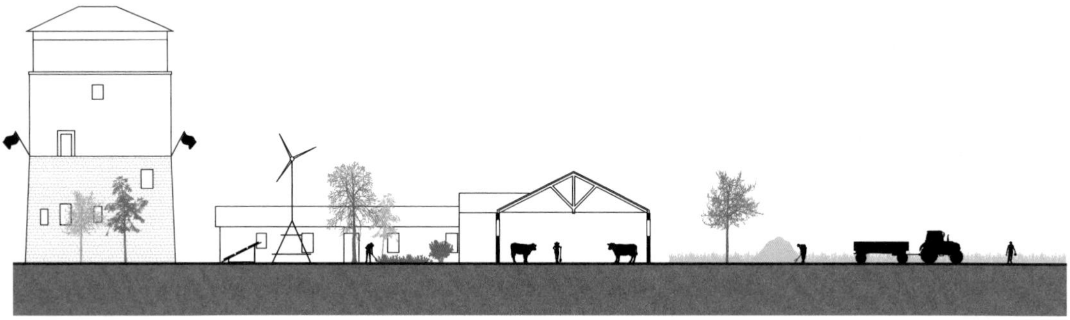

2. The site is illegally occupied to preserve the agricultural function.

3. The Agricoltura Nova is legalized as a centre for agricultural production and social activities.

Local Flexibility
Instruments: dynamic biodiversity management, guerrilla gardening, community shares, converting tradition

Initiators: young student squatters
Completion: 1977–today
Programme: environmentally friendly agriculture with a social focus
Website: http://www.agricolturanuova.it/storia-2/

Environmental crises lead to a reconsideration of the relationship between cities and their green surroundings. How can urban expansion be brought to a halt, protecting its surrounding ecology? How can a flourishing countryside contribute to the quality of urban life? Cooperativa Agricoltura Nuova, an active community of organic farmers close to the suburbs of Rome, is experimenting with answers to those questions. The cooperative started illegally in the 1970s and now focuses on organic farming in combination with urban programmes such as food-festivals and social care.

Rome is the largest agricultural municipality in Europe, both in terms of farm land and in terms of the quantity and quality of the land's products. In the late 1970s many agricultural cooperatives were established in the periphery of the city by young, unemployed people, for instance Agricoltura Nuova, Cobragor, Il Trattore, Coraggio, Capodarco and Mistica. Today, the result of those initiatives is unique in the framework of peri-urban agriculture: stimulating organic farming, creating hundreds of jobs, also for disabled people, and protecting the landscape.

The Agricoltura Nuova is a one of these cooperative farms on the outskirts of Rome, founded after a group of 30 young people occupied former agrarian land that had been vacant for 25 years in 1977. In doing so, they opposed the region's urbanization process in the form of a planned residential district for 6,000 inhabitants. The goal was to preserve the agricultural function of the farmland near the city and to create jobs for young people. Thanks to the support of residents of neighbouring communities and institutional actors such as the farmers' and trade unions, environmental organizations and the communist party, Agricoltura Nuova was able to exist for 20 years despite being illegal. In 1996, the operation was finally legalized through an official lease agreement with the City of Rome, securing a long-term place in the heart of the newly created Decima Malafede Regional Park.

Today, two areas totalling 250 hectares are farmed under the name Agricoltura Nuova. The cooperative started out with 180 hectares. This land is still owned by the City of Rome. The extra 70 hectares have been leased from the Santa Catarina Religious Conservatory since 2006.

The Agricoltura Nuova is characterized by a mixture of different agricultural activities. In addition to fruit and vegetable production, sheep, cows and pigs are bred. Furthermore, the facilities include an apiary, a dairy, a brewery, a mill and a weaving shop. The products are sold to customers in an on-side pizza restaurant and farm shop. The production has been certified organic since the late 1980s.

The Agricoltura Nuova also organizes numerous social activities. The grounds are used for festivals and have grown over time to include facilities such as a campground and playground areas, a riding school and an information centre about renewable energies. Community gardens are used to promote the care and inclusion of vulnerable adults such as people with disabilities or refugees, as well as hosting educational activities for children. With this focus, the Agricoltura Nuova has established itself as an important social actor in the region.

Organizational

Initially, the cooperative farmed its land according to market demand, which resulted in monocultural farming. However, this type of farming did not lead to the necessary profitability, so the cooperative members decided to diversify. For this purpose, a variety of original cultivated plants as well as native animal species were deliberately included in their dynamic biodiversity management. Chemical substances or genetically modified species are strictly avoided, thus protecting the quality of natural assets such as soil and water as well as the worker's health. The diversification of the farm was further accompanied by a switch from wholesale to direct sales, which proved to be more profitable in subsequent years. In addition, the conversion led to the closure of material cycles for the most part, so that the farm produces hardly any waste. Organic waste, for example, is used to feed the farm animals or to produce compost and fertilizer, which in turn provides nutrients for the soil. In parallel, more and more non-farming activities have been organized in order to develop further sources of income and to strengthen the role of the farm as a social actor in the local community.

Legal

The Agricoltura Nuova started as an illegal occupation. The cultivation of the land can be seen as large-scale guerrilla gardening and was intended to show an alternative to the planned urbanization process of the ecologically valuable land. In the 20-year struggle for recognition of the cooperative's land rights, the existence of the cooperative was repeatedly threatened. Only through the broad support from civil society and political actors could legalization finally be achieved. The municipality asked the cooperative to leave the land several times. However, the cooperative received support from the local district as well as the Lazio Region, which for instance pushed for a change in the zoning plan and the creation of a regional park, both of which aimed to secure the cooperative's existence in the long term. Finally, an agreement was drawn up between the mayor's office and the construction industry, which stipulated that the occupied land would be designated for agricultural use and that the construction of buildings would only be allowed outside of this land. With the 1996 lease agreement, the cooperative had to retrospectively pay the rent for the previous 19 years of illegal occupation and received its legal status.

Financial

The Agricoltura Nuova started with the goal that all members jointly own and cultivate the land and share the corresponding costs as well as profits. Nevertheless, the financial situation at the beginning was so tight that only contributions from families and friends of the occupants could keep the cooperation afloat. To this day, the cooperative approach is characterized by its members jointly managing the land, with each of the members having one vote. Over the years, contract workers have also been hired. All profits of the Agricoltura Nuova are distributed to members and workers in the form of wages and reinvested in the production. Especially in the early years, salaries remained very low, as most of the cooperative's income was invested in improving the farm.

Despite general difficulties of small farms, the financial situation of the Agricoltura Nuova has stabilized, due to a stable group of consumers and supporters of the farm, who appreciate the high quality of the products as well as the social orientation of the farm. Today, the non-agricultural activities such as the restaurant business or educational services contribute significantly to the financial success of the farm.

Spatial

The members of the cooperative quickly began restoring the abandoned buildings on the site. The cooperative's composition of mostly young people is also leading them to re-engage more with agricultural professions, while the industry is largely lacking in young workers. The increasing focus on further processing of the goods produced also results in the strengthening of classic local professions such as baker and confectioner. For reasons of environmental protection and the highest possible level of self-sufficiency, the cooperative members also had an early focus on the development of environmentally friendly energy sources on the site. Photovoltaic systems, a windmill and rainwater collection systems were installed as early as the late 1970s. Thus, to this day, the Agricoltura Nuova contributes significantly to the protection of the surrounding area, which is a stronghold of biodiversity and a natural source of water for the city of Rome.

AGRICOLTURA NUOVA
6

IKEA Store, Vienna, Austria

From a conventional building block to a building accommodating a park

1. When a building block is about to be demolished, local residents express the desire for a park here.

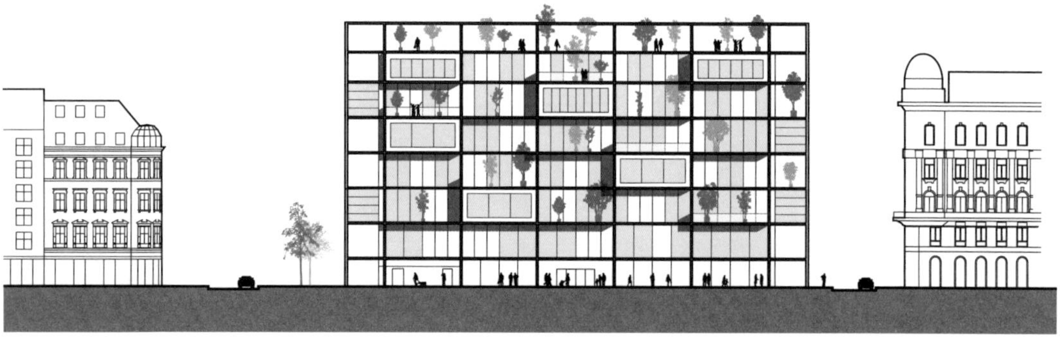

2. Trying to be a good neighbour, IKEA builds a flexible building that has the features of a park.

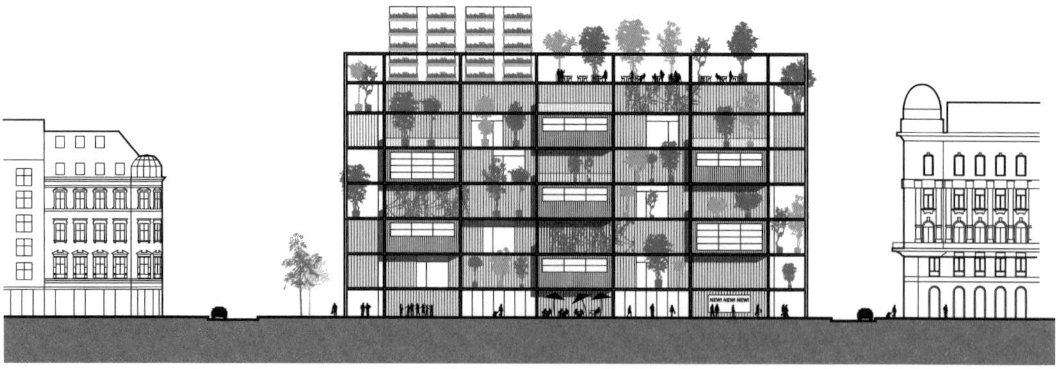

3. The flexible building structure is further developed, contributing to its direct surroundings in many ways.

Use-driven Flexibility
Instruments: dynamic biodiversity management, sustainability protocol, privately financed public assets, microclimate modification

Initiators: IKEA
Completion: 2021
Programme: IKEA store, pharmacy, hair salon, bakery, hostel with 345 beds, public roof
Design: Querkraft
Website: https://www.ikea.com/at/de/stores/wien-westbahnhof/

As urbanization continues to spread out and densify, the availability of green spaces in cities is becoming increasingly scarce. In response, buildings could take on a greater role in providing these essential green spaces. The IKEA store in Vienna shows that incorporating green features into building design, such as green roofs and even entire green facades with trees, the building can offer the important benefits a park would offer to a city like improved air quality, meeting space, reduced urban heat island effect and increased biodiversity.

In recent years, Ikea faced a challenge in the Austrian market as their traditional big-box stores on the outskirts of cities did not commercially perform as well as expected. Austrian consumers favoured smaller shops that were more centrally located and easily accessible by public transportation. When Ikea expressed interest in building a new store in the heart of Vienna, it was initially met with scepticism. Rather than another shopping destination, the city's residents wished for a park where people could meet and relax. To address this challenge, Ikea decided to experiment with a new type of store, one that would be car-free and easily accessible by public transportation. As the major objective, IKEA therefore told the architects: 'we want to be a good neighbour'.

The company chose a spot at the end of Mariahilferstrasse in the Westbahnhof area of Vienna, close to a major transportation hub and popular shopping destination, where until recently a conventional building block had been situated. Ikea collaborated with Austrian architect querkraft to create a building that would fit the urban environment, be environmentally sustainable and serve as a community space, rather than just a shopping space. The resulting structure is a distinctive gridded building made of glass and steel with a green accessible roof and trees spread over different levels, providing insulation and helping to regulate the building's temperature.

The building is designed to be thoroughly sustainable, with solar panels on the roof and an advanced waste management system that sorts and recycles waste, reducing the amount sent to landfills. In addition, the store also features smart lighting and an irrigation system. Smart lighting uses motion sensors and daylight harvesting technology to reduce energy consumption by automatically adjusting the lighting levels based on the presence of both natural light and people in the space. The irrigation system uses rainwater collected from the roof to water the plants in the building's community garden, reducing water consumption and the strain on the city's water resources.

In addition, the building's core structure aims to be flexible and a good addition to the neighbourhood. The design is structured with a simple concrete base and a 'balcony' structure around it. The architects sought to incorporate balconies into the design of the commercial spaces, inspired by the idea that balconies were previously only found in residential buildings. The flexible frame can be considered as a kind of shelf, which can always be used in different ways. Its shelf-like structure increases the site's flexibility through the ability to adapt to new functions in the future.

Ikea Westbahnhof opened in 2021 and quickly became a popular destination for Vienna residents and tourists alike, offering not only furniture shopping but also successfully serving as a community space. As a vertical park, Ikea Westbahnhof represents an experiment in retail design and sustainability. On top of the environmental perks of the design, the rooftop is a social meeting place, being free and accessible to the public outside of the store's open hours. Like most open rooftops in Vienna, they serve drinks and food. Across the 26,200 square metres, the building also includes multiple cafes on different levels. Some of the exterior balconies are accessible as well and offer seating and viewpoints. The trees create a cooler and less dry environment in and around the building.

Its innovative design, sustainable features and community-focused approach have helped to reshape the way consumers think about Ikea and simultaneously added significant value to its urban context. Its sustainable design has already inspired other retailers and developers to prioritize eco-friendliness in their own projects, and the success of the store allowed Ikea to open similar stores in other cities around the world.

Organizational

Not only did the store's design address the challenge of meeting the community's desire for a park-like space, but it also had numerous other benefits for the surrounding community. The green roof and trees on different levels promote biodiversity, providing a habitat for wildlife. Open spaces promote different types of environments including bird nests, with a total of thirty nesting spots to ensure that local bird types such as kestrels and swifts can reproduce. There are well-equipped beehives and a good variety of plants for the bees. To further support biodiversity, IKEA Westbahnhof collaborated with nearby schools to build insect hotels, that were placed around the building. The company made sure to emphasize this focus through species diversity in the selection of plants, different vegetation structures, a species-rich herb layer and habitat structures.

Legal

Ikea initiated a competition to find architects who could align with their sustainability goals. During the Idea Contest Phase in 2017, they worked in collaboration with Greenpass, a Vienna-based expert on sustainable real estate, who provided them with a monitor for measuring the environmental impact of the building focusing on six urban domains: climate, water, air, biodiversity, energy and costs. With these key categories, IKEA could monitor the building's efficiency with thorough calculations that acted as a sustainability protocol for the company. This new quality verification was also acknowledged within the BREEAM assessment system for key indicators such as microclimate and biodiversity. The project achieved an 'Excellent' rating in this category, further highlighting its success.

Financial

Based on the demands of the municipality, the privately financed new city store provides private open spaces and communal areas, all of which are tailored to the preferences of local residents and users, designed to be accessible without barriers. In the upper two floors of the IKEA store, there is a hostel with 345 beds, which brings life to the building even outside of regular opening hours. On the ground floor, there is an arcade with a pharmacy, a hair salon and a bakery. IKEA wanted to include the businesses previously located in this building to deliberately generate a mix of uses. There is a publicly accessible 1,800-square-metre rooftop terrace where IKEA and the hostel operators also offer gastronomy services, but there is no obligation to consume. This arrangement is permanently established in the urban development contract. The idea of creating an urban 'park-structure' was well received by the municipality of Vienna. After the construction of the building, the architects and owners saw that the building had a positive impact on the neighbourhood, the building even has its own small fan club. Although the neighbourhood hadn't exactly requested an urban park, the accessibility and noncommittal concept of the store is highly appreciated by local residents and tourists.

Spatial

A total of 160 trees on the building contribute to a more pleasant microclimate. On a hot day, they can cool the surroundings by up to -1.5°C. Additionally, they improve the air quality in by converting carbon dioxide into oxygen, and, for example, by blocking dust, and cooling and humidifying the air. With its green roof, IKEA's new store helps to improve insulation and air quality, provide shade and reduce the urban heat island effect.

HEILBORN APOTHEKE
IKEA

IKEA

Seestadt Aspern, Vienna, Austria

From an abandoned airfield to a circular and climate-adaptive city quarter

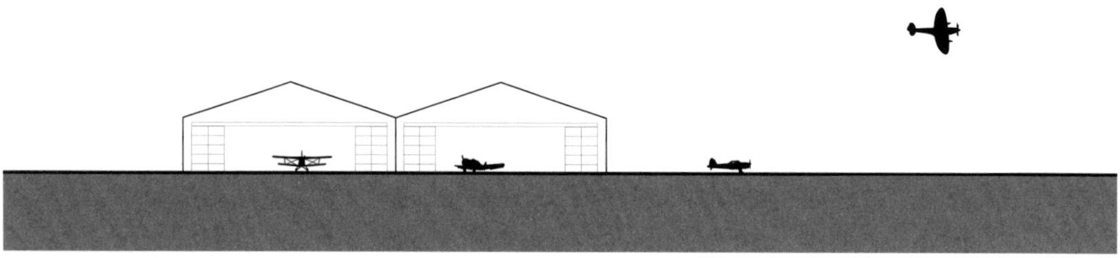

1. An airport terrain was closed and designated as residential area.

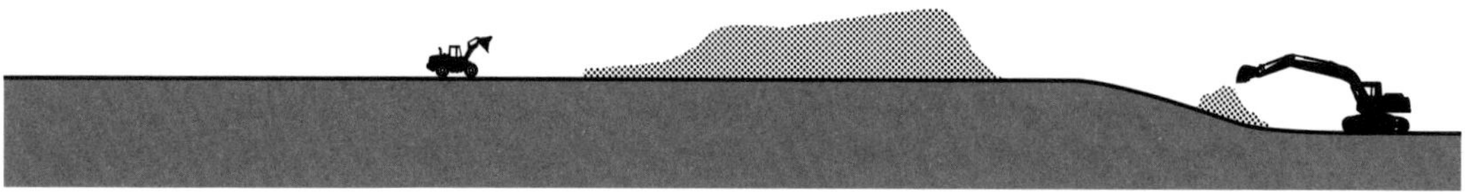

2. Local land is being redistributed, leading to a central lake surrounded by varied residential areas.

3. The city of Seestadt Aspern grows stepwise, each time implementing the latest insights regarding circularity and climate adaptation.

Use-driven Flexibility
Instruments: empowering local communities, purpose-specific freezone, free public transport, rooftop benefits

Initiator: City of Vienna
Design: Tovatt Architects & Planners and others
Completion: 2009 – present
Programme: urban district to be inhabited by over 25,000 people.
Website: https://www.aspern-seestadt.at/en

Many European cities are characterized by strong population growth and face the challenge of providing new space for housing, jobs and (social) infrastructure in a very limited time. At the beginning of the 2000s, Vienna decided to take the radical step of building a new urban quarter under the name of Seestadt Aspern. This new district for more than 25,000 inhabitants is located on the site of a former airport and is intended to meet the requirements of a climate-adaptive and socially inclusive residential district.

The agricultural village of Aspern was incorporated into the municipal area of the Austrian capital Vienna at the peak of the Viennese modernization in 1905, establishing an airfield northeast of the historic village. The airfield lost importance in the postwar years and was completely closed in 1977.

The abandoned northern part of the former Aspern airfield was acquired by the municipality of Vienna in 1992, which decided in 2003 to commission the development of an urban master plan. Under the leadership of the Swedish planning office Tovatt Architects & Planners and the German project development office N+ Objektmanagement GmbH, the Masterplan Seestadt Aspern was developed, which was adopted by the municipal council in 2007. The plan envisages the construction of a new urban district on the 2.4-square-kilometre site in a multi-phase development ending in 2028. Approximately 11,000 apartments for more than 25,000 people as well as workspaces are aimed to contribute to the rapidly growing city of Vienna. With these dimensions and planned investments of over 5 billion euros, Seestadt Aspern is one of the largest urban development projects in Europe. The master plan's defining elements are a centrally located lakeside park including an artificial lake, which gives the district its name. The excavation work for the lake began in 2010. Almost all the materials from the excavation (around 1 million tons) were processed on site into building materials for the surrounding constructions, primarily for road works. Not having to transport these materials has so far saved around 6,000 tons of greenhouse gas emissions. The typically Viennese building blocks are designed for a mixture of uses. Only in the east of the area larger mono-functional commercial zones are planned. The goal is to create an urban district in which living and working, education and culture, shopping and leisure are all within a short distance of each other. The central component of the traffic development is the extension of the U2 subway line.

The 'Am Seebogen' quarter is one of the quarters of the International Building Exhibition (IBA) Vienna 2022, which focused on new social housing. In this area, 80 per cent is reserved for residential use, while the remaining 20 per cent is designated for office space. In the already realized part south of the lake, the focus has been on the implementation of climate-adapting redesign measures in public spaces, since a high degree of sealed surfaces leads to the formation of heat islands in the area.

Organizational
The development of Seestadt Aspern is linked to ambitions to strengthen local communities. Publicly used facilities such as the central swimming lake and community-operated projects such as the Madame

d'Ora community garden or the Seestadtpark promote social exchange and active participation of all the different residents in the neighbourhood. The district management acts as a contact for the residents and manages a neighbourhood fund, where residents can initiate micro-projects totalling 3,000 euros per year themselves. In addition, residents are given the opportunity to help shape the design of the neighbourhood. Assemblies, in which communities of residents plan, design and organize themselves together, play a central role. So far, ten such assemblies have become active in the development of Seestadt and have developed building sites according to their individual needs and possibilities. One of these is Que(e)rbau, which promotes living for unconventional types of families and creates an inclusive living environment. Another focus lies on the advertising slogan 'Seestadt is female'. This stands for the decision to name all streets in the new district after women, thus increasing the proportion of Viennese streets named after women from 5 to 7 per cent. This highly symbolic measure is intended to make women's historical achievements more visible, to include them in the city's collective memory and ultimately to empower female citizens.

Legal

One of the central goals in the Seestadt Aspern is to reduce motorized individual traffic to a minimum. To achieve this goal, one of the measures taken is reducing the number of available parking spaces to make it less attractive to drive a car. Normally, the law in Vienna says that there has to be one parking space for every 100 square metres of usable living space. However, the parking space regulation of the Vienna Garage Act allows fewer parking spaces if a (very) good public transport connection can be proven in the corresponding planning area. In Seestadt Aspern, the number of required parking spaces could thus be reduced by 30 per cent. In addition, builders of car parks in the area were obliged to pay a fixed amount per parking space into a mobility fund as a result of the reduced parking space obligation. This money will be used to support projects that reduce the mobility pressure from Seestadt on the surrounding areas and encourage residents to choose environmentally friendly means of transport.

Financial

As a further instrument to reduce car traffic and to achieve the targeted modal split of 40 per cent cycling and walking, the SeestadtFLOTTE bike rental system is operated in Seestadt. Currently, 34 e-bikes and 18 conventional bicycles are available for individual trips with a guaranteed minimal carbon footprint. The bicycles can be rented and parked at fixed bike stations. In 2022, there were seven such bike stations plus one additional electric cargo bike station. With the expansion of Seestadt, the network of rental stations will also be expanded to 26 bike stations and two cargo bike stations in the final development stage. Bicycle rental is only possible with a SeestadtCARD. The registration fee of 10 euro is waived for residents of Seestadt. Until further notice, the SeestadtFLOTTE system is available free of charge. The sum of the measures to reduce car traffic leads to a level of motorization in Seestadt that is significantly below the overall Viennese average.

Spatial

Many projects in Seestadt Aspern feature an innovative use of roof space. All parking garages, for example, are covered by roofs arranged as public squares or gardens. Also, the mixed-use building at the corner of the Janis Joplin Promenade and Anna Bastel Gasse and the educational campus of Seestadt are covered by terraced roofs.

Opened in 2015, each of the elementary school classrooms in the educational campus is directly connected to a south-facing, partially green roof terrace. The highest roof surface of the main building, on the other hand, is largely equipped with solar panels, which is common practice in Seestadt. Photovoltaic systems installed on roofs play a central role in the goal of 100 per cent electricity and heat supply from renewable energy sources in Seestadt. In addition, sports activities have also found their place on rooftops. On the car park next to the U2 terminus, five football fields and an associated gastronomic facility are operated under the name 'Andi kickt'. The multitude of roof uses shows what intelligent utilization of rooftop benefits can look like in practice.

The People's Pavilion, Eindhoven, the Netherlands

From ordinary waste towards a temporary people's pavilion

1. A big and empty square is designated to be part of the Dutch Design Week.

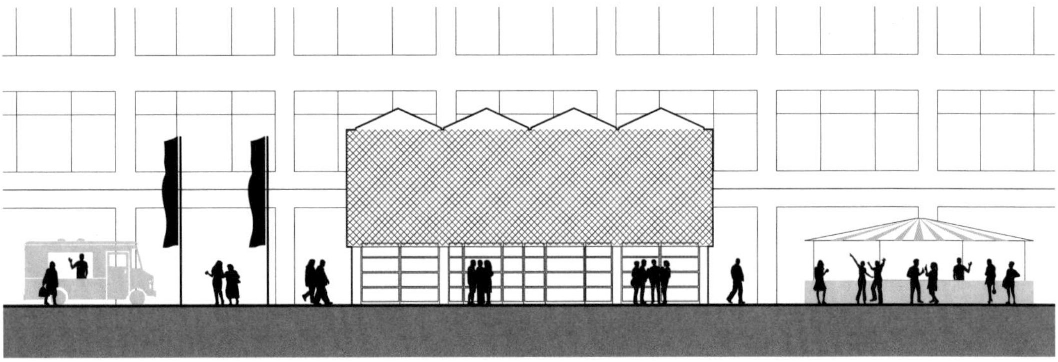

2. Being built with only borrowed materials, a temporary and experimental pavilion arises.

3. After demounting the pavilion, all borrowed materials are brought back to their owners.

Use-driven Flexibility
Instruments: reused materials mediator, material passport, upcycling, re-interpretation

Initiator: Dutch Design Week 2017
Design: Overtreders W, bureau SLA
Completion: 2017
Programme: central meeting space for the Dutch Design Week of 2017
website: https://www.overtreders-w.nl/en/peoplespavilion

The rising costs of raw materials, their inevitable finiteness and the large environmental footprint of the processes turning them into proper building materials, pose major challenges to building industries. Experiments with innovative building methods, such as the reuse of materials and associated alternative business models are necessary to come to a future-proof, circular building industry. Because of their limited lifetime and less strict regulation, temporary buildings are very suitable for these experiments.

The annual Dutch Design Week is the largest design showcase in northern Europe, featuring over 2,600 designers from all over Europe who present their ideas on various topics, including the future of architecture and design in the face of the climate crisis. The exhibition takes place in more than 110 locations in Eindhoven, some of which are existing venues, while others are temporary outdoor pavilions. The People's Pavilion, built to exist for only a few weeks on the occasion of the Dutch Design Week in 2017, was designed by Overtreders W and Bureau SLA as a statement of the circular economy, a building where no materials would be lost in the process. The pavilion served as the central meeting place during the Dutch Design Week for up to 600 people at a time. The architects adapted this way of building by only 'borrowing' materials that had to be returned to their owners in an unaltered condition after their use in the pavilion. Therefore, a key element of the pavilion's design features reversible connections that eliminated the need for nails or glue. This design ensured that the materials retained their initial condition and could be returned to their owners after having been part of the pavilion for a few weeks.

A primary element of the design was the colourful panel facade of the pavilion, created from plastic waste materials such as PET bottles. Donated by local Eindhoven residents who, by doing so, got rid of their personal waste, the locally sourced waste could be repurposed into a valuable building element. The innovative use of recycled plastic waste as the primary material for the panel facade of the pavilion is a remarkable aspect of the design. The architects took a conscious decision to utilize locally sourced waste, thereby providing an environmentally sustainable solution. This approach not only prevented the plastic waste from becoming landfill, but also provided a waterproof and easily processable building element. Through the repurposing of the plastic bottles, the designers were able to create a striking visual effect on the facade, with the colourful panels contributing to the overall aesthetic appeal of the building. They produced approximately 9,500 colourful tiles and returned them to the local residents as a souvenir from the Design Week after the building was disassembled. Thus, the People's Pavilion succeeded in the aim of a zero-waste outcome. The success of the People's Pavilion at the Dutch Design Week demonstrates that the impact of building can be very minimal and that circularity in its design can be a viable and sustainable approach to both temporary and lasting structures.

Organizational
Significant adjustments had to be made to the design process to bring this vision to life due to the

uncertain availability of materials. A concept sketch had to be presented to wholesalers and other partners to persuade them to join the project and lend out the materials. With each confirmed material the building process changed to incorporate the new opportunities. This meant that the design had to be flexible enough to accommodate unforeseen materials that were discovered and borrowed during the course of the project. This going back and forth during the adjustment process took place at every stage of the design, including the construction phase itself, to ensure that the project could successfully incorporate newly available materials.

The architects tackled the challenges of using 'borrowed' elements by collaborating with various companies and relying on the help of the residents of Eindhoven. They worked with Arup and the Technical University of Eindhoven to validate their calculations and experiment with this unconventional building approach. Together with these two organizations, they developed models and structural material samples to test the statics and propose designs to various material suppliers. To obtain the necessary wooden beams and concrete columns, the architects contacted construction companies and made agreements to borrow the materials. The lower facade was a remnant of the renovation of webshop bol.com's headquarters and was returned after nine days for use in a new project. For the upper part of the facade made of plastic tiles from household waste, the architects partnered with Govaerts Recycling, to shape and create the tiles.

Each aspect of the building had to be measured carefully and planned precisely to keep all the building elements in their original state, so that everything could be returned as it was received. The architects used a system of over 350 tensioning straps to connect each element of the building to the others. The foundation of the 8-metre tall building was set by twelve prefab concrete pillars, which were connected to steel rods and an outer glass facade salvaged from a demolished office building. For the interior, they used borrowed composite timber beams that held everything together. The glass roof was borrowed from a local greenhouse supplier, providing beautiful natural lighting.

Legal

By carefully registering each borrowed element of the building and keeping an overview of all materials, linking them to a customized material passport, the architects were able to ensure that all parts could be returned to their owners after the Dutch Design Week was over. Even the interior elements such as furniture and lighting were borrowed for a few weeks and carefully registered, so everything could be returned without any waste.

Financial

Items were reused in subsequent construction projects, adhering to the circular economy principles and upholding their value throughout the supply chain. As the materials were returned in their original condition, their financial value remained almost unchanged. It could be argued that their value increased after being used in the pavilion, as the unexpected way they were used as a proper building material enlarged their future using possibilities. Being part of a useful, high-profile building structure, their value was at least promoted for a few weeks, giving them a higher value than they would possibly have had otherwise. This Pavilion raises the question of what market value could come from 'rented' materials in the built environment.

Spatial

Designing a building with materials and resources that are to be borrowed and to be returned in an unchanged condition asks for an unorthodox way of looking at materials and building products. The wooden elements, for example, were temporarily tied together with straps, forming the beams that carry the roof. A positive effect of the pavilion being a showcase for reuse was that this improvisational way of building was made explicit. By using broad, black tensioning straps, that stood out against the wood, they were explicitly part of the architecture as interior ornaments.

The process of turning plastic waste such as PET bottles into facade tiles also asked for an innovative production process. Developed by a commercial company called Pretty Plastic, the Pavilion functioned as a showcase, not only showing the sustainable, waterproof and fireproof qualities of the product, but also showing how beautiful the reuse of plastic can be, leading to a palette of different colours expressing the various origins of use that the materials had before.

Cité Maraîchère, Romainville, France

From an agricultural food-producing area to an urban food-producing area

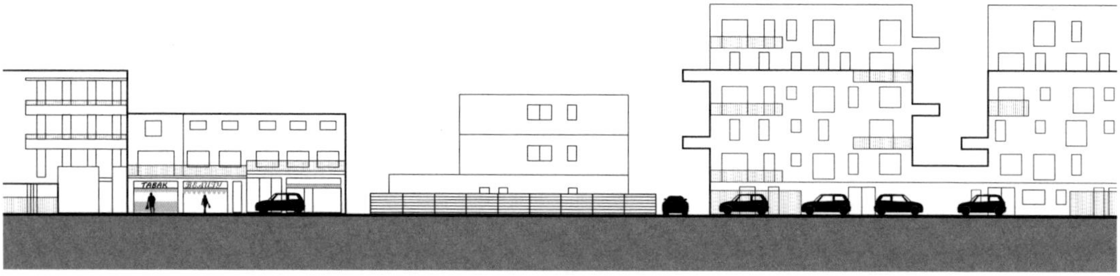

1. Being encapsulated by Paris, all remains of its agricultural past disappeared in the municipality of Romainville.

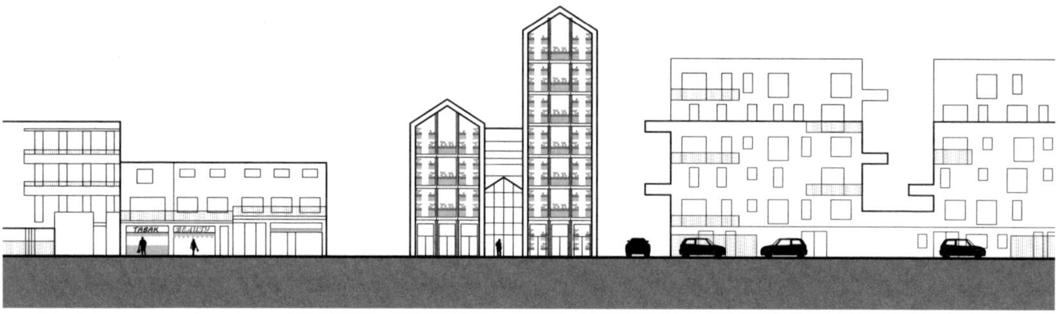

2. On an open spot in the city, the municipality decides to build an experimental greenhouse.

3. The local community rediscovers the private production of food, the neighbourhood is becoming greener and greener.

Use-driven Flexibility
Instruments: circular supply chains, customization, social currency, densification

Initiators: ACTES, Ile-de-France Region, Greater Paris Metropolis, Seine-Saint-Denis Departmental Council, AgroParisTech
Designers: ilimelgo architects
Completion: 2008
Programme: laboratory for urban food production
Website: https://www.lacitemaraichere.com/

As our current food consumption leads to significant greenhouse gas emissions and waste, we must look for ways to reduce its negative effects. Cité Maraîchère, accommodated in two major urban greenhouses in the east of Paris, shows that food can sustainably be produced in highly densified urban areas, promoting a circular food chain and a more responsible food consumption. Also on the local scale, the benefits are surprisingly impactful, such as a higher social cohesion, better environmental awareness, an improved local economy and last but not least: better food.

For a long time, Romainville, a municipality within the urban tissue of Paris, used to be an agricultural area, a characteristic that got lost over time, when urban sprawl took over. This is why the city has been trying to revive its agricultural identity for several years already, by, for example, encouraging the development of urban agriculture. Various food-related projects came to life, such as the temporary use of urban brownfields in Romainville or the temporary organic farm in Bobigny.

The project of the Cité Maraîchère was initiated by AgroParisTech (a research institute in agronomy), and started with both high sustainability and social ambitions, namely the reintroduction of agricultural activities in the city and the creation of new employment such as urban farmers, zero waste mediators and compost guides. Being a part of the larger framework of the Agence Communale de la Transition Écologique et Solidaire (ACTES), the Cité is a laboratory for sustainable practices, providing grounds for research and practical urban agriculture experiments. The Cité brings to light new ways of producing sustainable and qualitative food, while making sure that fresh, healthy and seasonal produce are easily accessible to everyone.

But the Cité is also a communal space, where people can meet and gather in the café-canteen, to enjoy a variety of organic, local and seasonal produce. The Cité also organizes activities around urban nature, sustainable eating, eco-citizenship, and other cultural, educational, scientific and culinary events.

Organizational
The Cité Maraîchère advocates for urban food production to complement traditional agriculture. The project shows that agricultural production is possible in urban settings, keeping food loops small and local. The building comprises two vertical greenhouses aiming to produce 12 tons of food each year. The Cité makes sure that its supply of local production is varied, with different types of fruits, vegetables and herbs, depending on the season, but also edible flowers, different types of mushrooms and microgreens. As a living laboratory, the Cité Maraîchère is still experimenting with its types of production, trying to optimize the supply and demand of food and to avoid mismatches.

The objective of the Cité is not financial profit. Though prices are not necessarily cheaper than traditional food supply chains, the production at the Cité Maraîchère is more sustainable and less expensive in terms of energy and water consumption. Rainwater is harvested and makes up around 40 per cent of the production's watering. The soil in which the food is grown was developed in a laboratory as a solution against soil pollution in urban contexts. AgroParisTech, a research institute developed a 'circular' substrate made of locally harvested compost, green waste and coffee grounds. This soil therefore has many big advantages, such as its local availability, low costs, high efficiency and natural components. Food preservation workshops are being held for local residents in order to reduce food waste.

Legal

In order to allow the development of agriculture in the urban context, the local urban plan of Romainville had to be revised, permitting constructions and projects with agricultural functions within the municipality borders. These changes in the legislation now allow agricultural production.

The food production is kept healthy thanks to a combination of strict internal and legal protocols, forbidding chemicals and imposing a seasonal and diverse food production with old and new vegetable types being grown. The rainwater harvesting tanks are regularly tested in order to verify the absence of bacteria before usage. Though the production of the Cité does not have the 'AB' (organic agriculture) label, since the food is not grown directly in the soil, it follows the same regulations. When agricultural production faces challenges, such as insects or pests, sustainable products are used, made from black soap or orange essential oil, for example. These solutions might be more time-consuming, but are more sustainable in the end and they work.

The complexity and innovative character of the Cité Maraîchère require a constant collaborative supervision of the project. Since the start, the municipality of Romainville put together a group of people with different backgrounds but with shared interests that follows and supports the development of the project on the long term. The group meets twice a year, dealing with all kinds of challenges concerning urban food production. At the same time, a scientific advisory group aims at improving the project of the Cité regarding educational, technical, marketing and employment issues. Both groups keep an eye on legal issues as well. Both legal threats and changes are monitored, analysed and provided with a solution or advice if necessary.

Financial

Since summer 2021, the Cité Maraîchère has been selling its food production to the inhabitants of Romainville following an innovative pricing scheme. The Cité wants to be inclusive, guaranteeing a qualitative food supply for all the inhabitants of Romainville. The municipality therefore set up a pricing scheme adapted to the financial revenue of the local residents. The scheme has three categories, offering up to 75 per cent discount on the produce.

Besides food production in urban contexts, the other main goal of the Cité Maraîchère is to be an example of socio-professional support by creating new jobs and enabling professional reintegration, by helping people who lost their previous employment in finding a new one. The Cité aims at creating 22 new local jobs, providing certified training in the fields of farming, eco-entertainment, catering and food services.

The Cité hosts cocreative, participatory workshops organized by both the residents and the representatives of the community of Romainville. The participatory workshops were held with the help of local experts in permaculture and urban agriculture. They resulted in the vitalization of outdoor spaces of the Cité Maraîchère, creating collective compost, a shared vegetable garden and a medicinal garden.

Spatial

The building of the Cité Maraîchère is split according to its functions: the ground floor hosts the most public functions such as a kitchen for workshops, seminars and pedagogical trainings, meetings and conferences. 90 square metres of the greenhouses are also accessible to the public for trainings and workshops. On the first floor, another 36 square metres are dedicated to meetings, exhibitions and workshops. The total food production of 700 square metres is growing in 753 containers that are not connected to the ground. In this way, the production can be stacked, saving on floor space.

The building itself was designed with agricultural functions in mind: volumes and materials were chosen in order to allow maximum indoor daylight and limiting weight. The food production area is divided in two aisles, maximizing the amount of natural daylight coming in. On the upper floors and in the basement, where mushrooms are grown, the production of food is very efficient. However, as the lower floors sometimes lack daylight, the yield is quite low. These floors will probably be reconverted to another type of production, requiring less daylight.

Atri, Sikhall Vänersborg, Sweden

From a remote forest to an off-grid building site

1. Many distant places in the vast forests of Sweden are suitable for habitation, but lack the right infrastructure.

2. Taking advantage of the landscape qualities, an experimental house is built, completely off-grid.

3. As the experimental house appears to be a success in many ways, more off-grid housing is realized.

Use-driven Flexibility
Instruments: circular supply chains, customization, life cycle finance, seasonal flexibility

Initiators: Niklas Dahlström & Anders Solvarm, Naturvillan
Designers: Naturvillan
Completion: 2022
Programme: Residential off-grid home
Website: https://naturvillan.com/

Underground infrastructure for energy, water and sewerage occupies subsoil space that is also claimed to make our cities greener and rainwater-resilient. Future transformation of existing infrastructure, enabling our cities to use new types of renewable energy and sustainable water management, puts even more pressure on our urban undergrounds. Off-grid building, that does not need large-scaled infrastructure, can contribute to lowering this pressure. Atri, an off-grid housing project in the woods of Sweden, shows not only how practical, but also how attractive off-grid living can be.

Atri, a glass covered human habitat, contrived by the designers of Naturvillan, is an example of a minimal-impact home that rethinks the aesthetics of what it means to be off the grid. The triangular glass and timber structure serves as a greenhouse covering the inner insulated cube that houses the living quarters. The living quarters have two floors, three bedrooms, two bathrooms, a kitchen, and an open-plan dining and living room. The living quarters are accessible from two sides of the greenhouse creating two 'patios' on either end of the greenhouse. The greenhouse is lined with raised beds for plants. The home is fitted with a multiple-circular system – wastewater recovery that is used to grow plants, trap heat, create and store its own energy. With our increasingly unstable and expensive energy on the one hand and a growing pressure on networks for energy supply on the other, Atri becomes an interesting alternative.

The house is built for a certain lifestyle. The circular systems are for the most part automated, however, there is some work to be done to grow food and potentially to generate heat in the winter. The heat in the winter comes mostly from the wood-burning oven, which requires human maintenance and a daily supply of wood.

Organizational

The house, inside the greenhouse, has been built to be operated completely off-grid. During summer, the solar cells provide electricity to the battery that drives the house and heats the water. In winter, a wood-burning boiler with a hob and oven provides heat and hot water. If necessary, there is a proprietary domestic power plant to recharge the battery.

Drinking water comes from the well on the property, and does not involve expenses. The principle is that nutrients and water in the wastewater are recycled and purified in the greenhouse's plant beds, where macro and microbiota interact with the plants' root systems. The grey-water system together with heat capturing help the residents to live self-sufficiently.

Due to its substantial plot of land there is potential to grow more food in the surrounding area. However, as Atri is located in rural Sweden, growing food outside is not possible all year around because of the harsh winter conditions.

Legal

Naturvillan and the municipality of Vänersborg worked closely together to build Atri. Sikhall, the area where Atri is located, does not have a strict zoning plan. The main concern was to adapt the building aesthetically and technically to the landscape in which it stands.

Atri has several features that are out of the ordinary, such as the eco-cycle system that utilizes nutrients from wastewater for the garden plants. As it is such an innovative system, extra information and explanation had to be provided to convince the building inspector. The eco-cycle system was in the end allowed and installed.

In Sweden, many homeowners choose to extend their houses with a conservatory, a glass-covered room. Atri takes this idea to the extreme. One of municipality's concerns was that Atri's living quarters were a little small and the space that is only covered by a greenhouse roof cannot be counted as liveable space. This can lead to a conflict when calculating the square metres. However, as one of the members of the municipality team pointed out: 'It requires a certain lifestyle to really feel comfortable in these spaces. At the same time, it is probably this change of lifestyle our planet needs from us. Compact, passive, and aware of the fact that we cannot go on living like we have been doing the last 100 years'. Overall, the municipality was enthusiastic about the project and in fact would welcome more projects of this nature.

Financial

The financial arrangement of this project differs from that of a conventional building. Building Atri requires a relatively large initial investment. But unlike conventional concepts, no external resources like energy and water have to be paid for during the period of use. As the chosen materials are easy to maintain, the exploitation of the house is virtually free of costs. Compared to conventional housing, living in this house gets cheaper by the year. After some decades, theoretically the house even starts earning money for the owner, if you compare its costs with those of living in a conventional house. As the founder of Naturvillan pointed out, it may be difficult to get banks on board for loans with a project that is as out of the ordinary as this one.

The metrics to calculate when this type of house has fully paid itself back, are different to a standard passive house because of the circular systems and the added value they bring. In Sweden, solar cells start earning back after seven years. Solar cells are the main source of energy in sunny months along with a heat-recovery system. These feed the battery, which in turn runs the house's automated systems and heats water for domestic use. The creators of the building estimate that in the dead of winter it may be necessary to run the backup battery for several hours every day to supplement the main supply of heat – a wood-burning oven in the kitchen. The backup battery can also be run from a proprietary domestic power plant in the winter months. Additionally, according to the architect, placing the living quarters in a greenhouse alone can save 30 per cent of energy.

Spatial

The insulated living quarters have a constant interior condition throughout the year. The microclimate in the greenhouse, however, does vary across the seasons. In wintertime, it captures heat from the insulated part that would otherwise be lost, resulting in a wintergarden climate. In the summer it captures heat from the sun. The surplus of heat is stored in in the battery, while the inhabitants enjoy the sun, protected from the wind by the glass facades. Because the microclimate in the greenhouse stays within a certain bandwidth, the residents can grow plants all year round and have a steady yield of fruit and vegetables. Sun exposure is scarce especially in winter months and therefore having a house inside a greenhouse is possible without making the indoor conditions too extreme.

Gent knapt op, Ghent, Belgium

From a housing stock in a poor condition towards an affordable and sustainably renovated housing stock

1. Many privately owned houses are in a poor state, being badly insulated and depending on fossil energy resources.

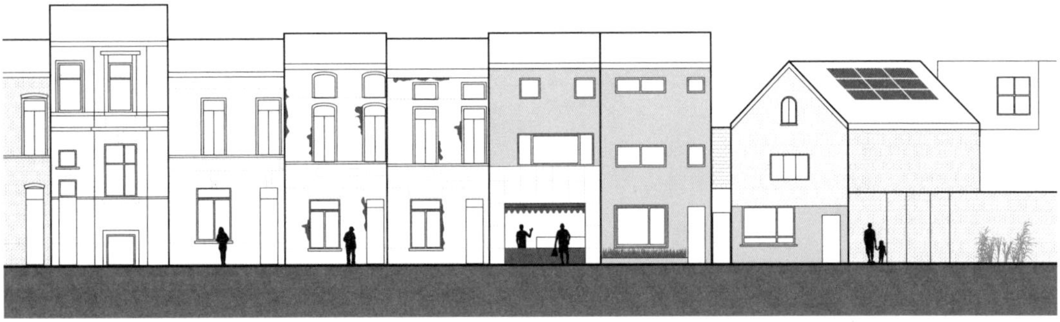

2. In close cooperation with residents, the 'Gent knapt op' programme manages to renovate more and more houses.

3. The renovated houses inspire other house owners to renovate their house too.

Use-driven Flexibility
Instruments: empowering local communities, law change motivation, recurrent housing fund, re-interpretation

Initiators: City of Ghent, University of Ghent and KU Leuven
Designers: various
Completion: 2018-2021
Programme: renovation of 100 homes
Website: uia-initiative.eu/en/uia-cities/ghent-call3

There is a strong need to upgrade the existing housing stock in order to reduce emissions related to heating and cooling demands. The 'Gent knapt op' programme shows that sustainability and social inclusion can – or even should – go hand in hand. Under this initiative, the Belgian municipality of Ghent creates incentives for homeowners that not only reduce the energy consumption of their property, but links these improvements to social, environmental and economic benefits.

Housing is a critical issue in Ghent. Like in many other cities, rising housing costs, housing shortages and substandard living conditions are major challenges. In addition, the city has a relatively high rate of people living in poverty (15.5 per cent). 'Gent knapt op' (translation: Ghent renovates) aims to address these challenges by enabling homeowners to invest in the improvement of their homes, thereby increasing the quality and sustainability of housing in the city. One of the key aspects is its focus on making housing more energy-efficient. Many homes in Ghent, particularly older ones, are poorly insulated, leading to higher energy bills and greenhouse gas emissions. The 'Gent knapt op' programme provides incentives for homeowners to invest in insulation, double glazing, energy-efficient heating systems and other measures to reduce their energy consumption and lower their carbon footprint.

The city of Ghent has a growing population, which has put pressure on the housing market, leading to an increase in housing prices and a shortage of affordable housing. This situation has made it difficult for many residents, particularly low-income households, to find adequate housing. They often end up in poor-quality housing with substandard living conditions such as poor insulation, inadequate heating and a lack of maintenance. This situation can lead to higher energy bills, health problems and safety issues.

The main objective of the initiative is to renovate 100 houses of low-income homeowners to make them safer, more qualitative and more energy-efficient with the use of a recurring fund. As an effect of the renovations, the general quality of living of the households and of the neighbourhoods are improving. Through the use of a recurring fund, public funding is not only used for a limited group, but can be used over and over again to fight this major urban challenge.

Another key aspect is its support for neighbourhoods and the local economy. The renovations carried out under the programme generate jobs for local contractors and suppliers, helping to boost the local economy. The increased quality of housing also leads to better social circumstances in the whole neighbourhood.

Organizational
Homeowners who do not have the resources to renovate their homes to a decent standard are the main target group of the project. These homeowners are sometimes called the 'captive owners'. In many cases, the houses were inherited or bought in poor condition because the owners couldn't afford to rent them and didn't qualify for private funding to renovate them. Access to funding and guidance allows the homeowners to renovate their properties into higher quality and more energy-efficient houses. The programme aims to be as socially inclusive as possible and to help homeowners regardless of their age,

ability or socio-economic status. A requirement is that the owners should live in the house themselves and have a relatively low income. The programme is not meant for landlords.

'Gent Knapt Op' not only provides funding, but also social support to participants as they go through the renovation process. By becoming a central part of the process and providing social support to the homeowners, the project is also able to boost their self-esteem, independence and social connections. The initiative not only improved the physical living conditions of those in need, but can also have a positive impact on their overall quality of life, taking away private concerns about maintenance and energy costs. It is known that people living in poor conditions do not easily invite other people, such as friends, neighbours or family, to their homes and easily get socially isolated.

These initiatives not only benefit the local community but also contribute to reducing energy consumption and greenhouse gas emissions. For example, the programme provides funding to carry out energy-saving projects, such as insulation or the installation of solar panels. Moreover, the programme provides information and education to residents to help them understand the benefits of sustainable housing and to encourage them to make informed decisions about home improvements. This approach helps to build awareness and knowledge among residents, empowering them to take an active role in creating sustainable and inclusive communities.

Legal

The programme both works as a stimulus for homeowners to act according to new regulations for more sustainability and advocates at a governmental level for policies and regulations that support sustainable housing and social inclusion.

For example, the programme has successfully advocated for the introduction of tax credits and subsidies for homeowners who carry out energy-saving renovations or invest in renewable energy systems. These incentives help to make sustainable housing more accessible and affordable for residents and encourage homeowners to make sustainable improvements to their homes.

The programme also advocates for regulations that promote social inclusion, such as accessibility standards for housing and regulations that require landlords to maintain safe and healthy living conditions for their tenants. 'Gent knapt op' works with local authorities to ensure that these regulations are enforced and that housing providers are held accountable for providing safe and adequate housing. Collectively, these efforts help to create a legal and policy framework that supports the programme's objectives and contributes to the development of sustainable and inclusive communities in Ghent.

Financial

The 'Gent Knapt Op' pilot project also introduced a new financial model, the 'recurring fund', to address the shortage of affordable housing in the city and ensure the sustainability of the project. The fund works by providing financial support (30,000 euros) to homeowners for essential renovation work. The homeowners then repay the original contribution plus interest only if and when the house is sold. This allows for longer-term continuity of the programme and provides an opportunity for more homes to be renovated in the future. It's a creative approach to tackling the shortage of affordable housing, and the project provides intensive social and technical support and community building as well as funding.

Another financial mechanism is the use of subsidies and low-interest loans to incentivize homeowners to invest in energy-saving renovations and other sustainable housing improvements. The programme provides funding for these initiatives through a variety of sources, including the city budget, regional and national funds, and private sector investments.

Spatial

'Gent knapt op' focuses on reactivating existing spaces. After living in their homes for a while, residents may not see the possibilities of renovating their own property any more. Therefore, technical counselling is part of the programme. Technical experts and architects help owners find the best solutions and try to renovate the spaces according to their spatial needs. Attics are not only insulated, but also turned into bedrooms or children's rooms, depending on the actual wishes of the residents.

The 'Gent knapt op' project has a community component with the potential to strengthen neighbourhood networks and increase participants' role in their neighbourhood and city. The project recognizes the role that social connections and a sense of community can play in promoting overall quality of life. The research consortium measured the level of participant involvement in their city or neighbourhood before and after the renovation, as this can provide valuable insights into the impact of the project. In addition, the increased opportunities for socializing in a newly renovated home, such as inviting over friends and family, may also contribute to stronger social networks.

Resource Rows, Copenhagen, Denmark

From waste out of a building to a building out of waste

1. The Carlsberg Brewery is demolished and afterwards, the Copenhagen Metro removes temporary structures such as scaffolding.

2. Materials are harvested and brought to the new construction site.

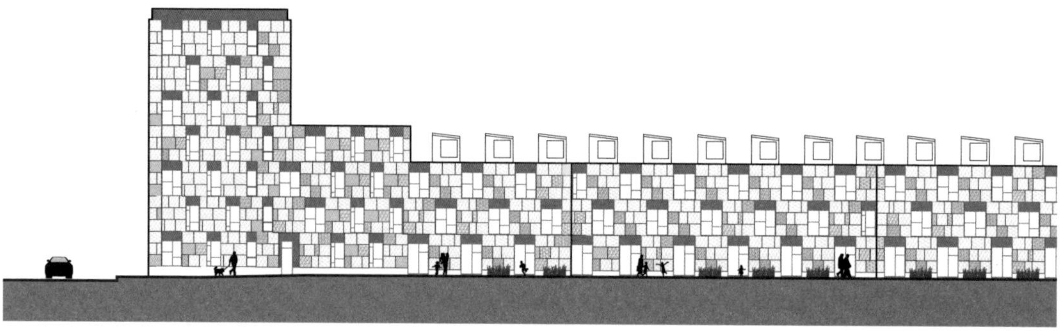

3. The Resource Rows project – a brand new housing block – refers of the city's past by showing its reused materials.

Time-based Flexibility
Instruments: circular supply chains, material passport, upcycling, re-interpretation

Initiators and designers: Lendager Group
Completion: 2020
Programme: 63 apartments and 29 terraced houses
Website: https://lendager.com/project/resource-rows/

If circularity should become the new standard for building, we need convincing, realized examples that show us how circular building is technically and organizationally feasible, financially affordable and ready to be scaled up. Resource Rows is a circular housing project in Copenhagen that transforms 463 tons of waste from nearby demolished buildings into new space. By upcycling bricks from the nearby Carlsberg Brewery and wasted wood from the Copenhagen Metro, Resource Rows proves that circular building can compete with regular prices, conventional qualities, strict guarantees and – on top of that – offers a whole new aesthetics.

Resource Rows is a housing block with 63 apartments and 29 terraced houses in the new development area Ørestad Syd in Copenhagen that demonstrates that it is possible to reuse bricks and waste wood in a new building without compromising on costs and aesthetics. The scheme is arranged around a shared courtyard and roofscape, with two rows of three-storey terraced houses book-ended by two five-storey apartment blocks. The facade features a unique pattern of brick tiled in different directions that pays homage to the character and history of the Carlsberg breweries, old schools and abandoned homes that they were reclaimed from. The 29 greenhouses in the courtyard and on the roofscape are made of recycled glass and window frames. Even the concrete TT beam-bridge across the courtyard connecting the two parallel terraces roof-to-roof is recycled, from a nearby factory.

Since it was no longer possible to recycle individual bricks due to the strength of the mortar, existing brick facades from various abandoned buildings were cut into square brick modules, which were then assembled as a patchwork facade for the new terraced houses. The panels were mounted in steel frames to form facade modules that were fixed to a composite concrete/timber superstructure. On brick level it saved 500 grammes of carbon per brick, which is 70 per cent. The combination of vertical and horizontal bricks and the offset surface gives the scheme an almost knitted texture.

In addition, large amounts of residual wood were upcycled as finishing material in the project's interior and for the rooftop community garden huts, much of it sourced from a construction site for a new metro station nearby. In the making of the new subway tunnels of Copenhagen's expanding Metro, 900 tonnes of larch wood was used in the transportation and construction of concrete tunnel elements for the new underground. 300 tonnes of it was reused in Resource Rows. On exterior wood, an old Japanese technique (yakisugi) was applied, charring the surface with fire to impregnate it, making it completely fireproof and resistant to fungus and insects without using any chemicals.

Organizational
As a true circular supply chain, Resource Rows has used waste as resources for its construction. Implementing this circular supply chain required restructuring the process of building material demolition and production, and reshuffling the roles involved based on an understanding of the traditional process and interests of the stakeholders involved.

The standard demolition process had to be reorganized in order to save the materials and be able to reuse these. Traditionally, a contractor will hire a demolition firm that tears down the building on the site and brings in a waste hauling company that then takes it all to the dump. Pieces of the building that could be salvaged, such as doors, windows, high-end finishes and large-scale materials, are often not preserved due to both an often tight schedule, lack of space to store the materials, and no knowledge of who would even be willing to purchase and reuse them.

The biggest challenge however was to convince the client and the main contractor that this was a viable solution; risk had to be taken out of the equation. Facing scepticism, Lendager Group restructured the business so it could function as architect, demolition contractor and materials manufacturer. Lendager set out to create the 'missing pieces', researching and sourcing recycled material, designing prototypes and finding partners to produce new building products from old. Delivering the sustainable materials themselves, they could eliminate the contractor's risk, while using some of the money in the budget to investigate how to make these new materials cost-neutral and as durable as regular products.

The narrow timeframe added pressure to develop and deliver these innovations as well as locate local various buildings at the end of their lifespan from which resources could be extracted. The time from finding a building to harvesting it, then preparing the materials to build with, involved a much smaller window than when a regular manufacturer had been used, who would have its products in stock.

Legal

The materials have been harvested and put into production by the architects. They have developed methods for scaling up the reuse of untapped resources in 'construction waste' to build new homes, using sustainable non-toxic and certified materials. Labelled and provided with an index that states the features relevant for their position in the new building project, it is easy to implement them into the new building. The recycled materials include facade bricks and aluminium, internal floors, exterior wood for terraces and decking and rooftop huts, including the windows.

Financial

Adding value and use to waste materials is at the core of this project. Resource Rows is using upcycled bricks and waste wood, a recycled concrete beam used as a bridge and old windows and waste wood as rooftop community garden huts with an allotment garden ambiance. Making circularity a realistic and financially viable alternative for the traditional building material production process is the ambition driving the architects. While the amount of existing and future waste material that could be upcycled into new construction is immense, upcycling practices will not scale up until pioneering projects like Resource Rows have tested and proven their economic and environmental merits.

The project was underwritten based on a conventional terraced house and apartment project meaning that all sustainability efforts had to fit in a conventional budget frame in order to be implemented. Resource Rows has an upcycle percentage of 29 per cent carbon dioxide emission saving per square metre (Life Cycle Assessment) and was still delivered for the same price per square metre as the equivalent block built traditionally. And although flat rentals were slowing in Copenhagen even before the Covid-19 pandemic, properties in Resource Rows were popular from the start. The project's low carbon footprint provided the catalyst to help client Nordic Real Estate Partners (NREP) differentiate itself from the competition. Urban dwellers appear to be increasingly looking to live a responsible life with as little climate impact as possible.

Spatial

The brick panels used on the Resource Rows project are just a more orderly version of what can be seen in many old historic walls, which are often made up of an eclectic layering of reused stone and brick. It was only with the development of new, harder, cement-based mortar in the 1960s that bricks could no longer be recycled efficiently. The bricks themselves crack before the mortar does, on demolition. For this reason, an innovative method was developed to cut out larger squares of brick masonry to form into panels, either by fixing them to a steel frame or bedding them into a thin backing layer of concrete.

Due to this new interpretation of the potential of redundant brick walls, these walls can now be reused, thus contributing to a more circular environment. This innovative approach makes it possible to recycle and give the bricks many lives instead of just one, while also getting a new building with history and character. These inherent stories also function as shared references binding the tenants closer together as residents of the old Carlsberg Brewery and the Copenhagen Metro.

41

Town Hall Extension, Korbach, Germany

From a modernist town hall made out of concrete to a contemporary town hall made out of that same, reused concrete

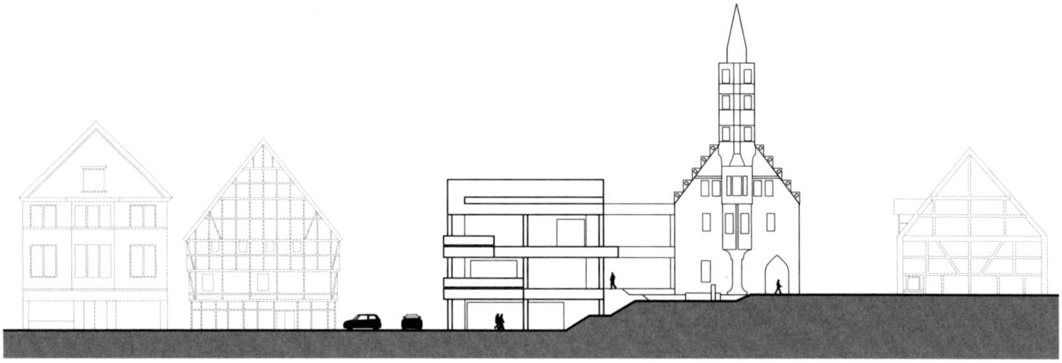

1. The modern and brutalist building structure of the Korbach Town Hall does not fit well into the medieval old town.

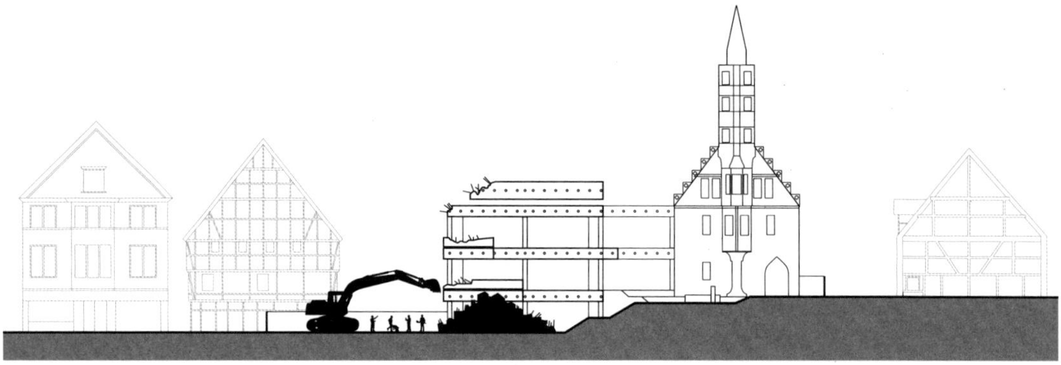

2. The brutal building structure is demolished and its building materials are carefully kept and inventoried.

3. A new town hall, that fits much better into the medieval old town, is built using the old town hall's materials.

Time-based Flexibility
Instruments: reused materials mediator, customization, upcycling, re-interpretation

Initiators: Municipality of Korbach
Design: heimspiel architekten Matzken Kampherbeek PartGmbB and Christian Thomann of agn Niederberghaus & Partner GmbH
Completion: 2022
Programme: Replacement of the town hall extension
Website: https://www.heimspielarchitekten.de/projekte/rkb/

Implementing the circular use of building materials by replacing worn-out buildings with new ones should be done with an open mind and without any prejudices. By redeveloping its town hall, the city of Korbach has shown how building materials can be radically different after being reused and how an architectural style can easily be set aside. A brutal modernist building was replaced by a contextual tailorized town hall with historic features, built with a significant part of the building materials coming from the building that had just been demolished.

In medieval times, Korbach was located at the intersection of two important trade routes. Due to this favourable location, Korbach's economy prospered and the population grew accordingly. In the vicinity of the original old town, new villages were built, which over time grew together with the old town. With the unification of the old and new town in 1377, the new joint town hall was built, which still characterizes Korbach today.

In the following centuries, the town hall building survived fires, economic decline and warlike conflicts in the town. In the early twentieth century, the tower and the southern arcade were added. At the beginning of the 1970s, in the course of a municipal redivision, several previously independent surrounding communities were incorporated into the municipality of Korbach, which led to a sudden increase in the number of inhabitants to around 23,000. As a result, the town hall was expanded with a spacious modern concrete building right next to the historic building, which provided office space for the higher number of administrative staff. However, the oversized structure of the brutalist building failed to fit well into the medieval old town. In the following decades, public resistance against the modernist architecture grew and the visible ageing of the concrete structure made the building even less popular.

The Korbach city council finally decided to redesign the town hall quarter and launched a Europe-wide realization competition in August 2016. In mid-2017, the joint design by heimspiel architekten Matzken Kampherbeek PartGmbB and Christian Thomann of agn Niederberghaus & Partner was chosen as the winning design. It envisaged the creation of a town hall ensemble consisting of the medieval building and two interconnected gabled buildings that would replace the 1970s extension. The new buildings jump back from the outline of the previous modernist structure and are parallel to the front facade of the medieval town hall building, creating space for a new town square. In order to ensure the visibility of the staircase gable of the historic town hall on the east facade, an originally proposed extension was not built. As a result, another proposed freestanding structure placed at a distance from the historic stepped gable facade was extended, for which the historic Brühmann House was demolished.

The central idea in the winning competition entry was the use of the demolished old municipal building as a source of materials for the new building. The aim of this circular process was to reuse as many materials from the previous building as possible for the new construction, thereby saving resources and closing material cycles. The construction project was realized in a three-year construction process starting in 2019. The new ensemble was officially opened in April 2022.

Organizational

The idea for the circular use of building materials was not part of the competition brief, but was brought in by one of the members of the winning design team, Anja Rosen, who was at that time also related to the Bergische Universität Wuppertal as a lecturer in building construction, design and materials science. The circular concept focused on the reuse of the mineral building materials – primarily concrete – which made up 95 per cent of the previous building. From this demolition material, a recycled material aggregate was produced, which could be used to manufacture new concrete. Before demolition of the old part of the building, concrete and bricks were analysed in a laboratory with regard to their recyclability. For this purpose, a representative sample of the material was examined, among other things, for its composition of harmful substances and categorized according to its aggregate. After a subsequent calculation of the quantities of recycled concrete that could be produced from the demolition material, the building was dismantled and the demolition material was separated, crushed, screened, washed and processed.

Legal

To judge if the obsolete concrete could be reused safely, the guidelines of the German Committee for Reinforced Concrete (DAfStb) were of central importance.

DIN EN 12620 regulates that only recycled aggregates that have no harmful effects on the environment, in particular on soil and groundwater, should be used for the production of concrete, which had to be confirmed by the laboratory testing. Additionally, DIN 4226-100 provides an evaluation scheme according to which recycled aggregates are to be categorized into four different types, of which only types one and two can be used for the production of concrete. Accordingly, the proportion of recycled aggregate in concrete must not exceed 45 per cent. In order to meet these legal restrictions, an extensive testing procedure had to be passed in a laboratory. These tests showed that the intended circular use of building materials would meet all restrictions.

Financial

From the very beginning, the entire project was designed to create added value from the demolition materials of the previous buildings and not to treat them as construction waste requiring costly disposal, as is the case in conventional construction practice. Through the urban mining process, 5,000 tons of the extracted demolition material was used to fill the foundation pit and create the subgrade, while another 1,000 tons was recycled and used as recycled concrete for floor slabs, ceilings, beams and exterior walls in contact with the ground as part of the structural framework of the new building. Recycled aggregates from 8 to 22 millimetres were used for this recycled concrete. For the facade, 260 concrete panels were manufactured with the help of this material as well. The demolition material obtained from the red roof tiles of the dismantled historic Brühmann House was added to these panels in order to obtain a slightly reddish colour. The 6,000 tons that were thus used directly for the construction of the new building represent approximately 62 per cent of the total 9,848 tons of mineral demolition material obtained. The remaining 3,800 tons were taken away for external recycling.

Spatial

The project shows how the designers succeeded in developing a concept in which the existing building was viewed as an urban mine for reusable materials, highlighting its material potential rather than its disruptive factor in the historic environment. Careful analysis showed what the potential of the materials was for reuse, thus leading to a material base for new buildings. And while they were built, these new buildings were already seen as stores of materials for the future. They were designed to be reused as easily as possible at the end of their life cycle. The exposed concrete elements of the new buildings were left raw to ensure better recyclability. The modular roof elements of the new pitched zinc roof were designed in such a way that they can be easily separated into different types of materials again in the future. Irreversible bonding or mixing of materials was also avoided.

Puukuokka Housing Block Jyväskylä, Finland

From carbon-dioxide-emitting buildings to carbon-capturing buildings

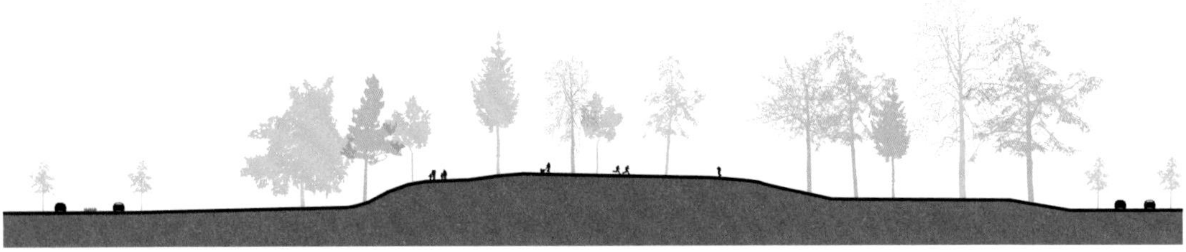

1. Jyväskylä has a natural hilly bedrock landscape with pine trees.

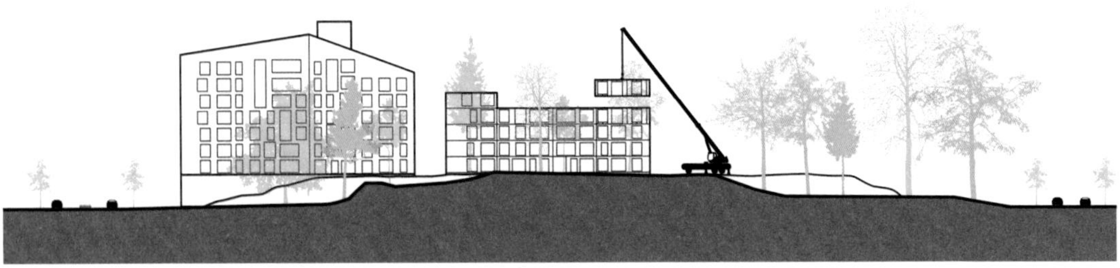

2. The eight-storey Puukuokka Housing Block is built with prefabricated CLT modular units, exploring the potential of this structural, biobased building material.

3. Based on the lessons learned building the first building, the other buildings are erected, completing the housing complex and respecting the site.

Time-based Flexibility
Instruments: innovation booster, customization, life cycle finance, modular building

Initiators: Lakea Oy housing developer, OOPEAA
Design: OOPEAA
Completion: 2018
Programme: housing (184 apartments, 14,000 m2), shared facilities (4,650 m2)
Website: https://oopeaa.com/portfolio/puukuokka-housing-block/

The Puukuokka apartment complex in Jyväskylä city in Finland shows that modular building can provide surprisingly good answers to many challenges our building practice is currently facing. The three buildings are made out of prefabricated CLT modular units. Based on biobased materials such as wood, this building method results in limited carbon dioxide emissions and a small ecological footprint. With a clever combination of only eight repetitive modular units, the entire complex offers affordable homes with a high quality for 184 households, from single dwellers of all ages to families with children.

CLT is an engineered wood formed by glueing together several layers of wood at right-angles to each other, making it much stronger and more rigid than normal wood. Manufacturer Stora Enso took advantage of these properties to develop a modular building system using only this material. These lightweight modules make up the building's main structural framework. Compared with typical concrete constructions, they can be installed in half the time, with far fewer weather-related delays. Thanks to this lightweight wooden modular construction method it was also possible to keep the machinery considerably light and small in size, minimizing the disturbance to the ground on the site and leaving most of the pine and birch trees undisturbed.

Completed in 2015, Puukuokka One was the first eight-storey wooden apartment building in Finland. It explores the potential of modular prefabricated CLT construction to meet the goal of providing high quality, environmentally responsible and affordable housing. Puukuokka Two was completed in 2017 and Puukuokka Three in August 2018. The three buildings together form a block that complements the Kuokkala neighbourhood in Jyväskylä, Finland. It puts an emphasis on the connection between the city and the surrounding natural landscape of hills and the lake. Together with the adjacent Kuokkala Church designed by OOPEAA in 2010, it forms a focal point for the neighbourhood.

The ambition was to create a building that combines the sense of warmth and privacy of a single-family dwelling with the semi-public character of the shared spaces of an apartment building. Each apartment is composed of two CLT modules, one housing the living room, the balcony and the bedroom, the other housing the bathroom, the kitchen and the foyer area. The apartments include a mix of studio flats, and one- and two-bedroom apartments. Each apartment has its own sauna and a balcony. The wooden balcony modules seem as though they have been scattered randomly across the court-facing facade, some protruding, others recessed. The interiors of the flats with recessed balconies are wrapped around the exterior space, their high glass facades and sliding doors seamlessly connecting the indoor and outdoor spaces.

In the interior, wood as a material is pleasantly present in the hallways as well as in the apartments themselves. The exterior of the building is also wooden – larch panels clad both the front and rear of the building. The side facing the road has been painted black, while the courtyard-facing rear facade has been left untreated and is covered with balconies.

The complex is built on a concrete foundation with indoor parking spaces on the basement level. To preserve the naturally hilly landscape of the site, as much of the bedrock has been left untouched as possible. The building follows the contours of the site to minimize disturbance to the underlying bedrock and existing vegetation. Wood is a locally available, renewable and recyclable material for construction. It also produces fewer emissions than for instance concrete and provides remarkable carbon storage. The goals set for creating an innovative concept for an ecologically and socially sustainable concept for multi-family housing were exceedingly well met and the project was realized within the set budget framework and schedule.

The Puukuokka complex has been extremely well received by the residents, who praise it for creating a comfortable living environment with an excellent framework for a friendly and social neighbourhood. It has been recognized with several awards.

Organizational

Housing developer Lakea Oy initiated this innovative approach to the construction process and realized it in collaboration with the City of Jyväskylä. The architect worked closely together with manufacturer Stora Enso to design a building that could serve well as a case study for what results prefabricated elements can yield while reducing the cost and construction time. At the start of the project in 2011 the Stora Enso concept was still in its preliminary stages. The close collaboration between architect and manufacturer has been important in developing many of the solutions applied in the final iteration of the Stora Enso Multi-Storey concept. In addition to collaborating to develop a system that meets the technical requirements, the role of the architect has been crucial in helping to streamline the overall management of the production process and in making it possible to achieve high quality in the end result. Puukuokka is an excellent example of productive collaboration between architects and engineers in developing a new concept that can be applied in other cases.

Legal

Fire regulations had previously prohibited buildings of this height being constructed from wood. But a change in Finland's building code in 2010 – largely prompted by the high fire-resistance of CLT – has now made it possible to build an eight-storey block with a wooden frame, as long as this load-bearing structure is coated and an automated sprinkler system is fitted. It has been estimated that, when realized in accordance with these regulations, a wooden apartment building is fifty times more fire safe than a similar apartment building made of concrete.

The urban plan has also been tailored to meet the needs of the building complex. Only part of the shared spaces is included in the calculations regarding the permitted building volume. The shared spaces thus have an open and spacious feel, while the floor space of the individual units has not been compromised on.

Financial

Puukuokka pilots a low-cost, low-risk financing model for homebuyers. After renting a flat for 20 years, the occupant becomes its owner. Before moving in, the future owner pays a modest down payment (7 per cent of the total value of the home). The remaining sum is covered by a State-guaranteed bank loan. The occupants pay off the loan in the form of rent over a 20-year period, after which the flat becomes their own. The sales price is negotiated and agreed upon when the lease is signed. This financial arrangement is not only financially advantageous for its users, but enlarges the sense of ownership from the beginning, leading to better maintenance of the property.

Spatial

Puukuokka explores the potential of modular prefabricated CLT construction to provide environmentally responsible and affordable housing of high quality. Puukuokka served as a pilot case to develop and test a CLT-based system of volumetric modules. The entire load-bearing structure and frame of the Puukuokka buildings is made of massive wood and composed of prefabricated volumetric CLT modules.

The 276 CLT modules were prefabricated in a local factory just an hour away from the site. The use of eight different module types enabled a large variety of apartment types. All the modules came with fully finished interior surfaces and all the necessary fittings, ready for installation. The use of these kind of prefabricated modules made it possible to cut the construction time on site down to six months per building and to reduce the exposure to weather conditions making it possible to achieve a higher quality in the end result.

The Triodos Bank, Driebergen-Rijsenburg, the Netherlands

From a bank for money towards a bank for materials

1. Although the Reehorst estate is very green, the estate is in a rather poor condition and needs maintenance.

2. The Triodos Bank building is built as a completely demountable bank for materials. The project adds new landscape qualities to the Reehorst estate as well as an increase of its biodiversity.

3. When the building is no longer in function, it is demounted, leaving no traces behind in its green surroundings.

Time-based Flexibility
Instruments: design output monitor, material passport, upcycling, biobased building

Initiator: Triodos Bank
Design and engineering: RAU Architects, ARCARDIS Netherlands BV, EDGE Technologies, Odette Ex (interior design)
Completion: 2019
Programme: Offices for the Triodos Bank
Website: https://www.triodos.nl/reehorst

With resources becoming increasingly scarce, there is a growing need to preserve and reuse materials as much as possible. Currently, the majority of buildings lose their material value after their demolition. The headquarters of the Triodos Bank show that changing our perception of buildings from the final stop in the production chain into banks of materials could be a great way to enhance reuse and preserve the material value.

Triodos Bank was founded in 1980 and focuses on sustainable investment, ethical banking and corporate social responsibility. A few years ago, Rau Architects were commissioned to plan and design the new Triodos Bank headquarters near Zeist, the Netherlands. The building was completed in 2019, and being a pioneer in sustainable thinking, Triodos Bank had set the goal to have it designed with a strong focus on sustainability, energy efficiency and environmental responsibility. What makes this building special is its ambitious, innovative and all-embracing approach to sustainability, which is prioritized in the construction, maintenance and future of the design.

Located within the De Reehorst estate, dating back to 1850, Triodos planned to preserve and strengthen the spatial, cultural-historical and ecological quality of the estate and its surroundings. The architects' land use plan reinforces the ecological structure of the existing landscape, providing a habitat for enables bats, birds and amphibians. The building was designed in an organic shape to adapt to the natural outline of the surrounding woods. An integral spatial plan let the office building serve as a new economic driver for the estate, which also accommodates a congress centre and a farm. Pavements at the terrain are mostly permeable to rainwater. The estate also has an area for growing vegetables. The office building contains a gross floor area of approximately 12,500 square metres.

As of today, the office building of Triodos Bank in the Netherlands sets new global standards in circular construction. The energy-neutral building consists of a wooden structure and a glass facade and is designed to be completely dismountable. The materials used are documented in detail in a digital material passport. It is a pioneering example of the principle of 'buildings as material depots', which is to design buildings in such a way that materials can be easily removed, making them a repository for resources and materials that can be stored for later (re)use. This approach is a critical step in advancing circular building design and can potentially mean significant progress, given that an estimated 40 per cent of the buildings expected to be in use in the EU in 2050 have not yet been constructed.

Organizational
By working in close collaboration with technical experts, the architects developed and made use of a well-balanced variety of emissions-reducing design elements, in order to predict the carbon footprint of the building and implement sustainable assets to make the building net zero. The building is designed with smart heat and cold storage. It is part of the local water cycle and a green roof helps reduce heat absorption and stormwater runoff. Additionally, 3,300 square metres of solar panels on the terrain provide around 506,000 kilowatt hours of solar power a year. The use of renewable energy to pow-

er the building as well as numerous bicycle parking spaces and electric company cars for car sharing, making it a truly sustainable and forward-looking project. The architects promoted emissions- reducing and sustainable assets with nearly every element of their design. Even with the materiality they chose assets like highly thermally insulated block windows, which regulate the temperature and the 2,623 cubic metres of wood store more than 1.6 million kilogrammes of carbon dioxide. The design choices result in the building having one of the lowest carbon footprints to date.

The building was also designed to be constructed with great respect for the surrounding nature. All material movements and work schedules were planned to minimize disturbance to wildlife and to maintain a peaceful environment. As a result of their efforts to be carbon neutral, the Triodos Bank building has received a BREEAM rating of 'outstanding' for its commitment to sustainability. BREEAM certification is held in high regard because it is completely independent, and the assessment is carried out by a third party. To prevent possible future waste of materials within the building, the structures have a high degree of flexibility, enabling various future uses with only limited necessary architectural changes.

Legal

This is one of the first buildings with a material passport to ensure that once the building is to be demolished, the materials are known and can easily be reused. To reimagine how valuable materials can be recycled, the architects and engineers developed a system to identify and track materials in a building. With a digital material passport, they established a database that can recover the position of materials. By documenting detailed information about the location, size and use of a building element, they give the material itself a form of 'identity' that makes them independent of their current use. The system developed is used during the engineering of the project. Thus, the Triodos Bank is a pioneering example of how materials can be 'stored' in a building and reused after the building's function is over: the building becomes a bank for materials.

To make the building's resources as recyclable and reusable as possible, the architects made every element easily demountable. Besides tracking and identifying all building elements in a detailed Material passport, the architects designed the building without wet joints, using a total of 165,312 screws to be able to completely dismantle the building after its use. Every item, including the screws, can be disassembled at the time of demolition. As they are digitally documented, their functionality and state after use are also ensured, and they can be reused without imposing a safety hazard.

Financial

Upcycled materials are recyclable materials with a value that does not devaluate, but can even increase when they are used or reused. The building was constructed using different kinds of upcycled materials. The easily demountable wooden structure parts, for example, keep their value as building materials after a future demolition.

The Bank offers safe and resourceful storage of materials that can be 'harvested' and upcycled in a new building in the future. This way, the architects created a space that reflects the bank's values, focusing on ethical and sustainable banking practices. Also the construction of the core of the building, with a concrete structure for the basement, is an example of upcycled materials. The concrete is made from recycled aggregates.

Spatial

The Triodos Bank is an exemplary biobased building which showcases the use of natural resources in its materials and design. Notably, the building's prominent use of wood in its structure is a striking feature. The laminated rafters and CLT cores are clearly visible, while the CLT floors are partially hidden by wooden tracks and climate-controlling ceiling elements. Most of the wood used for the furniture and flooring is locally sourced, further emphasizing the building's sustainability.

In the interior, wooden furniture elements are combined with wall-covering natural textiles, giving the interior spaces good acoustics. The insolation of the roofs is reinforced by a layer of soil, for natural rainwater retention and as a good base for plants and insects.

Atelier LUMA, Arles, France

From a former industrial production site to a laboratory for bioregional production

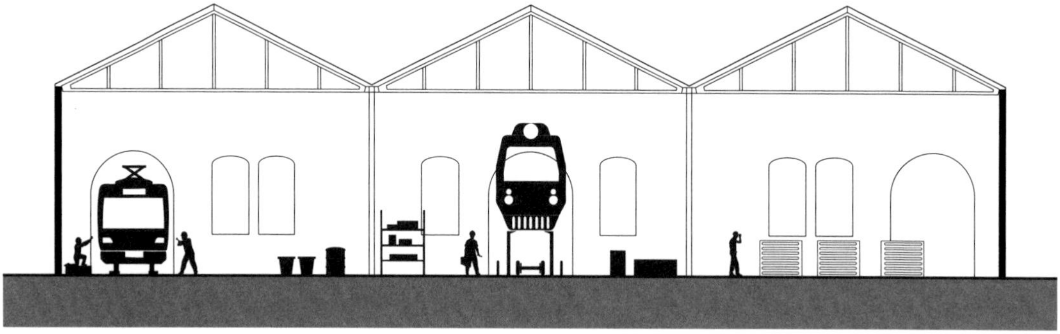

1. The Magasin Electrique building is part of an industrial railway site in Arles.

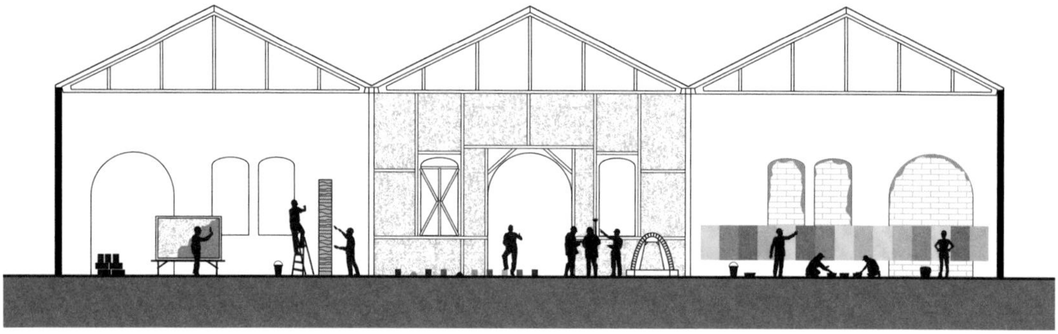

2. After a period of vacancy, atelier LUMA uses the building as a research and prototyping lab for bioregional materials.

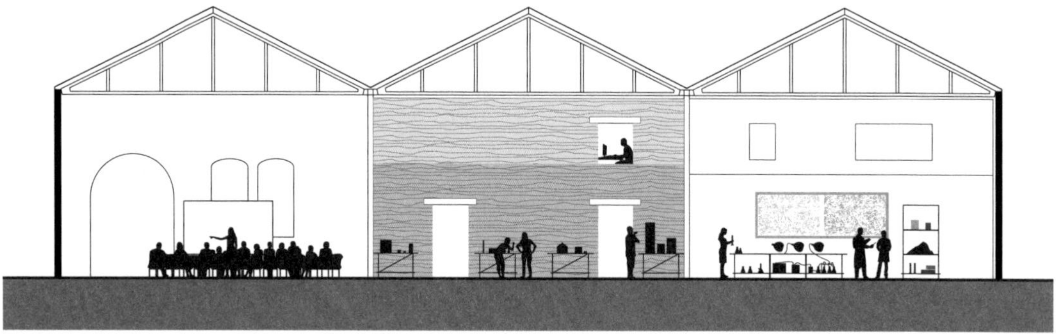

3. The resulting building remains a space for experiment and, consequently, will never be finished.

Time based flexibility
Instruments: circular supply chains, sustainability protocol, subsidy, biobased building

Initiator: Maja Hoffmann
Designers: Atelier LUMA, Assemble, BC architects & studies
Completion: 2023
Programme: Programme: design and material research laboratory, offices and a multipurpose space
Website: https://www.atelier-luma.org/

Now that the globalized market of building products is increasingly in trouble because of its growing environmental footprint and insecure costs, building materials that are locally found, harvested or produced are getting rediscovered. By investigating the resources of the Camargue bioregion and by connecting different fields of local expertise, Atelier LUMA is developing fundamental ecological, economic and social alternatives. Its projects are implemented locally while their principles can be replicated in other contexts and regions. The renovation of the 2,000-square-metre Le Magasin Électrique is the biggest manifestation of their work so far.

Located at the Parc des Ateliers in Arles, the former industrial site Le Magasin Électrique has been renovated and reused as the home for Atelier LUMA, a pioneering material and design laboratory, which is part of LUMA Arles, an experimental cultural center located in the South of France. Le Magasin Électrique is built and equipped with the results of Atelier LUMA's research, focusing on bioregional design practices. Almost every raw or recycled material was sourced and processed within 70 kilometres from the site. Its door handles, for example, are made of salt. Its walls are made of sunflowers. Its furniture is developed based on Atelier LUMA's research around textile and invasive plants. Broken roof tiles were reused in the floor, embedded in a slick surface of polished terrazzo. Rice straw, sunflower stems, salt, soil and limestone waste all find their way onto the site of the former railway electrical shop, reimagined as thermal and acoustic insulation and rammed earth interior walls, among other things.

Le Magasin Électrique is a research and prototyping space that consists of a biolab, wood, ceramics, textile and DTP workshops, office spaces, a dye house, a materials-testing lab and a functional plant garden. The Agora, a large central space in the building, hosts temporary exhibitions and events open to the public. On site, visitors can discover the technical and aesthetic research carried out and immerse themselves in the history of this pilot rehabilitation. At the heart of the approach, one can find the valorisation of traditional know-how, collective experiments on the site, the development of materials rooted in the Arles bioregion and the creation of a local and international network of expertise to share knowledge.

Le Magasin Électrique is the manifestation of a new kind of low-carbon, bioregional architecture that takes cues from ancient practices. Like in medieval days, it is based on an experimental and open way of designing by prototyping on the site, testing it and in this way discovering what can be used in the new building. The end result was not based on a predetermined total design, but was the unexpected outcome of a number of experiments each with their own result. In this sense the process was more important than the outcome. Atelier LUMA, Assemble and BC architects & studies jointly decided on the programming and the design, while doing research by prototyping on the site. The renovation of the site enabled the implementation of Lot 8, a long-term research project for a bioregional architecture, guided by principles of locality and sustainability and connecting with the region's landscape and people. The construction site, a large-scale prototype, brought together many local partners and was the occasion for collective workshops and training sessions on the materials and techniques developed. The resulting building is a true living lab, a space to experiment in and in that sense, it is a building that will never be finished.

Organizational

Atelier LUMA is deeply connected to its geographic and cultural environment: the Camargue region, the Alpilles mountains, and the Crau plains. Atelier LUMA's work began with a cartography of the different industries, plants, resources and waste products in the region identifying streams of materials and local knowledge. Atelier LUMA engaged an extensive network of scientists, institutional and industrial partners to research bioregional resources of the Camargue region, in order to develop building materials. Mainly sourced from agricultural and quarry waste streams in the region, different resources were collected, studied and developed.

For the rammed earth – compressed earth blocks and earth mortar – Sarragan debris sand and Nimes demolition waste were used. These materials were used for the load-bearing internal walls in the building and gave them their characteristic white colour. Earth (base layer) plaster was composed of the orange clay slurry from Vallabrix as well as Sarragan's debris sand. The resources were wet, mixed, sprayed, compressed, smeared and/or cured in order to discover their potential as a building material. This resulted in both handmade and lab testing. Those deemed to have potential were further developed into full-scale validated prototypes, with the involvement of the executing craftsmen and contractors. The validation happened through different sets of norms (German, French, European). In the end, six building materials were developed and validated.

Legal

The method of Atelier LUMA can be seen as the manifestation of a sustainability protocol based in the Camargue bioregion aiming to promote a sustainable production and consumption model of closed regional and biobased loops. These shared goals of Atelier LUMA formed the basis for the selection of all the partners involved. From the designers and the farms and quarries to the craftsmen who helped with the optimization of the production processes and the renovation of the building.

Financial

Atelier LUMA is funded by Maja Hoffmann, a Swiss art patron and heiress to the Roche pharmaceutical fortune. Hoffmann grew up in Arles, where her father, Luc, was a pioneering naturalist who fought to conserve the region's Camargue wetlands and cofounded the World Wildlife Fund. She sees Atelier LUMA as a means of continuing his work.

In 2004, Hoffmann founded the LUMA Foundation (Zurich) as a vehicle for her ongoing artistic commitments, followed by LUMA Arles (France) in 2013, an experimental and cross-disciplinary platform dedicated to the production of exhibitions, art and ideas, research, education and archives. The LUMA Foundation includes a resource centre designed by architect Frank Gehry; various industrial buildings renovated and converted by architect Annabelle Selldorf; and a public park designed by landscape architect Bas Smets. The site's main building, by Gehry, opened in the summer of 2021, and uses tiles made out of salt that were produced by Atelier LUMA. Le Magasin Électrique, where Atelier LUMA is housed, was completed in May 2023.

Spatial

All of Atelier LUMA's research themes are related to biobased building. A team of 30 researchers – with backgrounds in product design, chemistry, sociology, biology, economics and engineering – has been studying everything from algae dyes to sunflower leather. Following extensive testing and certification, many of these experimental materials were used in the actual building.

With its Algae Lab, Atelier LUMA is working on the production of biopolymers that can be used as biodegradable plastics. The Camargue Cane workshop explores how Provencal cane, which is found in abundance in the south of France, can be processed to produce a pulp from which you can make paper or even large laminated panels. The Smart Fiber Factory uses the agricultural waste of the local rice production, processing its fibres to create high-quality biostratified materials, using the entire waste stream. The Atelier's Sunflower Company only uses the waste from sunflower cultivation for different products, one of them being the earth plaster that was used in the building. It contains the chopped stems and piths of the Camargue sunflower waste. While the strong stem fibre gives structure, the soft and elastic pith provides for a lightweight aggregate, resulting in a porous and elastic plaster which absorbs sound at the same value as PUR foam acoustic panels, reaching an α of 0.7 (tested in ENTPE Lyon).

Crèche Justice, Paris, France

From an unused spot to a circular building for the neighbourhood

1. Rue Justice has some neglected corners while the neighbourhood lacks social facilities such as childcare.

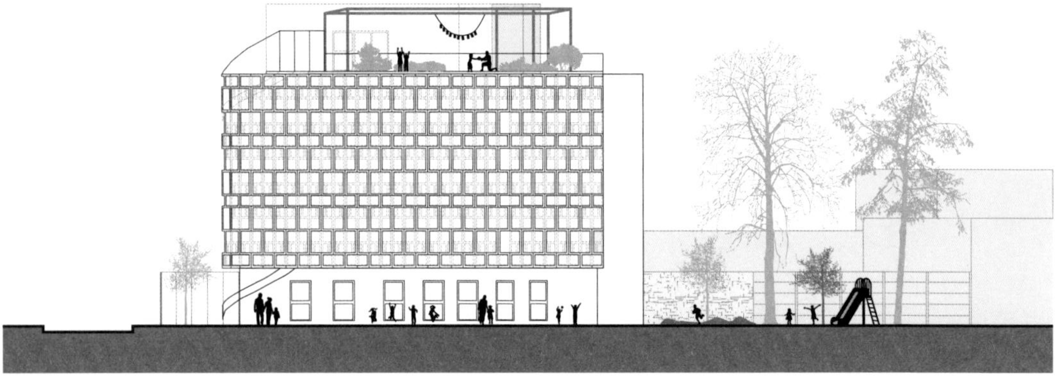

2. The desired nursery is realized in a circular and flexible building structure.

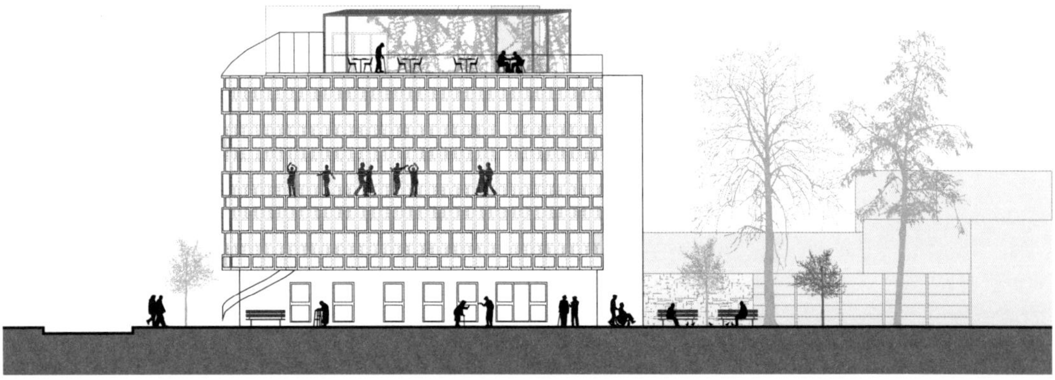

3. Having a flexible building structure, the building can easily change into a facility for elderly people.

Time-based Flexibility
Instruments: reused materials mediator, sustainability protocol, life cycle finance, rooftop benefits

Initiators: Mairie de Paris, Ville de Paris – Direction du Patrimoine et de l'Architecture Service de la Petite Enfance et Environnement Social, BERIM, AGI2D
Design: BFV Architects
Completion: 2021
Programme: Childcare centre for 140 children
Website: https://bfv.team/en/projects/faire-plus-avec-moins

Like many other cities, Paris is trying to find ways to reduce the environmental impact of the building sector. The Crèche Justice, a nursery in the 20th district of Paris, shows that many ambitions for more sustainability can be achieved by densifying existing urban tissue with flexible building structures made out of circular and reused materials.

The Creche Justice is an initiative of the municipality of Paris, who wanted to add this social facility to the densely populated 20th arrondissement at the east side of the inner city. The Creche, named after the street it is located in, the Rue de la Justice, is considered by the municipality as an essential social service in a neighbourhood full of young families. Having good local childcare contributes to social inclusion as it potentially provides young families with a dual income and makes young women financially independent.

The possibility to densify the urban tissue with the public facility arose when two separate plots were joint, one owned by a housing corporation and one in use as a small strip of public vegetation. As the initiator and future owner, the municipality of Paris saw a chance to realize a building project meeting many sustainability goals. In France, the building sector is responsible for 44 per cent of the energy use and 25 per cent of the carbon dioxide emission. The RE2012 national sustainability law, which constrains the use of energy in building projects, tries to reduce the footprint of the building sector. The Paris municipality demanded a building design that was more ambitious than these legal restrictions. The building was not only to have a low energy usage, it also had to be partly circular and have a flexible structure, so that different future uses would be possible.

The chosen design met all those ambitious sustainability goals. Trying to find the best fit in its tight location, the five building floors are all exactly the same size, while originally, the programme asked for more variation between the different floor sizes. The additional benefit of this straight building volume is that it stimulates an economic, repetitive use of building materials. To provide sufficient outside spaces – which are crucial for the intended programme – each floor has a generous outside terrace. These terraces are covered with reused oak doors, that function as sun protection, fall-through protection and relate the building to its surroundings with the right scale.

For the building's structure predominantly drywall construction was used, with load-bearing facades made of precast concrete with integrated insulation. This construction method implies a strict stacking of levels in an elementary form. A simple grey paint on the exterior facade and a pore sealer on the interior facade finished the concrete's raw appearance. The interior is made of wooden partitions, minimizing the use of gypsum boards. Material choices are sober and simple. The interior partitions have dry connections, allowing for maximum flexibility in the building and preparing for a future reuse of these materials.

Organizational

The building was initially designed with a wooden facade. However, no suitable supplier could be found until the project team saw an opportunity at a nearby construction site: 621 corridor doors were about to be disposed of because they did not meet the new building regulations.

Bellastock, an expert in material reuse, conducted a study on the feasibility and viability of the reuse of these wooden doors, finally guaranteeing a proper implementation of old materials into the new design. The oakwood doors were first stored in a warehouse for ten months. The storage period was crucial as it had to match the construction schedule. Subsequently, a carpenting company took care of the preparation of the interior doors as outside facade elements. The doors were repaired with wood filler. The paint was sanded off and the doors were reassembled in order to make facade modules with a one-floor height (3.2 metres). By attaching them onto a steel frame, the assembly only took ten days. The door knobs were reused in the interior as coat hangers. In the end, 60 per cent of the 621 doors were reused.

It was a real opportunity to find these doors, since oakwood could never have been used here, because of its high price. This reuse process ensures a very strong and durable facade cladding. Besides that, the repurposing of old doors reduced the costs significantly.

Legal

The project brief, initiated by the Mayor of Paris, set high sustainability ambitions, asking for innovative ways to build with circular materials whilst keeping the budget tight. This stimulated the use of circular materials.

Though the building was designed in accordance with the RT2012 law, setting limits to the primary energy of buildings and asking for bioclimatic architecture, it is, in some aspects, more ambitious. Limiting the emissions caused by the construction process, the project anticipated much tighter regulations. In order to reduce the amount of building materials, the building had to be designed as efficiently as possible. Great attention was paid to the choice of materials, reusing as many as possible, maximizing the use of wood and making sure that all interior finishes were healthy (with no VOC emissions) for the building users.

Financial

The building's design ensures reasonable operation costs thanks to simple installations and easy maintenance of building systems and facades.

The whole building is designed to be adaptable to different usages over its lifetime, ensuring the relevance of its construction over the years and preventing its obsolescence. The nursery has quite a compact shape, ensuring an efficient use of heating. Windows on opposite facades allow for good natural ventilation, and maximize the amount of daylight inside, reducing the need for artificial light.

On the roof, a pergola supporting the solar panels creates an additional sheltered outdoor play area, on the 194-square-metre planted roof terrace. The building's optimal exposure enables a good energy performance, and the solar panels of the roof power the interior installations, as well as the outdoor lighting. Solar boilers provide additional heating for the water used in the kitchen and in the bathrooms.

Spatial

As the programme of childcare requires an excellent quality of outdoor space and the surrounding space of the building is limited, creating this space was a challenge in this project. The rooftop is arranged as a playground and at each level, huge terraces are attached to the main structure of the building. The rooftop accommodates a roof garden, compensating the little green spot that the building was built upon. The solar panels on the roof provide the building with shelter on sunny days.

Off-grid house in the forest, Småland, Sweden

Circular housing blocks De Punt, Amsterdam, the Netherlands

Adaptable mixed-use building De Kleine Omval, Amsterdam, the Netherlands

Nature-inclusive residential area Weespertrekvaart, Amsterdam, the Netherlands

About the Authors

Temp.architecture was founded in 2011 by Maarten van Tuijl and Tom Bergevoet. The firm focuses on design and research. Its name is based on the concept of time: the firm works from the conviction that time is a crucial factor for reaching sufficient, sustainable design solutions. Temp.architecture works on assignments that vary in size, from renovation and interior design to planning projects on an urban scale. Recurrent themes are flexibility, transformation, circularity and climate adaptation. Though the first designs of the firm were not executed, for instance the temporary extension of the Amsterdam Olympic Stadium, recent designs were realized, such as the entrance area of the Amsterdam UMC hospital and the social housing block Diderot. Currently, the firm is preparing the realization of their designs for the nature-inclusive residential area Weespertrekvaart and the circular housing blocks De Punt. Temp.architecture often works in close collaboration with technical experts and other designers. The Flexible City book series, of which this book is the third, forms a continuous dialogue between the theoretical knowledge of the firm and its daily design practice.

Tom Bergevoet (1972, Utrecht) is an architect, researcher and writer. After obtaining his Master's degree in Architecture from the Delft University of Technology, Tom worked for SANAA (Tokyo), OMA, Architectenbureau Koen van Velsen, and Architectuurstudio Herman Hertzberger, where he helped design the multifunctional Tivoli Vredenburg music centre in Utrecht. Tom is guest lecturer at the Faculty of Architecture and the Built Environment at the Delft University of Technology and the Academy of Architecture at the Amsterdam University of the Arts. Tom believes that good architecture contributes to its environment in many ways, giving significance to the public realm, reinforcing social and ecological networks, leaving a modest ecological footprint and, last but not least, being highly appreciated by its users. In collaboration with other designers and researchers, Tom recently worked on the design of the entrance area of the Amsterdam UMC hospital and the book publication *The Flexible City.*

Maarten van Tuijl (1972, Amsterdam) is an architect, publicist and an expert for the EU Programme URBACT. He is also a visiting guest lecturer at the Delft University of Technology and a number of academies. Maarten graduated as Master of Science in Advanced Architectural Design at Columbia University in New York. After working for Rafael Vinoly, Dok architecten and UN Studio, he collaborated with the Japanese architect Naoko Hikami at na-ma architecture on various projects till 2011. Maarten has been a member of the Dutch Repurposing Team and Lead Expert for the URBACT sub>urban network. Working closely together with Lead Partner Antwerp, Oslo, Vienna, Dusseldorf, the Area Metropolitana Barcelona, Brno, Casoria, Baia Mare and Solin, on the transformation of their post-war urban areas. Maarten enjoys looking for the most suitable solution for complex challenges together with others, also taking quality of life and beauty into account as important goals.

About the Reporters

These reporters were a great help to the authors writing this book. All interested in the themes of the book in their own way and all familiar with another part of Europe, the reporters initially collected and proposed numerous possible projects and examples. Partly based on this input, a balanced selection could be made of analyses, instruments and example projects from all over Europe, highlighting the themes of this book in different ways. Subsequently, the reporters did detailed research on the selected projects and cowrote the texts together with the authors.

Tallula Oellerich (1998, Berlin, Germany) is a Berlin-based interior and spatial designer. She studied at the Glasgow School of Art and Pratt Institute in New York. With her bachelor thesis centred around *The Flexible City; Sustainable Solutions for a Europe in Transition*, her core focus lies in sustainable planning and reinventing modular architecture. Since graduating, she has worked at Studio Aisslinger and curated exhibitions at Haus der Statistik in Berlin. In 2022, she relocated to New York to explore international developments in reshaping urban building systems and advancing material reuse. She is currently pursuing a Master's degree in Interior Architecture.

Joseph Siebenaler (1999, Luxembourg) studied Architecture at the Glasgow School of Art and University of the Arts in Berlin, and is now studying the Urban Policy dual-degree at Sciences Po in Paris and LSE in London. Both creative and practical, Joseph combines the artistic experience of his studies with technology-based solutions and creates work independent of his studies. He is particularly interested in the spatial conditions of European cities, using a variety of representational methods to investigate and communicate these qualities and to propose striking new possibilities.

Aurélie Griveaux (1996, Créteil, France) is a French Architect. She studied architecture and landscape design in France, and has a Master's degree in Architecture, from the Delft University of Technology. Her academic work focuses on gender concerns in India. After graduating, she cofounded MOR Studio, an architecture and engineering office, focused on sustainable architecture. She now works at ZUS. As an architect, Aurélie focuses on user-centred design and inclusivity. She strives for the creation of more biodiverse and resilient environments, focusing on people as much as other living organisms.

Niklas Scheuer (1997, Berlin, Germany) is specialized in urban research, planning and design. He holds a Bachelor's degree in urban and regional planning, a Master's degree in urban studies, and is currently pursuing a double Master's degree in urban design and architecture. He has studied at Technical University Berlin, University of California at Berkeley, and six universities in Brussels, Vienna, Copenhagen, and Madrid. Currently based in Shanghai for a one-year residency at Tongji University, his primary interests lie in urban tourism and mobility research, sustainable urbanism and housing as well as urban analytics.

Anna Tsagkalou (1991, Athens, Greece) is an architect/sustainability engineer and cofounder of MOR Studio. She graduated from National Technical University of Athens (NTUA) and continued her studies at TU Delft where she obtained a Master's degree in Building Technology. Anna believes in an integrated design approach, where climate and energy performance-driven design are used as integral tools for creating sustainable architecture. In addition to her architectural and research projects, which primarily concentrate on building transformations and the application of digital tools to quantify sustainability, she actively participates in events and publications to raise awareness about sustainable design.

Paulina Szuba (1994, Stalowa Wola, Poland) is an architect, designer and researcher. In 2015, she started her career, gaining professional experience working for both international and Polish architectural firms. In 2018, she obtained a Master's degree in architecture. Since then, she has been working together with one of the biggest architectural firms in Poznan, where she designs mostly high-rise and residential architecture. In 2020, she founded her own studio GASPA, collaborating with other firms in the architecture and graphic design field.

Anna-Marie Mašková (1996, Prague, Czech Republic) is a designer and researcher. Circular economy, future-proof circular design and renovations are the focus of Anna-Marie's work. Thanks to her varied education, she is experienced at designing across scales from interior to urban. She holds Master's degrees in Urban Design and Building in Development from University College London and a Bachelor's degree with honors in Interior Architecture from the University of Brighton. In 2021, Anna-Marie joined the Master's programme in Architecture at the Academy of Architecture in Amsterdam. In the coming years, she strives to expand her experience in circular architecture, in addition to researching the socio-economic impact of the climate crisis.

Acknowledgements

This book was made possible thanks to financial support from the following

The Creative Industries Fund NL
Dutch Ministry of Interior and Kingdom Relations
Agenda Stad
City Deal Public Space
City Deal Circular and Conceptual Building
Van Eesteren-Fluck & Van Lohuizen Stichting
Waternet
Regional public water authority Amstel Gooi en Vecht
City of Amsterdam
Temp.architecture

This book could not have been written without contributions from the following

Koen Haer
Frank Reniers
Bart Stoffels
Gertjan de Werk
Sybren Bosch
Kasper Spaan
Lara Rodenburg
Joyce van den Berg
Bas Horsting
Lejla Duran
Katrine Øhrberg
Vera Noldus
Joan Caba Roset

The drawings (maps, elevations, sections and other) in this book are interpretations by the authors of actual analyses, projects and situations. The texts are the result of extensive research of different sources by the authors and the reporters. The authors and the reporters have made a great effort to describe the projects and subjects both factually correct and to place them in the wider perspective of the book.

The text about the Klimatilpasning Kokkedal was written with the help of Realdania and is based on the following sources: Klimatilpasning Kokkedal: Evaluering af de vandtekniske aspekter by Ole Fryd and Marina Bergen Jensen, 2018; Klimatilpasning Kokkedal: Erfaringer og anbefalinger fra et partnerskab by Dorthe Hedensted Lund, 2018

We gratefully acknowledge the assistance of many others who are not named here, especially those who contributed to our previous books, which were the base for this book. We would also like to thank those who helped the reporters and us to describe the example projects in Chapter 4 and those who made pictures available to us.

Several publications by the authors preceded this book

De Flexibele Stad; Oplossingen voor leegstand en krimp (2013)
The Flexible City; Sustainable Solutions for a Europe in Transition (2016)

We would like to thank our colleagues at Temp.architecture who worked on the graphic visualizations in this book

Lisa Paramzina
Alexandra Shilova
Kevin Groothuis

Photocredits

Thierry Kinet: 76
Copernicus Land Monitoring: 77
Lars Gruber: 78
Delphine Mathy: 79
Saliampoukou Olga@photolgaphy_: 80
Cirkelstad: 81
Ensapl - HABITER2030: 82
Joyce van den Berg, Gemeente Amsterdam: 83
Jeroen Broeckx: 84
Atelier Loidl: 88
City of Gothenburg: 89
Buro JP: 90
CELL: 91
Wikimedia Commons: 93
Roman Keller: 94
Nottingham City Council: 95
David Boureau: 96
Elena Rosa: 100
freepik / @ wavebreakmedia_micro: 101
Nils Petter Dale: 102
Malta Public Transit: 103
Municipality of Athens: 104
Radu Malasincu: 105
Zala Strojin Božič: 106
Ponderosa Templeton: 107
GRIMSHAW: 108
Anders Rajendiram: 112
Victoria Tomaschko: 113
Francesco Jodice: 114
Laura Guerrero-Ajuntament de Barcelona: 115
baubüro in situ ag, Foto: Martin Zeller: 116
Jan-Kees Steenman: 117
Andreas Muhs: 118
IBA Hamburg GmbH / bloomimages: 119
Frederik Beyens: 120
In-situ: 129
Karolina Samborska: 130
Steffen Stamp for Realdania: 135
DEL RIO BANI: 139, 140
Åke E:son Lindman: 145 (top)
PatrickDegerman: 145 (bottom)
Katja Effting: 149, 150
Hertha Hurnaus: 159, 160
Temp.architecture: 165 (top)
Stadt Wien/Christian Fürthner, stand 2019: 165 (bottom)
Filip Dujardin: 169
Jeroen van der Wielen: 170
Poltred studio: 175 (top)
Ilimelgo architects: 175 (bottom)
Marcus Eliasson: 179, 180
Hanne Van Assche: 185
Rasmus Hjortshøj: 189, 190
ARGE agn heimspielarchitekten: 195 (top)
Caspar Sessler: 195 (bottom)
Mikko Auerniitty & OOPEAA: 199, 200
Ossip van Duivenbode: 205
Adriaan Deweerdt: 209 (top), 210 (top right, bottom left), 211 (top right, bottom right)
Joseph Halligan: 209 (bottom)
Victor&Simon / Joana Luz: 210 (top left), 211 (bottom left)
Laurens Bekemans: 210 (bottom right)
Jean-Baptiste Marcant: 211 (top left)
Côme Bocabeille: 215
Temp architecture: 216 (top right)
Wouter Jansen: 216 (top left)
Scofo: 216 (right, second from the top)
Parallel: 216 (bottom), design by Temp.architecture with Architecten Cie, Flux Landscape Architecture and Raumplan
Martin Wengelaar: 217

Credits of graphic schemes, sections and drawings: Temp.architecture

Credits

Text copyrights
Tom Bergevoet, Maarten van Tuijl

The authors share their copyrights with the following reporters for the indicated texts:

Tallula Oellerich
Chapter 3: Databased Policies; Material Passport; Emission Limitation; Demolition Ban; Life Cycle Finance; Soil-sensitivity
Chapter 4: Ikea store; People's Pavilion; Triodos Bank

Anna Tsagkalou
Prologue: Heat Stress
Chapter 3: Empowering Local Communities; Innovation Booster; Social Currency; Biobased Building; Converting Tradition

Joseph Siebenaler
Prologue: Greenhouse Gas Emission
Chapter 3: Dynamic Biodiversity Management; Reused Materials Mediator; Purpose Specific Freezone; Law Change Motivation; Upcycling; Recurrent Housing Fund; Rooftop Benefits
Chapter 4: Sara Cultural Centre; Gent knapt op

Paulina Szuba
Prologue: Soil Pollution

Niklas Scheuer
Prologue: Waste Excess
Chapter 3: Holistic Approach; Circular Supply Chains; Car Ban; Community Shares; Privately Financed Public Assets; Free Public transport; Subsidy; Microclimate Modification; Densification; Modular Building; Re-interpretation
Chapter 4: Seestadt Aspern; Rathaus Korbach; Cooperativa Agricoltura Nuova

Aurélie Griveaux
Chapter 4: Les berges du Rhône; Cité Maraîchère; Crèche Justice

Anna-Marie Mašková
Prologue: Biodiversity Decline
Chapter 3: Guerrilla Gardening
Chapter 4: Atri

Copy editing
Jean Tee
Image research
Tom Bergevoet
Maarten van Tuijl
Tallula Oellerich
Anna Tsagkalou
Joseph Siebenaler
Niklas Scheuer
Aurélie Griveaux
Anna-Marie Mašková
Design
Sanne Beeren
Printing and binding
Wilco
Paper
Munken Lynx 120 gr and 240 gr, Arctic Paper
Production
Marja Jager, nai010 publishers
Publisher
Marcel Witvoet, nai010 publishers

nai010 publishers is an internationally orientated publisher specialized in developing, producing and distributing books in the fields of architecture, urbanism, art and design.
www.nai010.com

nai010 books are available internationally at selected bookstores and from the following distribution partners:

North, Central and South America – Artbook | D.A.P., New York, USA, dap@dapinc.com

Rest of the world – Idea Books, Amsterdam, the Netherlands, idea@ideabooks.nl

For general questions, please contact nai010 publishers directly at sales@nai010.com or visit our website www.nai010.com for further information.

Printed and bound in the Netherlands

ISBN 978-94-6208-832-0
NUR 648
BISAC ARC010000

The Flexible City; Solutions for a Circular and Climate Adaptive Europe
is also available as e-book:
ISBN 978-94-6208-833-7 (e-book)